Televising Queer Women

Televising Queer Women
A Reader

Second edition

Edited by
Rebecca Beirne

Dana Heller's "Out for Life: Makeover Television and the Transformation of Fitness on Bravo's *Work Out*" was previously published in *Continuum: Journal of Media and Cultural Studies*, vol. 22 no. 4 (August 2008): 525–535. Reprinted by permission of Taylor & Francis.

First published in hardcover in 2008 by
PALGRAVE MACMILLAN®
in the United States – a division of St. Martin's Press LLC,
175 Fifth Avenue, New York, NY 10010.

Where this book is distributed in the UK, Europe and the rest of the world, this is by Palgrave Macmillan, a division of Macmillan Publishers Limited, registered in England, company number 785998, of Houndmills, Basingstoke, Hampshire RG21 6XS.

Palgrave Macmillan is the global academic imprint of the above companies and has companies and representatives throughout the world.

Palgrave® and Macmillan® are registered trademarks in the United States, the United Kingdom, Europe and other countries.

ISBN: 978–0–230–34098–5

Library of Congress Cataloging-in-Publication Data is available from the Library of Congress.

A catalogue record of the book is available from the British Library.

Design by Newgen Imaging Systems (P) Ltd., Chennai, India.

First PALGRAVE MACMILLAN paperback edition: September 2012

10 9 8 7 6 5 4 3 2 1

Printed and bound in Great Britain by
CPI Antony Rowe, Chippenham and Eastbourne

Contents

Acknowledgments

My sincere thanks to the contributors to this volume: Allison Burgess, Mónica Calvo-Pascual, Tanya R. Cochran, Maite Escudero-Alías, Dana Heller, Melissa M. M. Hidalgo, Sue Jackson, M. Catherine Jonet, Kelly Kessler, Whitney Monaghan, Candace Moore, Jennifer Moorman, Marnie Pratt and Laura Anh Williams. I am especially grateful to Mónica Calvo-Pascual, Maite Escudero-Alías, Sue Jackson, M. Catherine Jonet, Whitney Monaghan, Marnie Pratt, and Laura Anh Williams for producing new contributions within a very short time frame. Thanks must also go to those contributors to the first edition who could not be included here because of issues of space.

Thanks to Robyn Curtis, Samantha Hasey, and Kristy Lilas at Palgrave Macmillan and Deepa John from Newgen Knowledge Works for their work on this edition, as well as to Brigitte Shull for her work on the first edition.

Contributors

Rebecca Beirne is a lecturer in Film, Media and Cultural Studies at the University of Newcastle, Australia. She is the author of *Lesbians in Television and Text After the Millennium* (2008), as well as a number of book chapters and journal articles concerning the representation of queer women in popular culture. She also is coeditor (with James Bennett) of *Making Film and Television Histories: Australia and New Zealand* (2011).

Allison Burgess holds a PhD from the Department of Sociology and Equity Studies in Education and the Graduate Collaborative Program in Women and Gender Studies at the Ontario Institute for Studies in Education of the University of Toronto (OISE/UT). She does research in the areas of sexuality, feminist poststructuralism, queer activist organizing, and popular culture.

Mónica Calvo-Pascual is a lecturer in the Department of English and German Philology at the University of Zaragoza, Spain, where she obtained her PhD on contemporary US literature. Her current research interests focus on the representation of trauma in contemporary fiction in English and on the gender component in compulsive behaviors like eating disorders and deliberate self-harm. Her latest publications include the volume *Chaos and Madness: The Politics of Fiction in Stephen Marlowe's Historical Narratives* (Amsterdam and New York: Rodopi, 2011).

Tanya R. Cochran is an associate professor of English at Union College, Nebraska. She received her PhD from Georgia State University and has published in the areas of popular culture and pedagogy studies, including *Investigating Firefly and Serenity: Science Fiction on the Frontier*, which she coedited with Rhonda V. Wilcox (London and New York: I. B. Tauris, 2008).

Maite Escudero-Alías is a senior lecturer in the Department of English and German Philology at the University of Zaragoza (Spain). She belongs to the competitive research team "Contemporary Narrative in English," which is currently working on ethics and trauma in contemporary fiction in English. She has published widely on her main research interests, which center on feminism, queer theory, cultural studies, and trauma studies, with a special focus on the affect of shame. She is the author of *Long Live the King: A Genealogy of Performative Genders* (Newcastle-upon-Tyne: Cambridge Scholars Publishing, 2009).

Dana Heller is professor and chair of the Department of English at Old Dominion University in Norfolk, Virginia. She is the author of *Hairspray* (Chichester: Wiley-Blackwell, 2011) and editor of the forthcoming *Loving The L Word: The Complete Series in Focus* (I. B. Tauris).

Melissa M. M. Hidalgo is an assistant professor of English and World Literature at Pitzer College in Claremont, California. She teaches classes in Chicana/o literature and cultural production, education and empire, and US cultural studies, with an emphasis on queerness, gender, sexuality, race, and desire. Hidalgo's current research project, Mapping Mozlandia, analyzes the relationship between British pop musician Morrissey and his largely Latina/o-Mexican fan base in Los Angeles and across the US Southwest.

Sue Jackson is senior lecturer in the School of Psychology at Victoria University of Wellington, New Zealand. Her research and publication work centers on young women's negotiation of sexuality, the ways sexuality is represented in girls' popular culture, and how girls make sense of media representations of femininity and sexuality. Currently her research centers on a three-year project, *Girls, 'Tween' Popular Culture and Everyday Life* supported by the New Zealand Royal Society Marsden Fund.

M. Catherine Jonet is an assistant professor of Women's Studies at New Mexico State University. She received her PhD in Critical Theory and Cultural Studies in 2007 from Purdue University. Her teaching and research interests include experimental literature/visual culture by women, literary graphic narratives, and representations of queer desire in popular culture.

Kelly Kessler is an assistant professor of Media and Cinema Studies at DePaul University, Chicago. Her work engages primarily with the American musical, television genre, and the mainstreaming of lesbianism in American media. Her book *Destabilizing the Hollywood Musical: Music, Masculinity, and Mayhem* examines the gendered and thematic evolution of the genre from the mid-1960s to the early 1980s. Her scholarship can also be found in journals such as *Film Quarterly* and *Cinema Journal,* and in other works, including *Feminism at the Movies* and *The New Queer Aesthetic on Television.*

Whitney Monaghan is a PhD candidate in Film and Television Studies at Monash University. Her dissertation focuses on queer girls and queer temporality in contemporary screen culture. Her research interests include the representation of queer adolescents in film and television, participatory fan culture, digital culture, and theories of time in film and television. Her work has appeared in the journals *Jump Cut* and *Colloquy,* as well as in the online film magazine *Screen Machine.*

Candace Moore is an assistant professor at the University of Michigan, where her work focuses on queer representation in media, primarily television. Moore's articles have appeared in *Cinema Journal; GLQ; Production Studies: Cultural Studies of Media Industries; Televising Queer Women* (1st edition); *Gender, Race, and Class in Television: A Critical Reader* (3rd edition); *Reading The L Word: Outing Contemporary Television;* and *Third Wave Feminism and Television.* Moore has also published extensively as a media critic for *Curve, Girlfriends*, and AfterEllen.com.

Jennifer Moorman is a PhD candidate in Cinema and Media Studies at the University of California, Los Angeles. Her dissertation focuses on women filmmakers in the adult video industry. An earlier version of her contribution to this volume was published in the first edition of *Televising Queer Women.* Her articles also appear in the edited volumes *Porn.com: Making Sense of Online Pornography* and in *Supernatural Teens: Essays on Magic, Mutation, and Adventure.*

Marnie Pratt is an instructor in the Women's Studies program at Bowling Green State University. In addition to her contribution to the first edition of *Televising Queer Women*, she has presented research on *The L Word* at several national conferences and has contributed chapters to a number of other edited collections. She also earned two of her university's research awards for her work. Besides *The L Word*, her interests include feminist and queer theory, media, popular culture, social movements/activism, and celebrity.

Laura Anh Williams earned her PhD in Theory and Cultural Studies at Purdue University in 2010. Her academic interests include Asian American literature, food studies, visual culture, and queer studies. She teaches for the Department of English and the Women's Studies Program at New Mexico State University.

Introduction: Queer Women on Television Today

Rebecca Beirne

When *The L Word* first screened in 2004, it was widely celebrated as a watershed moment for lesbian culture and representation, but it also was critiqued on a number of fronts. Perhaps unsurprisingly, the media engaged in a form of communal amnesia about the forms of queer female representation that had come before the Showtime series, effectively overstating its "newness" and the extent to which the world of lesbian representation on television had changed. In recent years, however, I have come to believe that things *have* changed. We have come a long way since the mid-1970s, when "every sexual minority in a network drama [in fall 1974] was a violent criminal" (Capsuto 107) and the media committee of an organization known as Lesbian Feminist Liberation, Inc., wrote an open letter to television stations protesting the screening of programs that "are detrimental to our fight for our civil rights and dignity" (Cotter). Although their demand of "no negative portrayal of lesbians on television until 12% of all the women represented on television are portrayed as lesbians" has yet to be met, today we have a greater number and variety of representations of queer women on television than ever before.

Now, in my classes, students volunteer that they snuck behind their parent's backs to watch *The L Word* at age 13. These young women and men clearly grew up in a different era of lesbian representation on television than my own. They had access to believable queer teen characters in teen programming in the United Kingdom such as *South of Nowhere* (on The N 2005–2008) and *Skins* (on E4 2007–, on MTV 2011), and even a series whose entire narrative revolved around the desires and adventures of a young queer woman in *Sugar Rush* (Channel 4 2005–2006). Queer cable networks in the US have primarily focused on gay male programming, but they also have also presented the lesbian-focused series *Exes and Ohs* (Logo 2007, 2011), and the (truly abysmal) made-for-television film *In Her Line of Fire* (Here 2006). In the UK, following on from the massive success of the pre-*L Word* lesbian-focused period drama mini-series *Oranges Are Not the Only Fruit* (1990) and *Tipping the Velvet* (2002), the two-part drama *Fingersmith* (2005) screened to large audiences on the BBC, and ITV produced the made-for-television film *Affinity* (2008). The BBC, the UK public broadcaster, even commissioned an internal study on representations of lesbians, gays, and bisexuals on its network, and the resultant "diversity strategy" (Geen) is well-served by the lesbian-focused serial drama *Lip Service* (2010–). Launching in the same year, the Canadian fantasy series *Lost Girl* (2010–) is the earliest big-budget series to feature a sympathetic bisexual female lead, albeit one who can kill or control with a kiss.

Nonetheless, the number of queer characters on television certainly does not reflect the proportion of queer individuals in real-life communities, and there are significant limitations on their representations. The relative absence of queer characters on television has made those queer representations that do occur all the more significant. Their potential to influence the wider population, who may never have knowingly met an actual lesbian or bisexual woman, sparks a profound investment in these images. For television can indeed produce powerful affective relationships. Diane Anderson-Minshall has commented on psychological studies "proving that people develop such intense relationships with people on TV that those characters act as our de facto friends, providing ancillary relationships that are so deeply ingrained in our psyches that when those people go away we actually grieve and when they reappear we feel intense joy" (11).

What impact, then, do those few lesbian characters we see on our television screens have? In the first edition of *Televising Queer Women*, Marnie Pratt saw the "importance of media representations for lesbian communities" as both "moving" and "profoundly troubl[ing];" she observed that this high level of investment in media representations is "tied to queer culture's long struggle with 'the closet' and visibility" (189).

This investment in queer characters is compounded by the historical specificities of television's treatment of such characters. As Steven Capsuto, Stephen Tropiano, and Larry Gross discuss in their excellent histories of queer representation on television, during the early years of television, even into the 1970s and 1980s, queer television viewers rarely saw themselves on the small screen. When they did, it was as monsters or victims, objects of revulsion and pity or perhaps as a one-off "lesson" in tolerance, never to be

heard from again. Queer representation on television has progressed sub-
stantially since these times, but this has not constituted a steady narrative of
progress; rather, it has been marked by advances and retreats, breakthroughs
and hiccups, sometimes even all within the same program.

Lesbian and bisexual women have a unique position in popular cultural
representation. Simultaneously fetishized and ignored, desired and dispar-
aged, they have historically been represented in popular culture as either oversexed sirens or sexless creatures whose lesbian life warrants nary a moment of
screen time. As the move into "positive" representations increased in the late
1980s and early 1990s, so did the tendency to desexualize lesbian characters,
coyly ignoring their relationships and intimate lives. Sasha Torres reads such
characters as Nurse Marilyn McGrath (Gail Strickland) on ABC's *Heartbeat*
(1988–1989), the first regularly recurring lesbian character on US television,
and other more minor lesbian characters, as "eas[ing] the ideological threat
of such 'feminist' programs by localizing the homosexuality which might
otherwise pervade these homosocial spaces" (179).

Discussing the first woman-to-woman kiss on US television, between
bisexual lawyer C. J. Lamb (Amanda Donohoe) and her heterosexual colleague Abby (Michele Greene) on *L.A. Law* (1986–1994) in 1991, Roseanne
Kennedy observes, "In comparison with the erotic scenes between the
straight characters, the kiss between C. J. and Abby is restrained to the point
of being asexual.... in the heterosexual world of *L.A. Law* a potentially sexual relationship between C. J. and Abby can only be represented as an issue,
at the cost of eliminating the sex" (Kennedy 133). This tendency to displace
or underplay lesbian sexual expression on television continued; it stands in
marked contrast to hypermarketed and hypersexualized, ratings-stunt kisses
between bicurious/heterosexual women characters on such programs as *Ally
McBeal* (1997–2002).

Roseanne (1988–1997) was likewise a significant series in terms of queer
female representation on television; it included a bisexual female character,
Nancy Bartlett (Sandra Bernhard), and it had Roseanne's mother Bev (Estelle
Harris) come out later in the series. *Roseanne* brought to public attention
the intense pressure on television producers not to include lesbian sexuality
when ABC requested that an episode that involved a female-female kiss be
edited or not shown. Only after Barr herself took a stand on the issue was the
kiss shown, and, as Suzanna Danuta Walters observes in *All the Rage: The
Story of Gay Visibility in America,* this *Roseanne* episode "truly represented
a radical departure in its cogent and sustained attack on homophobia and
exploration of the shifting parameters of sexual desire" (69).

Also in the 1990s, enormously popular sitcom *Friends* (1994–2004)
included lesbian characters Carol (Jane Sibbett), ex-wife of primary character

Ross, and her partner Susan (Jessica Hecht). In keeping with the marginalized representation of many queer characters on television, however, they were not central to the narrative. As Kelly Kessler points out in "Politics of the Sitcom Formula," Carol and Susan were "For the most part...utilized solely as a vehicle for Ross' fatherhood, paranoia, and wisecracks" (134). The lesbian secondary characters on *Mad About You* (1992–1999) were equally problematic, promoting "the targeted heterosexual audience's identification with the characters" through "heterosexual standards of beauty, the invisibility of the lesbian community, the desexualization of the couples' relationship, and the erasure of political struggle" (Kessler 143).

In the context of these barely present representations, it was subtextual representation, absence, that marked the cult lesbian television classic of the 1990s: *Xena: Warrior Princess* (1995–2001). The show was a campy, pseudomythological series featuring a strong ex-warlord protagonist and her supportive storyteller sidekick (and honorary Amazon princess) Gabrielle. It is easy to see why the series was popular among lesbian viewers, as the show coyly lent itself to romantic/sexual readings of the Xena/Gabrielle relationship. This subtext offered a space for queer viewers to actively participate in rewriting the narrative via lesbian fan fiction, which in turn influenced the show towards stronger lesbian entendre. As Jeanne E. Hamming argues, "the cache of Xena/Gabrielle slash fiction which has grown out of the show's reliance on open secrecy has led to a circuit of productive desire between the creative forces behind *Xena: Warrior Princess* and the writers of *Xena* slash." Such open secrecy, however, once again codes lesbianism as something televisually undepictable. As Elyce Rae Helford notes, keeping its female homosexuality as "subtext means the series never has to 'out' its characters and the producers never have to risk the censure and eventual cancellation that might happen with an overtly lesbian program" (141).

The mid to late 1990s saw the outing of queer characters on television: they became not only less subtextual but more numerous. The coming out of comedian and actress Ellen DeGeneres and her character Ellen Morgan on *Ellen* (1994–1998) was, and in many ways still is, roundly celebrated as the most important event in lesbian television history, even prompting a key website focusing on queer women in popular culture to be named Afterellen.com. Not all, however, are comfortable with the embrace of Ellen's media ritual as a defining moment of change, or with the unambiguous narrative of progress suggested by such views. Anna McCarthy notes the contradictory nature of such celebrations of *Ellen* as a first: "[w]riters in the gay press and entertainment news would affirm the status of the show as a first, then generate long lists of queer people of all sorts who had appeared on television in decades past" ("*Ellen*" 593). Susan J. Hubert sees the much-vaunted coming out as "largely a media created event" wherein "Ellen's supposedly contro-versial attempt to push the limits of acceptability actually reinscribe[ed] con-ventional sexual politics" (31). The cancellation of the series once it became "too gay" is legendary, and in the context of hit series such as *Will & Grace* (1998–2006), which featured gay male characters, it serves as a reminder that progress is rarely evenhanded in representing all LGBT people.

Despite critiques of the discourses surrounding the famous coming out, DeGeneres's more contemporary work remains a subject of analysis within the discipline. Jennifer Reed sees DeGeneres, in her new incarnation as a daytime television show host (further discussed by Candace Moore in this volume) as continuing "to perform a specifically lesbian identity, that speaks to gay and lesbian, or queer literate viewers as well, and thus must challenge heteronormativity at some level" (Reed, "Public Lesbian" 34). Response to DeGeneres as a talk show host has certainly not been uniformly positive, and she has been "criticized by the gay press for soft-pedaling her lesbian-ism" (Lo, "The Incredible Story" para 8), though her willingness to address queer political issues has expanded in recent years, as Candace Moore dis-cusses in this volume.

One of the most popular television series in contemporary academic dis-course, *Buffy the Vampire Slayer*, also depicted queer women in the form of primary character Willow (Alyson Hannigan), and her lovers, witch Tara (Amber Benson) and potential slayer Kennedy (Iyari Limon). As Edwina Bartlem observes, the series did "present some empowered images of lesbians in the process of coming out, in long-term romantic relationships and as part of an alternative family unit," but it did not do so entirely without difficulty. Jes Battis notes that the "most prevalent critical reading of the Willow-Tara relationship is one wherein magic and lesbian sexuality are conflated" (36), and, as Edwina Bartlem points out, while "the spectacle of lesbian sex as a form of magic is romantic, it is also problematic as it perpetuates the nor-mative, homophobic notion that lesbian sex is not real, physical or visually presentable." Tanya Cochran (chapter 3 in this collection) explores the ways in which representation of the actresses in other media influenced readings of their relationship.

Although it is certainly tempting to do so, one must be careful not to view increases in lesbian visibility on television as inherently progressive. Nicki Hastie made the astute observation in 1994 that "As lesbian charac-ters explode onto the TV screen and 'lesbian' stories hit the headlines, it is imperative to question the gaps between visibility and empowerment" (38), an argument that is still relevant today and that in one way or another per-vades the scholarship surrounding the representation of queer women on television. For example, scholars Didi Herman and Jenni Millbank have both persuasively argued for the significance of the representation of queer women on *Bad Girls* (ITV 1999–2006). Herman goes so far as to postulate that the series stands in contrast to other television shows, which depict lesbian or gay characters that remain within a heteronormative framework (*Ellen, Will & Grace, Buffy*), instead signifying "a homonormative perspective, such as that found within gay and lesbian literature and independent cinema, [which] represents gay and lesbian identity as normal, natural, good and unremarkable in and of itself" (144).

The advent of *The L Word* has, however, undoubtedly been the most productive force in fostering academic responses to queer women on television. The series, shown on Showtime, a premium cable channel, revolves around a group of largely lesbian and bisexual women living in Los Angeles. The series has been hailed as groundbreaking in its representation of queer women on television. The publication in 2006 of *Reading The L Word*, an anthology edited by Kim Akass and Janet McCabe, brought together responses to *The L Word* by both academics and journalists, and a further collection *Loving the L Word*, edited by Dana Heller, is to be published in 2012.

Despite a significant number of essays that celebrate the series as a breakthrough, the critical response to *The L Word* has been by no means uniformly positive, as the series raises many problematic issues. As Samuel A. Chambers observes "*The L Word* produces a paradox...it takes a cast of mostly lesbian characters yet still manages to mimic, support and even reify the norm of heterosexuality" (89). Conversely, M. Catherine Jonet and Laura Anh Williams have argued that *The L Word* is "a restive text that recasts not only the history of lesbian representation, but also attempts to disrupt identitarian notions of queer women," destablizing heteronormativity and critiquing male privilege ("Everything Else Is the Same" 161).

Whatever side one takes, *The L Word* is not, as some would have it, the celebratory endpoint of the journey of queer women's representation on television. Much as *Ellen* did not unequivocally and unproblematically change the face of the representation of queer women on television, neither has *The L Word*. The series is, however, does represent a step forward, a move closer to the goal of representational abundance demanded by Lesbian Feminist Inc. back in 1975.

Although *The L Word* is still placed firmly in the "adult" category, inroads are slowly being made into representing queer characters on television for young people. Even though young queer characters appearing on teen-oriented programs in the 1990s sparked demands from the religious right to grant a special "homosexual content" label (Epstein 60), the representation of such characters has continued and, indeed, has flourished, as was observed at the outset of this introduction. Queer teen characters have also made their presence known on daytime soaps; Bianca (Eden Riegel) on *All My Children* (1970–) is a prominent example. The prime-time teen ensemble drama *The O.C.* briefly depicted a lesbian relationship, as examined by Allison Burgess in chapter 6 of our present collection. Other series directed at teens have also increasingly represented queer teens in recent years. The Canadian tween series *Degrassi* (1987–1991), long recognized for its willingness to tackle issues considered taboo in children's programming, in its new manifestation as *Degrassi: The Next Generation* (2001–), depicted young queer characters, both male and female.

The UK's Channel 4, known for their queer content with *Dyke TV* (1995–1996) and *Queer as Folk* (1999–2000), broke new ground with *Sugar Rush* (2005–), centering around Kim (Olivia Hallinan), a self-described "fifteen-year-old queer virgin obsessed with my best friend and her magnificent tits" (1.2), who spends the first season lusting after her straight best friend, and spends the second season in an on-again off-again lesbian relationship. Whitney Monaghan further discusses the series in this anthology (chapter 11). *Sugar Rush* is daring in the rampant desires it ascribes to its young female heroine, both for queer television and for television directed at a teen market. Although its "young adult" status might be somewhat compromised by its late timeslot, it was awarded the 2006 International Emmy Award in the "Children and Young People" category.

While desire is foregrounded in *Sugar Rush*, US series *South of Nowhere* explicitly highlights the question of identity, albeit a more fluid conception of identity than is usual for television. Central to the series narrative is the blossoming relationship between main characters Spencer (Gabrielle Christian) and Ashley (Mandy Musgrave), and Spencer's Catholic mother's homophobic reaction to their relationship, which by the end of the second season has turned to a certain degree of acceptance. An unwillingness to name bisexuality occurs in this series much as it does in both *The L Word* (see chapter 8 by Jennifer Moorman in this volume) and *Queer as Folk* (see Beirne, chapter 4). Despite Ashley's early assertion that she is "not into labels" (1.1), the series shifts to both of the girls generally describing themselves as "gay," despite Ashley's complicated relationship with her ex-boyfriend Aiden (Matt Cohen).

Alongside the growth of queer teen characters, there have also been openly queer women on so-called reality TV. These have included openly queer contestants on series like *Top Chef* (Bravo 2006–), *America's Next Top Model* (UPN/CW 2003–), *Australia's Next Top Model* (FOX8 2005–), and *Survivor* (CBS 2000–). The central participant on *Workout* (Bravo 2006–2008), Jackie Warner, was a lesbian lead. The series depicted her relationships in full, including her tense relationship with her homophobic mother, which was a key subplot. The next reality show to focus on lesbians, *The Real L Word* (Showtime 2010–), trod the same "educational" terrain as *The L Word*, while offering a curious but strangely intriguing interrogation of the good and bad in lesbian relationships.

Issues of conflating reality and representation complicate lesbian and bisexual representation on reality television. Such texts as *The Real L Word* purport to represent a kind of truth about lesbianism, established through the season-1 episode-commencing direct-to-camera interview montage, which seeks to define who lesbians are, what they want, and what they do. This tactic is also deployed by British reality series *Candy Bar Girls* (Channel 5, 2011) with its tagline: "Real lesbians. Real Lives. No clichés." The "real lesbians" of *The Real L Word* are suspiciously similar to its more clearly scripted predecessor, reinforcing established tropes of lesbian identity on television: the affluent betrothed couple (Nikki and Jill), the player (Whitney), the bitch (Rose), the quirky romantic (Mikey), and the woman stuck in a kind of coming out, dealing with parental disapproval of her sexual identity (Tracey).

Perhaps the strangest element of the series, however, is its sexual display, which goes beyond that of many other examples of reality drama. In "It's My Party and I'll Cry If I Want to" (1.7), for example, there is a scene that graphically portrays Whitney and Romi having what appears to be "real" strap-on sex. While Showtime is no stranger to soft pornography in its programming, this "realness" would seem to blur the boundaries with hardcore in a manner that may not be possible with a heterosexual couple or gay male couple on reality TV. The actresses later claimed to have been unaware of the cameras, but this incident was no doubt the impetus for turning Romi from a secondary character in the first series to a primary one in the second. Indeed, the only remaining first-series primary cast member, Whitney, was the one who let the cameras all the way into the bedroom. The purpose of the show seems quite clear: much like *The L Word*, it positions itself within a kind of educational voyeurism. What kind of visual economy is evoked here? Is this an example of television's new openness about lesbian relationships and sexuality? Or is it more of the same display of lesbian sexuality for the titillation of audiences, straight and gay alike?

The likelihood of the latter being the case is strongly supported by the second season, which depicts explicit lesbian sex far more frequently than did its predecessor. The series features one couple attempting to have a baby (yet another trope of lesbians on television) who do not have sex on camera, and a whole bunch of messed-up twenty-somethings who enthusiastically do. Which brings us back to old arguments about positive and negative representation, particularly fraught when lesbian representation on television has been represented with such polarity: by turns oversexualized or desexualized. As discussed later in this anthology (chapter 10), Sue Jackson's interviews with high school students revealed their conception of the television trope of the "hot lesbian" as the dominant mode of representation, yet the "hot lesbian" was a character that was not perceived to be a "real" lesbian.

How is one to determine positive or negative representation without recourse to audience? And won't audiences diverge in their responses, depending on a wide array of factors? One can easily read *The Real L Word* as straightforward sexploitation. And yet it is strangely transfixing in its revelry in and openness about the (admittedly constructed) lesbian experience, offering multiple points of recognition and identification.

Lost Girl (Showcase 2010–), a Canadian fantasy series based in a world populated by supernatural beings, offers as its protagonist a bisexual succubus, who "feeds" by draining sexual energy from humans. Although at first this seems little different from such bisexual killers as Miriam Blaylock in *The Hunger*, such concerns are somewhat ameliorated as the series progresses. Lauren, the human female love interest of Bo (Anna Silk) teaches her to control her power; sex is seen as positive when it is revealed as a way for Bo to heal (even from gunshot wounds), and she learns that her sexual "chi" can also be used to breathe life back into the severely wounded or recently departed. The likeability of the character, her genuine feelings towards both a werewolf man *and* a human woman over the course of the first two seasons, and the overall narrative trajectory of Bo's refusal to choose a side in other respects, creates an interesting portrait of female bisexual desire, which is not problematized intradiegetically and is remarked upon only by her sarcastic sidekick. And although Bo's encounters with women are generally fleeting in the first season, the frustrated romance between Bo and Lauren is intensified in the second.

Rounding out 2010 was *Lip Service*, the first lesbian-scripted drama in the few dry years since *The L Word*, *Sugar Rush*, and *Exes and Ohs*. As it follows the lives and loves of a group of women in Glasgow, the series seems less caught up in explaining lesbianism to its audience than its forbears were. Instead, the lesbianism of its characters is in many ways incidental to the narrative, with the exception of some secondary plots. The "search for identity" that forms a key character arc, for example, is about being adopted, not about lesbian sexuality. A certain (admittedly glamorous) gender ambiguity is seen in primary character Frankie (Ruta Gedmintas), and, although *Lip Service* still represents dominant notions of beauty, the costuming and casting are more realistically inclined than *The L Word* is. At the time of writing, the second season is currently screening. While the melodrama quotient has been definitely been upped, the series has thus far continued to represent lesbian characters whose lesbianism is neither an "issue" nor the theme of the series.

Putting together the first edition of *Televising Queer Women* in 2006, I felt a certain urgency about soliciting further discourse on queer women's representation on television. When well over half the papers submitted were focused on *The L Word*, which was appropriate in light of its currency, I was struck with a certain dissatisfaction about what this reflected—an existing limitation in the kinds of queer female representation on television that was of sufficient complexity for in-depth analysis. Revising this text for its second edition has been a challenge for a number of reasons, not least of which was the sheer volume of new representations that have emerged in only five short years. Although it would be impossible to address everything, the new chapters included herein offer scholarship that diversifies the original content: an audience study from New Zealand (chapter 10, Jackson); a chapter on lesbian representation in Spanish soap operas (chapter 13, Escudero-Alías and Calvo-Pascual); a chapter addressing lesbian representation on reality television (chapter 12, Heller); and an interrogation of queer teen girl representation (chapter 11, Monaghan).

Of the chapters carried forward from the first edition, those that were focused on series complete at the time of writing have been updated where relevant, but remain predominantly the same (Moore, Kessler, Cochran, Hidalgo, Burgess, and Beirne). Other chapters, such as the ones on *The L Word* (Pratt, Jonet and Williams, and Moorman), have been significantly revised or rewritten in response to developments in the later seasons. I know that I would have liked to have included so much more—the possibilities for potential subjects for research on queer women in television have blossomed to a point I could not have conceived of in 2008. I am, however, content in the knowledge that the field of study is growing every day. I envisage that, should I have the wonderful opportunity to revisit this collection in another five years, the televisual terrain will once again have changed—I hope, radically so. Perhaps I am too optimistic, but I cannot help but feel that the future is bright for the televising of queer women.

CHAPTER 1

Resisting, Reiterating, and Dancing Through: The Swinging Closet Doors of Ellen DeGeneres's Televised Personalities

Candace Moore

In 2005, gushing to *The Advocate* about her girlfriend, comedienne Ellen DeGeneres, television star Portia de Rossi said: "[Ellen] was so courageous and loud in '97, and now she is doing something that is more subliminal. She's changing the world, she really is" (Kort 40). De Rossi subtly articulated the difference between Ellen's 1997 "coming out"[1] and Ellen's daily dance into America's living rooms as a beloved daytime talk show host who "happened to be" gay. LGBT (lesbian, gay, bisexual, transgendered) activists and media critics slightly disagreed following the initial launch of Ellen's talk show in 2003, asserting that Ellen soft-pedaled her lesbianism on *Ellen: The Ellen De Generes Show* to find widespread acceptance (Lo, "The Incredible Story;" Virginia Heffernan, "The Perils" E5). As *New York Times* critic Virginia Heffernan put it: "Ms. DeGeneres no longer wants to talk about being gay, so she discusses pleasant: décor, holidays and the fridge" (E5). Host of a mainstream variety show that wowed NBC network executives by pulling in impressive numbers of its targeted demographic—women ages 25 to 54 (Deeken 30; Schnuer S1)—and hyped as having an "everywoman approach," DeGeneres often avoided the topic of her own homosexuality and actively closed down conversations in which the very word or concept came up during the show's first two seasons.

By queer theorist David M. Halperin's standards, these early on-air avoidance strategies symbolically placed Ellen firmly back in the closet. As Halperin interprets it, "To 'closet' one's homosexuality is also to submit one-self to the social imperative imposed on gay people by non-gay-identified people, the imperative to shield the latter not from the knowledge of one's homosexuality so much as from the necessity of acknowledging the knowl-edge of one's homosexuality" (29).

In a press conference prior to her talk show's launch in 2003, Ellen DeGeneres was explicit about the fact that discussion about her sexual ori-entation would not likely get much airtime: "People know I'm gay. There's nothing to talk about. It's part of who I am, and [the audience] knows that...I don't know how that would ever come up in a conversation [with a guest]" (quoted in Champagne). Since DeGeneres's Johnny Carson–styled show was organized around interviews of A-list celebrities promoting their own films, albums, and television shows, it seemed logical that the talk show would not revolve around the fact that she's gay. Criticism was instead directed at how Ellen demonstratively deflected mention of queerness in the show's early seasons, since, contrary to her predictions, it did come up. These punctuated "returns of the repressed," followed by quick deflections, served Ellen's act and had productive outcomes.[2] By first resisting talking about it, Ellen actually successfully framed queerness in her long pauses and her obvious redirects while forming a firm connection with audiences of varied ages, sexes, and sexual preferences, setting the groundwork for her current ability to speak openly about her wife, Portia, and to address LGBTQ issues on air.

In June 2008, the Supreme Court of California briefly overturned the state's ban on gay marriages; California reversed the decision months later, with the passing of an amendment to the California Constitution, Proposition 8, in November 2008, which defined marriage as between a man and a woman. That same year, a Harris Poll found Ellen DeGeneres to be "the most popular television personality, dethroning Oprah Winfrey" (Atkin 24). By 2008, a fixture in daytime's television schedule five years after the show's launch, DeGeneres stepped up her discussions of LGBT issues on her talk show, first with a teary-eyed discussion of the hate-based shooting of a gay teen, Lawrence King, on her February 29th episode of 2008: "It starts with laughing at someone [because they're gay], and then it's verbal abuse, then it's physical abuse, and it's this kid Brandon killing a kid like Larry" (*Windy City Times* 19). Then, in May 2008, when the California Supreme Court first overturned the ban on gay marriage, Ellen publicly announced on her show that she and Portia de Rossi (also on set) would tie the knot, causing her studio audience to break into a standing ovation.

The following week, on May 22, Ellen confronted presidential nominee John McCain on his anti-gay-marriage position, calling the idea that "we are not all the same," an "old way of thinking" (Johnson 6). Ellen also spent $100,000 of her own money to create a commercial begging Californians to reject Proposition 8 (Mitchell), and she shared photos of her August wedding with her studio audience and with readers of *People* magazine.

Although Ellen's attempts to shift opinions on same-sex marriage did not ultimately bear fruit at the polls in 2008, she has continued to discuss her married life with Portia on her talk show since then. As TV reviewer Ken Tucker noted in 2010, "She teases her audience about her private life— "This is something I've never revealed because it's personal and it's new: Portia and I dim the lights and get a couple of glasses of wine, and we watch football"—and the fans love it because she's neither hiding anything nor doing what her more conservative audience base might consider pushing an agenda" (Tucker).

Recognizing that Ellen has since incorporated Portia into opening-act chatter about her horses, wedding day, and home life, this essay interrogates Ellen's initial largely implicit social contract with daytime TV not to "bring up" her lesbianism on what has become one of America's highest-rated daytime talk shows. Rewinding, this essay traces multiple queer appearances and disappearances of Ellen DeGeneres on television from 1994 to 2005 to contextualize how Ellen adopted subliminal tactics to win the mainstream audiences with whom she is again out today. I will look back at early (pre-coming-out) episodes of ABC sitcom *Ellen* (1994–1998) and at the opening of an HBO stand-up comedy special, *Ellen DeGeneres: The Beginning* (2000), for clues as to what was enunciated and what was purposely left unsaid about character Ellen Morgan's sexuality and about Ellen DeGeneres's real-life lesbian sexuality, as well as what has been, through dance or physical humor, *performed* about both.

Not verbally addressing queer identity during her talk show's early seasons was understandable from DeGeneres's personal perspective. Her career all but collapsed not long after the glow of her public coming-out party died down. "To come out," according to David Halperin, "is precisely to expose oneself to a different set of dangers and constraints, to make oneself into a convenient screen onto which straight people can project all of the fantasies they routinely entertain about gay people, and to suffer one's every gesture, statement, expression, and opinion to be totally and irrevocably marked by the overwhelming social significance of one's openly acknowledged homosexual identity" (30).

Following Ellen DeGeneres's self-outing, her private life (with ex-girlfriend Anne Heche) became unbearably public—their love affair's ups and downs became unending fodder for gossip columnists and paparazzi, who stalked the new couple. Ellen's groundbreaking sitcom was summarily canceled the next year, due to advertiser pullouts, public attacks from the religious right, and, arguably, sabotage by the ABC network itself in imposing parental advisories because of the show's portrayals of same-sex romance. Such advisories were not, of course, placed on programs that tackled more explicitly sexual subjects with heterosexual leads (Gross 162). Through these trials, DeGeneres became an important icon of political courage for the LGBT community, even though she candidly stated that she had neither intended her coming out as a political statement nor had she wished to become a poster woman for the queer cause. To an interviewer at *Time*, she admitted in 1997: "I never wanted to be the spokesperson for the gay community. Ever. I did it [came out] for my own truth...I didn't do it to make a political statement...I did it selfishly for myself and because I thought it was a great thing for the show, which desperately needed a point of view" (Handy 86).

Well into its second season, Ellen's talk show persona on *Ellen: The Ellen DeGeneres Show* still linguistically sidestepped the word or concept of homosexuality. However, she actively performed queerness through what implicitly "exceeded" her stand-up jokes and sit-down talk, and, physically, through the ritual action of her daily dance sequence. Through these methods, perhaps DeGeneres worked to escape being such a convenient screen for hatemongers or bearing the responsibility of being a spokesperson for all of gay America, while she still maintained the *televisibility*[3] of queer identity.

Demonstrating how Ellen's coming out, her return to the closet, and her coming out once more become enacted again and again, ad infinitum, on television, my textual analyses involve queer ruptures on the then primarily heterosexual text of Ellen's Emmy-winning daytime talk show during its first two seasons. I see being in the closet and being out as performances that are constantly negotiated socially—either actively resisted or reinscribed—rather than one-time denials or declarations of sexuality that hold, and in this essay I highlight ambiguous moments in the early run of DeGeneres's show. In specific instances, De Generes gestured rhetorically or symbolically to her sexual preference, absurdly omitted or redirected possible discussions of homosexuality, or was subtly or not so subtly called out as gay by her celebrity guests.

In a 2005 essay in *Feminist Media Studies*, Jennifer Reed examines Ellen DeGeneres's different "lesbian personas" on network television, including her character on the short-lived CBS sitcom, *The Ellen Show* (2001). Reed argues that "in all of these incarnations, DeGeneres has performed a lesbian persona corresponding to a distinct set of terms and strategies in the socio-performative politics of same-sex desire. That is, each season of these shows has corresponded to separate, identifiable moments in the politics of the representation of same-sex desire" (25). I agree generally with Reed's assertions, but will seek here to examine televised manifestations of Ellen less in terms of the particular representational moment or historical context during which each is broadcast, and more in terms of the varied performative rhetorics she uses, given different televisual genres (sitcom, variety show, comedy special), modes of address (in character, performing/dancing oneself, stand-up), and formal contexts (prime-time network television, daytime network television, pay cable television). Although Ellen certainly speaks and acts differently in different formal contexts, I demonstrate how two recurring elements—discursive skirting and physical outing—act in dialogue in her various televised performances.

Repetition and reiteration were (and still are) a central theme in Ellen's show, with her daily dances, recurring verbal noises, and catchphrases. I ultimately argue that Ellen's many repetitious behaviors also serve as multiple self-outings. In 2001, Anna McCarthy ("Ellen") suggested that perhaps queer visibility on television was only permissible as spectacle; such televisibility became dangerous to heteronormativity when it presented queer lives and loves as "quotidian" (597). By repeatedly dancing to the same songs and expressing the same verbal tics over and over again, Ellen sought in the opening sequences of her talk show to present the out of the ordinary repeatedly, until its very performance, occurring daily, became unalarming and even infectiously celebratory.

During her ritual opening dance, Ellen looks into the camera, directly addressing the audience, and then follows by breaking the proscenium arch, dancing out into the pulsating, cheering, similarly dancing live studio audience. Her daily dances, set to a handful of uplifting disco, hip-hop, and R&B songs, with their awkward, nonchoreographed moves, together with her wide, toothy grin, seem to proclaim a message of self acceptance: *This is me! I'm great just the way I am, and you can be great just the way you are too!* Her dance moves themselves evoke nostalgia for the gay-steeped, seventies-era culture of disco. While Ellen does not remind her audience of her queerness over and over again verbally (though since 2008 she doesn't avoid the subject, either), Ellen does repeat acts that are both absurd and permissible, causing the most bizarre squawks and awkward dance moves to become a commonplace sight, and a site for pleasure.

Subliminal Rituals

While de Rossi's claim that Ellen was "changing the world" might represent the overstated rhetorical flourish of the then newly lovestruck, de Rossi's use of the word "subliminal," meaning "below the threshold of conscious perception" (*Webster's II New Riverside University Dictionary* 1154), to describe what Ellen was "doing," astutely points to the very *liminality* of Ellen's ritualistic daily dance performances.[4] To put it in other terms, de Rossi is here distinguishing between a *media event* and a repeated *media ritual*. A *media event* is a one-time, idiosyncratic phenomenon that acts as an exception to the usual rules of both television flow and content, and, if planned, is often surrounded by quite a bit of promotional hype (Hubert 31; Anna McCarthy, "Ellen" 593). A repeated *media ritual* also temporarily upends or stretches convention (only to reinstate it); however, it is less outwardly eventful. In fact, it gradually becomes perceived as a part of the normal flow, and signifies through repetition over time or through multiple broadcasts (Couldry 24). The media event punctuates the Nielsen's ratings; the media ritual has the potential to slowly, rather than rapidly, shift consciousnesses through a process of slow audience acclimation to and reinforcement of difference.

Susan J. Hubert called the controversy over Ellen's coming out episode "largely a media-created event;" she noted that "advertising spots went for premium rates, some for as much as 20% more than Ellen's usual $170,000 fee" (31). In "Ellen: Making Queer Television History," Anna McCarthy lists three reasons *Ellen*'s coming-out episode constituted a media event: (1) it was hailed as a first, (2) it altered the flow of the network schedule, and (3) it was described as television history (593). McCarthy argues that although this episode was an initial ratings draw to the network because of the publicity surrounding its bold "step ahead" during a liberal-progressive timeline of television history, the show itself was branded a failure the next season, when it followed television's changing trend in the 1990s from the episodic to what Horace Newcomb called the "cumulative" form (13). The result, *Ellen*'s 1998 practice of mixing in one-off episodes with episodes that advanced overarching plots about Ellen's lesbian love life in a serial fashion, was troubling to Disney-owned ABC, as Anna McCarthy noted in "Ellen:"

> [ABC's president, Robert A.] Iger explained that *Ellen* "became a program about a character who was gay every single week, and...that was too much for people." This statement is noteworthy for the way it opposes queer identity and televisual seriality...Its fear of a quotidian, ongoing lesbian life on television suggests that although the network could support queer television as a spectacular media event, it could not sanction a lesbian invasion of serial television's more modest form of history making, the regularly scheduled weeks of televisual flow. (596)

Ellen DeGeneres now broadcasts an "ongoing lesbian life" that fits into the regular flow, by appearing as a known gay woman on the air each day, every week. She's arguably the woman whose performance of gayness has most saturated the public sphere, given the maelstrom of media coverage on her sexual preference. Indeed, as host of the talk show, DeGeneres is in a relatively prominent position of power, and one in which, rather than being caught up in the "incitement to discourse," prodded to "confess," with her otherness continually under inspection, she controls the discourse (Foucault, *The History of Sexuality* 3–13). On screen, Ellen interrupts, pauses, shifts the subject, she shuts down conversations, she starts them and stops them, *she* formulates the questions. This is not to say that DeGeneres does not perform under the behind-the-scenes control, guidelines, and even potential censorship of the production company and network for which she works; however, her onscreen position of authority and the public's acceptance of her as figurehead are nevertheless meaningful symbolically. Therefore, when examining the meaning of Ellen DeGeneres's performance as host, rather than jumping to label her in or out of the closet, we should consider that her performances may mean something entirely different symbolically—subliminally, if you will—than they do on the level of literal, the explicitly said or not said.

To better grasp Ellen's performance on a symbolic as well as a linguistic level, we must consider her *formal ritual actions* in dialogue with her scripted and improvisational speech. In *Media Rituals: A Critical Approach*, Nick Couldry explains that

> [Rituals] by their repetitive form reproduce categories and patterns of thought in a way that bypasses explicit belief. On the contrary, if made explicit, many of the ideas apparently expressed by these rituals might be rejected or at least called into question; it is their *ritualized* form that enables them to be successfully reproduced without being exposed to questions about their content." (24)

In order for ritual actions to effectively cloak, but still deliver, content, they must be repeated; this repetition allows ritual actions to take on an ambiguity that serves to protect symbolic meaning from becoming surface meaning. Ellen's coming-out dance has been similarly repeated in the first fifteen minutes of every show (from season 1 on), unanchoring its meaning, while effectively performing the extraordinary in the everyday, the queer outside the closet. Literally dancing *out* into the audience, she provides an effective performative pun.

Encoding/Decoding the Dance

When asked in 2005 why Ellen DeGeneres didn't then address her homo-sexuality on her talk show, lesbian actress and screenwriter Guinevere Turner (*Go Fish*, *The L Word*) declared emphatically,"How could you dance like that and not be gay? That's a way of saying with every opening repre-sentation, I'm gay!" (Turner, personal interview). Marusya Bociurkiw, in a 2005 critical essay published in *Canadian Woman Studies*, concurred with Turner's view that Ellen's lesbianism is palpable in her dancing:

> As the music, usually hip hop, is played, Ellen's body is on display in a manner that is decidedly not heteronormative. Here DeGeneres displays the grace and confidence that her accessible, self-deprecating "kook" act disavows. DeGeneres looks like a butch lesbian dancing alone, in a club. (176)

These interpretations of Ellen's now-branded dance moves are just that, individualized readings of a polysemic text. Furthermore, "what a dyke dancing looks like" is a nearly impossible thing to put one's finger on. Just as lesbians are a diverse, rather than homogeneous group, composed of women of varying ethnicities, cultural backgrounds, styles, classes, gender presenta-tions, and so forth, their dance moves likely vary enormously. However, as a general consensus remains among these readings that "something's queer" here, I try to show, through examining prior precedents of Ellen expressing herself physically—whether through physical humor or through dance—that not only does her opening dance with herself (and thus with the viewer) represent a daily declaration of queer identity, but that she has coded it to mean exactly that.

Rather than revisit the coming-out media event of the "Puppy Episode" of *Ellen* (4.22 and 4.23, April 30, 1997), which has been explored in depth by Anna McCarthy, Susan J. Hubert, and Steven Capsuto, among others, I will concentrate instead on two pre-coming-out episodes from the second season of *Ellen*—texts that, like her talk show, operate doubly. In "The Fix Up" (2.5, October 19, 1994), Ellen's dance moves are first foregrounded, and in "Thirty Kilo Man," part 1 and 2 (2.23, May 10, 1995; 2.24, May 17, 1995), her character has a heterosexual love affair that reads as unmistak-ably queer.

Elevator Music on Early Ellen

Early *Ellen* is best described as ABC's version of *Seinfeld*'s sitcom about noth-ing, since both half-hour shows center around known stand-up comedians and their witty banter about insignificant, repetitious, or everyday matters with friends. During the three seasons prior to Ellen DeGeneres's/Ellen Morgan's doubly momentous 1997 coming out, Ellen's character on the middling-rated sitcom was consistently stuck in a weekly cycle of dates-gone-wrong with guys, who, for an array of incidental and sometimes extravagantly bizarre reasons, just don't fit for Ellen. In "The Gladiators" (2.19, March 1, 1995), for instance, Ellen's new beau, Nitro, a gladiator from the then-popular television show *American Gladiators*,[5] is snapped away from her by an ultra-buff woman (Ice), leading Ellen, the bookstore owner, to jealously beat the pumped-up woman to a pulp with a padded lance.

The sitcom's season with the most overtly heterosexual story lines, the second, is also the season with the most queer subtext. Disney would not okay the idea of Ellen Morgan's coming out until more than a year later, when blatant hints began to be worked into the weekly scripts (Gross 157). Ellen's obsessive man-shopping in season 2 is painted by the writers and producers as downright absurd, but what will serve as the alternative isn't quite clear yet either (it turns out to be asexuality, in most of season 3, before Ellen faces her queer identity). A journalist for *The San Francisco Examiner*, Joyce Millman, caught on early. In the spring of 1995, in a column entitled "The Sitcom That Dare Not Speak Its Name," the television critic prematurely outed Ellen Morgan: "As a single gal sitcom, *Ellen* doesn't make any sense at all, until you view it through the looking glass where the unspoken subtext becomes the main point. Then Ellen is transformed into one of TV's savviest, funniest, slyist shows. Ellen Morgan is a closet lesbian" (B1).

Season 2's episode "The Fix Up" (2.5, October 19, 1994) opens with Ellen inside an elevator—the enclosed space that arguably acts as the show's metaphorical stand-in for a closet. Ellen's adventures in or while waiting for an elevator are a recurring trope on the show. Given the sitcom's frequent meta-references to sitcom history (see McCarthy, "Ellen" 607–614), perhaps this trope, seen throughout the second season, is also a tip of the hat to the historically common "meat locker" sitcom scenario, wherein people with differences get stuck in a small space, often a meat locker or an elevator, and overcome their differences (Sconce 104–105). In this case, the elevator's only other passenger exits and, finding herself alone, Ellen openly acknowledges the R&B playing over the loud speakers, Aretha Franklin's "Respect," by first tapping her feet, then swinging from side to side and lip-synching. As the song builds to crescendo, Ellen is observed flailing, rocking her head along to the words, and jumping into the air, landing with thumps. As audience members, we are in anticipation for the elevator doors to suddenly open and for Ellen to be found out. Instead, Franklin's rousing tune halts abruptly and a male authoritarian voice comes over the loud speakers.

"Excuse me ma'am, this is Security," the voice interrupts. "Please refrain from jumping in the elevator."

The camera offers a shot from above, looking down at Ellen, as she immediately looks up to the speaker, with a petrified deer-in-the-headlights acknowledgment that she's being surveyed. She then cradles her head down in her hand, in embarrassment, before the camera cuts away.

This scene might be read as being divorced from any queer subtext, as merely silly high jinx in an elevator, with Ellen as the 1990s Lucy Ricardo, always getting herself into a new kind of trouble. However, the larger text of the sitcom suggests that the elevator is a contained closet, within which Ellen Morgan can finally release herself and be happy with who she is, until she is again reminded, reprimanded by a voice from outside, that others do not approve of her lifestyle. This is particularly suggested by the content of the dialogue between Ellen and her mother that immediately follows, and furthermore by the theme (failed heterosexual dating, what else?) of "The Fix Up."

In the scene that follows, Ellen's mother asks her a question over coffee that recurs, rephrased, throughout the series: "So, are you seeing anyone these days?"

When Ellen's answer implies no, her mom continues in full fuss mode: "I just worry about you. You're not immortal...I just want you to be happy."

Ellen retorts, "You know, it's possible to be happy without a man."

"Must you joke about everything?" her mom returns, and then promptly tries to fix Ellen up with someone she grew up with. Described by Ellen as the "weird" kid in the neighborhood who ate bugs, the character, it turns out, has matured into an adult man who isn't peculiar at all; in fact, Ellen seems to find him quite charming. In a plot reversal, he ends up finding Ellen entirely "weird," through the usual comedy of errors. "The Fix Up" is a stereotypical example of the pre-coming-out plotline, wherein events beyond Ellen's control, but generally propelled at least partially by her neurotic behavior, spiral, causing Ellen ultimately to be rejected by her possible heterosexual love interest, rather than force the thirty-something to own up to the fact that she's not truly interested in the first place. There are also instances where Ellen rejects men; these generally involve Ellen's discovery that the man she thought was a dreamboat has an impossible-to-stand trait.

The "date that always goes wrong" plot is finally frustrated and complicated in the two-part season 2 finale, "Thirty Kilo Man" (2.23 and 2.24, May 10, 1995 and May 17, 1995). The first part of the finale opens in Ellen's apartment, with Ellen's mother asking her about her plans for the weekend.

When Ellen makes a joke about getting a "Chia Date," so that she can sprinkle it and "watch it grow," Ellen's mom pulls out the claws: "You know what the problem with you is, Ellen? You're too picky. You always look for a man's faults. Greg was too nice, Roger watched too much TV, Carl was a drag."

"Drag king, mother," Ellen corrects, "I know I nitpick..."

As the episode continues, Dan, a man she was interested in during an earlier episode but rejected after discovering that he delivered pizza for a living, returns from Italy with a new, more prestigious job. The first ever return "beard" is also the one that actually ends up in bed with Ellen. A "next-day" scenario finds Ellen strutting out from her bedroom in a robe, hair mussed, puffing on an imaginary cigarette. Dan emerges, fully dressed and primped, and she kisses him, mumbling, "no fair, you brushed your teeth."

"Sorry," he practically sings. They touch their way into the living-room and in full soap-opera pitch Dan gushes: "I never want this feeling to end. Ellen Morgan, I think I'm falling in love with you."

In this scene, Ellen is scripted and choreographed into the position of the stereotypical man in a classic romance, who swaggers out of the bedroom; Dan is the stereotypical woman, who rushes to say effusive things, to say "I love you" right away.

Later, when Dan comes back from work, Ellen backs him into the couch and gets on top, kissing him. His beeper starts to vibrate in his pants; she pauses to say "What's that?" and then keeps kissing him, pressing into him, moaning, "You are such a considerate man!"

She grabs the cordless phone from the coffee table. "Okay, it stopped. What's your number?" This joke on his beeper as vibrator, a device implied as more pleasurable than perhaps his penis, again with the classic roles switched (Ellen as the "horny" one), plays on the notion that, although he is a man, they are in a "lesbian" affair. This joke is toyed with even further in part two of the finale, when he figuratively "brings a U-Haul," moving in with her right away, and they spend all waking moments together. In their every dialogue and physical interaction, Ellen plays butch to Dan's femme, and the season uses the potential of their hetero-homo romance continuing as a cliff-hanger to the next season.

Here the sitcom *Ellen* playfully *queers* heterosexual scenarios, since it cannot yet show a queer one. Ellen's otherness is continually the underlying gag. In "Three Strikes" (2.21, March 29, 1995), Ellen, forced under court order to live with her parents, is forced to wear a dress by her mother. As she walks through work, the laugh track goes wild; Ellen in a flowery dress in which she looks awkward is a joke in and of itself. Ellen Morgan's queerness, and, really, Ellen DeGeneres's queerness, is what always exceeds the text, both with her dates that don't work, and with the one, Dan, that does.

Heterosexual Talk

Ellen's closeted verbal discourse around the topic of her sexuality on the early seasons of *Ellen: The Ellen DeGeneres Show* functioned similarly to the coded scripting of her pre-out counterpart Ellen Morgan, on *Ellen*, setting up yet another coming out: open discussion of her own lesbian marriage and of other explicitly queer topics on the talk show. I have focused so heavily on the most heterosexual-themed (closeted) run of her earlier fictional show as a comparative tool, in order to put these episodes in dialogue with telling discursive moments on season 2 of her talk show.

Generally, when the topic of her own sexuality was broached in early live shows, Ellen DeGeneres would defer the question within a heterosexual paradigm in which straight desire was the main point of reference, the norm. Like a pre-"Puppy Episode" Ellen Morgan, who couldn't seem to find the right man, Ellen DeGeneres as a fledgling talk host rarely enunciated the nature of her desire on air, but always enunciated, rather, *what her desire was not*.

Two live tapings of *Ellen: The Ellen DeGeneres Show* from 2005 demonstrate this point. In a November 10, 2005, interview with Jake Gyllenhaal, the young actor appears on stage with 400 white roses for Ellen to congratulate her on her 400th live talk show (episode 3.49).

When they sit down together, Ellen immediately declares Jake "cute" and gives him a publicity suggestion: "more shots with your shirt off," she says, showing a clip of him naked from the waist up in *Jarhead*.

Her studio audience, mostly women, cheer at the top of their lungs.

"You should take it off right now," Ellen urges. "You don't have to…It's only going to help you." Gyllenhaal unbuttons his top button, then closes it again. "It's my 400th show," begs Ellen. "Roses are sweet and everything…I'll give 'em back if you'll take your shirt off." Gyllenhaal turns bright red and laughs, clearly bashful.

Ellen here mimics Rosie O'Donnell's passing as straight. Rosie O'Donnell, who came out as a lesbian *after* her popular television talk show wrapped, perfected passing by regularly harping on her ambiguously sexualized obsession with *Top Gun* star Tom Cruise. Gyllenhaal is verbally worshiped like Cruise; however, Ellen camps the faked crush even further, demonstrating her passing clearly as shtick. Acting similarly as a facilitator for straight women in their fantasies, DeGeneres's playacting has a distinct difference from O'Donnell's: DeGeneres's homosexuality is a known secret—a secret the audience knows in an iconic way—and she trades on this knowledge to make her interaction funny.

"It's not for me," Ellen asserts, looking Gyllenhaal in the eye, smiling. He can barely talk; he refuses to budge, but good-naturedly. "It's not for me!" she insists again, making it clear, as if he didn't get it the first time, that she's not trying to sexually harass him; *besides, she's gay.* They share an understanding glance.

"Are you single right now? I should ask that. Not for me, again, *I don't care*, but the women in the audience want to know."

After the commercial break, Gyllenhaal loosens the collar of his shirt and exposes the top of his chest.

The sustained tease of Gyllenhaal's potential strip that never happens acts as a promotional para-text for the 2005 film *Jarhead*. Ellen even spells this out: "if you want to see what the rest of that looks like you have to go see the movie *Jarhead*." Ellen focuses entirely on *Jarhead* and on her flirtation with Gyllenhaal about taking off his shirt. She gives his other about-to-released-film, *Brokeback Mountain,* an ever-so-quick mention at the end, but does not ask Gyllenhaal one question about this "film with Heath Ledger" (as she summarizes it), nor does she mention that the film deals with a homosexual romance between Gyllenhaal's and Ledger's characters.

While implying that her own homosexuality gives her the social mobility to be so openly cheeky with him, without it constituting any kind of gender upheaval or sexual come-on, Ellen has, in this exchange, played butch to Gyllenhaal's femme, much like Ellen Morgan did with Dan, placing him in the position of the looked at, the desirable one. She pimps Gyllenhaal, inverting gender roles, using sexuality and gender against access of sexuality. She insists, however, on her lack of desire and does not name why it is that she's not attracted to him—that is supposedly understood, it goes without saying.

Gyllenhaal gets visibly uncomfortable with his position as object, but becomes visibly more comfortable when Ellen finally asks if he's single, since "the women in the audience want to know," because she's offering him the space of normal heterosexual identity by default. Therefore, she intelligently also skirts the question of *his* sexuality. Here Ellen comes out through negation, although a denial of a heterosexual desire for one person does not necessarily imply homosexuality. The way she addresses the subject matter is very crafty—to those that do not want to be reminded of the nature of her desires, she does not dare speak its name; to those that do, she is, at least, honest.

In a special event edition of *Ellen: The Ellen DeGeneres Show* that aired on November 30, 2005, celebrating Ellen's 25th anniversary as a stand-up comedian, a similar incident takes place (3.63). Ellen's anniversary special revolves around clips shown from Ellen's career as a stand-up comedian, allowing her to poke fun at her many bad haircuts. Guest celebrities visit who vouch for Ellen's beginnings. Jay Leno, for instance, discusses getting Ellen her first gig on *The Johnny Carson Show*, a show that obviously inspired her own. Her first Carson appearance was featured most prominently during the hour, and the fact that she was the first female comedian ever invited to be interviewed by Carson after her act was underscored.

Ellen has played assorted on-screen and onstage roles during the course of her career, portraying an actress and television personality as well as a stand-up comedian. In fact, she is perhaps *most* famous for her role as Ellen Morgan on *Ellen*. Strangely, however, her sitcom was conspicuously missing from this retrospective. (Consider, for instance, a retrospective on Jerry Seinfeld that would fail to mention *Seinfeld*.) By focusing only on Ellen's stand-up career, not only were her sitcom and her coming out conveniently occluded from the history of Ellen that the talk show offers, but no clips with *any* gay content were shown. Ellen rehistoricizes herself as a stand-up comedian first and foremost, and an asexual one at that.

David Spade joins Ellen on this episode, and we learn through their conversation that they met 20 years earlier when the two traveled comedy circuits together, Spade opening for Ellen's headlining act. Spade admits a secret: "We used to do some of these gigs together...I had a big crush on her...then I got the news."

Ellen becomes visibly embarrassed and just laughs for a long while, while Spade turns it into a joke: "What it was, was the fact that you had a Walkman...and a *sweet* mullet."

"I thought you were adorable," Ellen finally responds. "No interest other than the fact that you were adorable. Although I did...I had a crush on you and you know it."

She goes right from this statement into a clip of David Spade's vintage comedy. Those of us in on the joke read David's crush on Ellen as real, and Ellen's crush on David as purely platonic.

Again, here Ellen discursively frames her queerness through expressing what she *doesn't desire*, and even that in a very mixed up way, as is evident in the statement, "No interest other than the fact that you were adorable." *What does that mean?* Ellen did not outright deny her homosexuality during the early seasons of her talk show; rather, when it came up, she deflected mention of "gayness" with the double-speak and coded strategies of her pre-coming-out sitcom character. At first, DeGeneres seemed comfortable expressing her nonheterosexuality on air (in a specific instance—so that it could be read as "She just doesn't like *him*"), but not her *homosexuality* directly.

John Limon points out that DeGeneres's strategy of "skirting" is not only admitted, but is defined, in her 1996 book *My Point . . . . And I Do Have One*:

> Someone recently wrote a letter . . . asking "Why does Ellen DeGeneres always wear pants and never skirts?" I'm guessing that the person who wrote that letter meant skirt, a noun signifying an article of clothing, and not skirt, a verb defined as, "to evade or elude (as a topic of conversation) by circumlocution." Because, if they mean the verb skirt, well, they're dead wrong. I'm always skirting. (DeGeneres 93; quoted in Limon 115)

Limon identifies DeGeneres's skirting as a form of "escapist art" that refuses "to put all kidding aside," and where "what is made visible . . . is evasion" (116–117). Her verbal skirts act as denials of reality that constantly rely on reality as their vanishing point. Rather than expressing information that can be pinned down or literally understood, she often replaces objective "truths" with tangential flights of fancy, distractions, and wordplay, while presenting the journey of the skirt itself as having *subjective* and transient values—of imagination, pleasure, and possibility.

Limon lyrically asks of DeGeneres's skirting: "Is knowledge of the body repressed or unlearned? Is the body itself decoded or disclaimed?" (121). He dubs DeGeneres "an inverse Lenny Bruce, whose shame existed to be displayed as pride" (121). The notion that DeGeneres's *pride* (with all of the meanings attached to that word) exists to be *displayed* as shame, as the case may be, is a savvy way to view beneath her early linguistic skirts. If skirting is DeGeneres's verbal strategy for, at least on the surface, distancing her comedy from the bodily, from *her* body and the material consequences of the world, while leaking other meanings, DeGeneres's physical displays, especially her dances, convey and rely on utter embodiment: the body engaged in ritual.

Interpretive Dance

As of this writing in 2012, Ellen brings up LGBT issues casually or even pointedly—often to advocate for gay marriage or to criticize hate crimes. Speaking about her gay identity, the particulars of her personal love life, her iconicity for the gay cause, and her coming-out sitcom and its cancellation, however, have been tasks constantly required of Ellen DeGeneres by the press years after *Ellen* was off the air. Both outing oneself and constantly being asked to speak about it, to re-out oneself, again and again, are patterned on the act of the confession. The confession, as described by Michel Foucault, is part of the "transformation of sex into discourse" and "the dissemination and reinforcement of heterogeneous sexualities;" both are "linked together with the help of the central element of a confession that compels individuals to articulate their sexual peculiarity" (*The History of Sexuality* 61). At some point then, Ellen's constant "incitement to discourse" serves only to show Ellen's sexual peculiarity, to highlight her otherness (Foucault 3–13).

Ellen's initial choice to deflect or redirect the question of her homosexuality in potentially heterosexual discursive terms on her talk show offered the comedienne one strategy to remove herself from the confessional paradigm, wherein an implied authority outside of herself (like the voice in Ellen Morgan's elevator), "the one who listens" (in the case of her show, the audience) was the implied judge or cheerleader of her private life. Instead, Ellen *performed* her queerness through her daily dances—illustrating both her control over what is expressed and her pleasure in expressing it. Here Ellen presents her queerness, individuality, difference, otherness, in an expressive act that broadcasts her self-love, and as part of a daily ritual that is ultimately not all about her. Her daily dance, which continues in today's broadcasts, also becomes a boundary-crossing ritual shared with all, where she encourages others (her studio audience and viewers at home) to join her—to get up and dance *themselves*. For Ellen, dancing with oneself becomes dancing with the watching world, fulfilling the wish of the final refrain of the 1980s Billy Idol tune, "Dancing with Myself:" "If I had a chance, I'd ask the world to dance." Dancing with oneself on television *presents* a dance *of* oneself to be received, shared, and potentially reciprocated.

Opening the stand-up special *Ellen DeGeneres: The Beginning*, which first aired on cable channel HBO on July 23, 2000, Ellen briefly addressed her coming-out saga before performing a dance about the very subject (set to disco music that devolves into chants of "nah nah, nah *nah*, nah"). A comedy special such as this one, on a pay cable network like HBO, offered DeGeneres a markedly less censored venue in which to express herself than was available on network television, either daytime or prime-time. In her introduction, Ellen gave an extremely telling speech that I'll end with, because I believe it not only introduces Ellen's specific dance performance that night, but frames why she established a discursive closet in early incarnations of her talk show, as well as why she established her soon-to-be-daily dance as out. Speaking her mind about what should be said, or not said, about her sexuality after *Ellen*, Ellen successfully encoded the media ritual of dancing that was later to appear on *Ellen: The Ellen DeGeneres Show* as a performance of queerness that expresses meaning where words have sometimes been found to fail:

> Since I made the decision to come out three years ago, my life has been very interesting…I knew that people would want me to talk about it. Some people may not want me to talk about it. So I went back and forth, trying to decide should I talk about it, should I not talk about it, and ultimately I decided: No, I don't want to talk about it. It's been talked about enough, what can I say? I feel it would be best expressed through interpretive dance.

Notes

1. Ellen came out as gay in real life on the cover of *Time* (April 14, 1997) and in character on the sitcom *Ellen* in the "Puppy Episode" (April 30, 1997).
2. In *The History of Sexuality,* vol. 1, Michel Foucault posits censorship as a discursively *productive* act, 12–13; 84.
3. I use the word *televisibility* to refer to instances of visibility on television by queer subjects.
4. Victor Turner asserts that the use of the word *liminal,* "of processes, phenomena and persons in large-scale complex societies…must in the main be metaphorical" (Turner, *From Ritual to Theatre* 29). Couldry recommends adopting Turner's term *liminoid,* meaning "liminal-like" (Couldry, *Media Rituals* 33). As *liminoidity* seems particularly awkward, I retain the word *liminality* here, intending it to be understood metaphorically.
5. *American Gladiators* (1989–1997, CBS) featured body builders competing against contestants on an obstacle course. Nitro was a regular gladiator and sometime cohost on the sensationalistic game show. Featuring *American Gladiators* on *Ellen* obviously served as an ABC-CBS cross-promotion.

CHAPTER 2

Mommy's Got a Gal-Pal: The Victimized Lesbian Mother in the Made-for-TV Movie

Kelly Kessler

The 1990s ushered in a proliferation of televised representations of gays and lesbians on American television. We all jumped up and down when *Entertainment Weekly* (*Will &*) *Grace*-d its cover with "A Special Report: Gay Hollywood 2000," depicting a happy cast of *Will & Grace*, a pleased (though then unemployed) Ellen, *Survivor*'s naked Richard Hatch, and a decontextualized Allison Hannigan/Willow of *Buffy the Vampire Slayer* (*Entertainment Weekly* cover, October 6, 2000). Along with this increasing collection of recurring gay, lesbian, and bisexual characters in weekly series, the often-ghettoized genre of the made-for-TV movie followed suit in depicting sexual minorities. Both broadcast and cable television answered the call for lesbian stories, airing films such as *Serving in Silence* (NBC, 1995), *Two Mothers for Zachary* (ABC, 1996), *Gia* (Showtime, 1998), *If These Walls Could Talk 2* (HBO, 2000), *The Truth About Jane* (Lifetime, 2000), *Common Ground* (Showtime, 2000), and *What Makes a Family?* (Lifetime, 2001). A noticeable trend in these films was their adherence to what some have critiqued in the television movie: the personalization of the political. Most specifically, network and nonpay cable channels tended to focus their lesbian narratives on issues of family, specifically motherhood. Even *Serving in Silence* often decenters the narrative of Grethe Cammermeyer's battle with institutionalized military homophobia to place the focus solidly on her interactions with and the strength of her four sons. Indisputably, occurrences of gay and lesbian characters in all facets of television had increased during this period; however, just what was at stake in such mainstream representations of the dramatized lesbian as matriarch?

In this chapter, I examine mainstream representations of the lesbian as victimized mother in the American television docudrama at the turn of the millennium, specifically *Two Mothers for Zachary* (1996) and *What Makes a Family?* (2001). Made-for-TV movies (hereafter MFTVM), in these cases based on real-life events, have suffered much criticism from those who question the political efficacy of the personalization of the political. However, these stories exceed the expectations of docudrama by troubling the issues of homophobic politics while addressing their audiences via an overt personalization of and manipulation by the films' narratives. These films still fall within a contested space; although their politics may skate past the criticism often leveled at their like, the heterocentric politics and economic imperatives of the post-network era still taint what could be seen as progressive representations.

While these films render explicit the pervasive homophobia and hypocritical notions of family that guide our justice system, they simultaneously construct a limited and legitimized notion of *The* Lesbian. By exploring the narratives, true stories, and popular reviews of these two films, I examine the possible ramifications of the clustered presentations of the victimized lesbian mother. What types of politics are rendered explicit in these MFTVMs? How do they use emotion to forward the goal of positive lesbian identification? What types of actresses continually portray them and how? By investigating the messiness of issues such as fact/fiction blurring, star persona, and class, I hope to add to the existing critique and commentary on the television docudrama. Finally, I uncover *The* Lesbian who, through her repeated representation and call for identification, becomes legitimized, while other types of lesbians are made invisible and/or inferior.

The Films

The two films I have chosen base their narratives on the true-life stories of women who have lost their children at the hands of a homophobic judicial system. *Two Mothers for Zachary* stars Valerie Bertinelli as Jody Shaffell, a lower-working-class Virginia woman who loses custody of her son, Zachary, to her mother, Nancy (Vanessa Redgrave), who disapproves of Jody's lesbian relationship and partner (Colleen Flynn). Starting with Zachary's birth and Jody's rejection of the biological father, the film follows Jody's hetero-party-girl shortcomings (indescriminate sex, heavy drinking, and child neglect), burgeoning lesbianism as she meets Maggie (Colleen Flynn), abuse at the hands of the local townspeople and the religious right, and courtroom ordeal as she repeatedly fights for and loses her son.

Screenwriter Linda Vorhees based the film on the story of Sharon and Kay Bottoms. Sharon lost custody of her son Tyler in March of 1993, after moving in with her lover, April Wade. Over the next five years, Bottoms repeatedly appealed for custody and for more flexible visitation than every other weekend from 6 p.m. Friday to 5 p.m. Sunday ("ACLU Fact Sheet"). All visitations must occur at Sharon's home, and under no circumstances may Tyler have contact, physical or by telephone, with Wade (Henry 16).[1]

What Makes a Family? tells the story of Janine Nielssen (Brooke Shields) and Sandra Cataldi (Cherry Jones). Janine and Sandra, after committing to each other in a public ceremony, decide to start a family. Shortly after the child's birth and christening, a doctor diagnoses Sandra (the biological mother) with systemic lupus. The film recounts the courtship, birth, and battle, with lupus in flashbacks as Janine relates the story to her lawyer (Whoopi Goldberg) and fights to regain custody of her daughter. After Sandra's death, her parents (Ann Meara and Al Waxman), who by Florida law are legally entitled to the child, petition for and receive custody of five-year-old Heather. The film examines Janine's battle for and eventual winning of Heather's guardianship.

This narrative is based on the story of Janine Ratcliffe and Joan Pearlman. After eight years of commitment, Joan gave birth to their baby, Kristin, in 1979, just prior to being diagnosed with systemic lupus. In 1984, Joan succumbed to the disease. Initially, the Pearlman grandparents signed over temporary guardianship to Janine, but shortly thereafter they covertly filed for adoption and attempted to prevent Janine from gaining any contact with her daughter. Over the next five years, Janine lost custody and eventually regained guardianship of the child, a groundbreaking occurrence in the infamously homophobic Florida (Price; Benkov 214–227).

Genre and the Docudrama

The MFTVM and associated docudrama remain contentious spaces on the television landscape. They came to prominence in the 1970s as networks realized that commissioning their own films was cheaper than purchasing the rights to theatrical releases. The first MFTVM aired on NBC in 1966. By the early 1970s, movies made expressly for television outnumbered those crossing from the big to small screen (Gomery, "Television" 125–126). Although the network MFTVM has waned in prominence, the genre finds a voice through endless Lifetime movies and broadcast and cable "special event" films, and these films still produce the same controversial blending of fact and fiction that their 1970s counterparts did. Scholars and producers alike have criticized and lauded the genre for its possible effects on the viewing public. For example, scholars such as Todd Gitlin argue that the MFTVM focuses on the personal effects of social issues. "The triumphs of American TV naturalism, in fiction as in the news, is [*sic*] the revelation of familiar figures visibly coping with public troubles, right here in the living room…But the price of familiarity is diminishment of the scale of things" (Gitlin 192). Douglas Gomery describes the genre as "[fulfilling] a particular need: topical entertainment reaffirming basic values and beliefs" (*"Brian's Song"* 87). The MFTVM negotiates the attraction of large audiences via topical narratives, the reification of societal norms, and the avoidance of overt political statement by "telling small stories" and focusing on tight, character-driven narratives (87–91).

Lawrence Jarvik argues, "by involving the audience directly in the social dramas on screen, the television movie serves to claim by its very fact of existence that ordinary folk must participate equally in the deliberation of the issues of our time" (80). The same "small stories" seen by some as manipulating audiences into uncritically accepting hegemonic social mores are seen here as Everyman's access to the social system. Furthermore, producers and writers have hailed the docudrama as a valuable educational tool. David Wolper, producer of the highly successful *Roots* (1977), replied to scholars who criticized the genre by suggesting, "…while you professors may feel that the audience doesn't learn everything from what they see, I feel we are generating at least the possibility that people will further look into the subject matter" (quoted in Jarvik 88).

Personalization and Politicization of the Lesbian Mother

As critics of the genre have noted, the television docudrama often reconfigures stories of social unrest in such ways that they can be understood as personal journeys or triumphs. By focusing on the trials and triumphs of the individual, pervasive social inequities are rendered invisible or deprioritized in light of the more compelling story of personal experience. I believe these two films—*Two Mothers for Zachary* and *What Makes a Family?*— take steps forward in the cross-pollination of the personal and the political. While they admittedly latch onto topical narratives of an oppressed minority and of family tragedies, they simultaneously embark on an investigation of the underlying and explicit politics that drive the stories. By evoking tropes of the mother-child bond, the primacy of the nuclear family, and the American judicial system, I believe this combination of familial and political investigation sets the scene for a more complete presentation of social injustice. Furthermore, the films' acknowledgment of their factual roots attempts a prohibition of emotional distanciation or dismissal of contemporary unjust politics as merely fictional.

Star Persona

One way in which MFTVMs create an emotional link to their protagonists is by the casting of popular actresses who have established themselves in the cultural consciousness as either similarly victimized or sympathetic characters. In *Stars*, Richard Dyer states, "Despite the extravagant lifestyle of stars...what is important about the stars, especially in their particularity, is their typicality or representativeness. Stars, in other words, relate to the social types of society" (47). Dyer notes how the popular construction of these stars leads audiences to identify with them in terms of desirable social types. Additionally, he explains how these constructed images then work to create fictional characters imbued with the characteristics associated with the performer's star image (126). The activation of social types and their encrustation in fictionalized characters described by Dyer occurs in the star persona of Brooke Shields in *What Makes a Family?* and also in that of Valerie Bertinelli in *Two Mothers For Zachary.*

Audiences know Shields from roles such as the innocent young castaway who discovers her "natural" sexuality in *Blue Lagoon* (1980), the sexy young Calvin Klein jeans model (1980), and the goofy yet sexy Susan in *Suddenly Susan* (1996–2000). Surrounding her *Blue Lagoon* and modeling success, Shields made several appearances on overly wholesome vehicles such as Bob Hope specials and *Circus of the Stars*. In addition, Shields has graced covers of magazines such as *People, US, Vogue, Sassy, Glamour,* and *Cosmopolitan.* These types of acting jobs and publicity solidly attach her to a wholesome, straight, sexy star image. Similarly, Bertinelli came to fame as everyone's favorite girl next door, Barbara Cooper, in the 1970s situation comedy *One Day at a Time* (1975–1984), and graced magazine covers such as *TV Guide, US, Young Miss,* and *People* during the run of the show. A top-rated sitcom, written/produced/created by Norman Lear, *One Day at a Time* showcased Bertinelli as a young, bubbly, pigtailed tomboy-cum-glamorous young woman. After the show ended, Bertinelli gained prominence as a major MFTVM actress with such films as *Rockabye* (1986), *Taken Away* (1989), and *In a Child's Name* (1991), all of which depict her attempting to retrieve a child in one way or another. Despite her 1981 marriage to rocker Eddie Van Halen, her acting roles combine to create the image of a wholesome victim.

For both actresses, their star personas aid in the creation of characters that beg sympathetic identification. As is evident in newspaper coverage of the films, their images cannot be separated from their performances or inclusion in the films. Reviewers refer to Shields as "far beyond her teen-star 'beauty' days," "playing against her goofily frilly type," and as "show[ing] here that she could be the first child star since Jodie Foster to become a real actress" (Smith A11; Wertheimer E10; Rosenfeld C1). Similarly, reviews refer to Bertinelli as both not being able to "disguise her magnificent cuteness" and "having thankfully lost a lot of her cutesy ways" (*Two Mothers and Others*," Y03; Vorhees 2). *Newsday* states that Bertinelli "has become a regular TV-movie diva over the years, playing a variety of roles while always retaining her essential Valerie-ness" (Kelleher 3). Originally defined as adhering to desirable mainstream values of fun, youth, beauty, vivacity, and righteousness, the subsequent roles of both stars would, according to Dyer, retain the values attached to their greater public image (126).

Even if described as surpassing them, the actresses still remain attached to their prior constructions. Consequently, both Bertinelli's Jody and Shields's Janine enter the diegesis with popular sympathy on their sides. Rather than representations of social pariahs and sexual deviants, their most popular performances were imbued with traditional American values. Consequently, by casting such well-known and established stars to play the roles of the main victimized lesbians, the films' creators release these stories into a social consciousness that must negotiate the tension between preconceived notions of the lesbian characters and traditional social mores connected to the actresses. Bertinelli's and Shields's personas thereby complicate the ongoing process of character/star identification or disidentification.

Mother-Child Bond

While, in the tradition of the television docudrama, these films investigate social problems (in this case sexual minority rights and homophobia) through the lens of personal experience, they simultaneously force an investigation of the politics that created these stories. In both cases, the films place a major focus on the American judicial system, each providing a critique of its homophobic politics and policies. I believe this critique possesses the potential to be effective— first, because of the films' humanization of the lesbian mother via her previously addressed star proxy and second, because of the protagonists' attachment to motherhood and estrangement by their own mothers. Textual and extratextual materials inextricably link motherhood to that which society deems as natural and necessary.

Attempting to further engage the viewing public, both narratives activate and renegotiate the notion of the mother-child bond. Despite the rising American divorce rate and the changing of gendered expectations regarding domestic roles, the naturalness of the interdependence of mother and child still stands at the center of American expectations of normative social relations. Consequently, the narratives tug at the heartstrings by throwing this social expectation into jeopardy. In both films, the relationship of mother and child comes into question in multiple ways, in terms of the lesbian as both mother and child. At the center of each story is a mother who may or may not lose her child; however, paralleling the threatened loss of her child is her symbolic loss of a mother. In both films, heterosexual mothers are depicted as maliciously damaging their children; because the heterosexual mothers' rejection of and damage to their daughters precedes and exceeds the circumstances surrounding the daughter's lesbianism, conservative viewers may be swayed to disidentify with the otherwise seemingly righteous mothers/grandmothers. Whereas removing the child from a "perverse" home may seem morally just to some, the heterosexual mothers' other actions may not be as easily defensible.

In the case of *Two Mothers for Zachary*, the grandmother, Nancy, claims her motives are to remove the child from an unhealthy home, but the film simultaneously constructs her as a mother who had herself failed to protect her own child. Shortly after moving in with Maggie, Jody seeks anger therapy from a psychiatrist, only to return home concerned with different issues. The narrative is unclear as to how she reaches this decision, but after the session she decides that she must confront her mother about the childhood molestation she suffered at the hands of her mother's live-in boyfriend, Harlan. Nancy initially refuses to believe the accusation, and upon Jody's threat to keep Zachary away from her house and from Harlan, Nancy pursues custody based on Jody's lesbianism, also accusing her of abuse. Shortly after the judge grants Nancy custody of Zachary, she denies Jody visitation.

> *Nancy*: I'm doin' this because I love Zach, because there is true love in my heart.
> *Jody*: You call this love. Geez, you're taking me to court. You're keeping my son from me. Mama, what about me? I'm still your daughter!
> *Nancy*: As long as you're with her, you're not my daughter.

Blatantly rejecting Jody, Nancy has now not only failed Jody during her childhood, but continues to play the natural role of supportive mother in Jody's adulthood unsuccessfully. Consequently, the narrative simultaneously positions Jody's unstable standing as mother and daughter, exemplified as she screams for her son, as her mother and police drag him away.

Similarly, *What Makes a Family?* presents Janine as the damaged daughter. Upon meeting Sandy, she describes an incident from her childhood when her parents, in a premature homophobic response, punish her for admiring a female classmate's hair, an act that she describes as causing lasting trauma. After this early establishment of her parents as unsupportive and homophobic, Janine discusses her lesbianism and impending motherhood with them. As she attempts to assume the role of mother, she becomes a rejected daughter. Her parents, portrayed as snobbish bluebloods and set apart from the rest of the characters by their social position and residence in an upper-class home, coldly reject her.

> *Father*: You come into our home and throw this in our faces!
> *Janine*: You're my family...
> *Father*: If you want to live the way you do, that's one thing, but don't you dare...You expect me to stand here and congratulate you, is that it? You want me to tell you it's okay? Well it's not!
> *Mother*: It's not natural, Janine!

Sandra's parents, who had stepped in early on in the film as her surrogate family, also hurl vicious homophobic slurs at Janine as they attempt to gain custody of Heather. After stating, "I always wanted another daughter" at the wedding, Mr. Cataldi explodes, "We do not want her around those kind of people!" after filing for custody of Heather following Sandra's death.

In both of these cases, the film uses the accepted normalcy of the mother-child bond and the repeated disruption of that normalcy through either the grandmother's dismissal of or attack of the daughter in order to draw an emotional response when the lesbian mother loses her child. She emerges as a double victim, not allowed to carry out her natural roles of either mother or of daughter. I believe it is this double disruption that encourages the placement of sympathy on the protagonists.

In both cases, the conflict comes to a head when the films embrace the highly manipulative visual tactics common to the MFTVM. In each film, the viewer sees the child painfully ripped from the arms of the mother after she loses custody. Both Zachary and Heather are removed forcefully from their mothers; with police officers in attendance, the grandparents surprise the actual parent and pull the child, screaming, from the actual mother. With much breast-beating and innocence-stealing (Zachary looks as if he has been awakened from a nap and Heather is just returning, still in leotard, from a ballet class), these scenes show the "natural" pained reaction of a mother losing a child, further establishing the lesbian as normal and the homophobic grandmothers as aberrant. By relying on this emotionally wrenching device, the films throw into question the ideological and judicial norms that allow the narratives to progress, surpassing the criticisms generally leveled at the MFTVM by scholars such as Todd Gitlin and Douglas Gomery, by placing causality beyond individual happenstance (Gitlin 192; Gomery, "*Brian's Song*" 89).

Troubling the Nuclear Family

The double victimization of the lesbian mother troubles the primacy of the nuclear family. Through a complete manipulation of the viewer's emotions, as described above, the narratives encourage the questioning of that which generally is accepted as normal, thereby throwing into question the abnormality of the lesbian protagonist. Each film systematically introduces the seemingly stable nuclear family, only to show its destructiveness and abnormality. Overtly constructed as the villains, the heterosexual biological parents of the lesbian characters encourage the viewer to cast a critical eye on expected norms. While the heterosexual families scream, shout, lie, and steal children, the lesbian mothers find stability, both financial and emotional, with their female partners. Closely resembling a storybook family, the lesbians pull themselves together and fight for their children. In both films, the nonbiological parent herself is constructed as the surrogate traditional father, functioning as the breadwinner of the floundering family.

In *Two Mothers for Zachary*, just after Jody loses custody, she and Maggie attempt to flee Virginia. While stopped at a rest area, Jody questions the logic of their actions and their ability to escape successfully. Asserting her commitment to her partner and their family, Maggie reassures of her ability to support them, saying, "You know me. People like me. I've got skills. I can find a job and take care of this family." Shortly thereafter, as Nancy snatches Zachary from his mother, while accusing Maggie of pretending to be his father, Jody shouts, "Maggie will make a better parent than you and Harlan could ever be."

A similar exchange occurs in *What Makes a Family?* when Janine orders Sandra, who is riddled with lupus and the side effects of its treatment, to quit her job. Sandra says, "Sweetheart, you can't support all three of us," to which Janine replies, "Yes I can. I'll work extra shifts at the hospital. We'll be okay. I promise." Furthermore, the film shows Janine's parents again refusing to help her regain custody of Heather, as they state, "The child is not blood to us or Janine. I'm sure she'll be better off with her family." A friend of Janine's scoffs and overtly critiques this notion, stating (in an almost soapbox-ish way), "I keep hearing about this notion of blood bonds making for a family..."

Juxtaposed with the behaviors of their respective parents, the uncompromising support that the nonbiological lesbian parents show for their children and partners uncovers the hypocrisy in the unquestioned belief in the superiority of biology over nurture. In both films, the nuclear families appear dysfunctional while the lesbian families appear loving and at least approaching capable. Again, the star protagonists and the associated narratives establish a preconceived notion of right and wrong, thereby positioning the legitimate relationship. In turn, the bad behavior of those representing the nuclear families (deception, backstabbing, and disbelief and disrespect of children) transfer easily into a questioning of their essential righteousness.

Judicial System

Aside from problematizing the notion of the nuclear family, these lesbian mother MFTVMs also turn their sights on the American judicial system. Driven by emotion, but more pointedly critical than the typical MFTVM, they resist a complete individualization and personalization of the problem of homophobia. While, in the tradition of the television docudrama, these films investigate social problems through the lens of personal experience, they simultaneously force an investigation of the politics that created these stories. This politicization of the personal occurs in various ways: by the bizarrely defined notion of "moral," by the injustice of the appeal system, and the implied subjectivity of the judicial process. In both cases, the films place major focus on the courts, providing a critique of their homophobic politics and policies. By connecting the sympathetic lesbian protagonist to the injustice of the robbed mother-child bond, these films frame the story around a critique of the judicial system. By juxtaposing legal policy with a constant evocation of the normalcy of family, the films uncover the hypocrisy implicit in the legal statutes that literally plucked these children from their mothers' breasts.

Two Mothers for Zachary reveals institutionalized homophobia in various ways. The film shows the victimized lesbian mother's inability to sufficiently defend herself when she discovers that the grandmother, Nancy, is demanding full custody of the child, rather than visitation rights. This discovery occurs seconds before the judge passes his ruling. Despite the revelations in court that Nancy's partner had repeatedly molested Jody and that the heretofore-estranged biological father requested that Zachary stay with Jody, the court grants Nancy custody, claiming neglect (based on sustained diaper rash and the practice of disciplining Zachary by standing him in the corner) in addition to perversion.

Evoking the injustices in their specific case and the system as a whole to their new lawyer, Maggie says, "Well aren't we the criminals. Too bad we're not fine upstanding straight citizens like all those wife beaters and child molesters. They've got custody of their kids, don't they!?" In a subsequent appeal, Jody wins custody, but Nancy's immediate appeal prohibits Zachary from returning home, highlighting the ease with which the child could be taken away, but the difficulty for the parent to regain custody. The injustice hits home as the film ends with Zachary in slow motion letting go of his mother's hand ("mama") as he takes his grandmother's ("maw-maw") and the title reads: "In February 1996, the juvenile and domestic court of the state of Virginia rejected Jody Ann's petition for custody based on changed circumstances." The title not only speaks to the reality, but also the timeliness of the case. The film aired September 22, 1996.

In a similar fashion, *What Makes a Family?* renders explicit the homophobia implicit in the legal system, overtly announcing the injustices through judges' rulings and lawyers' statements. In one session, the judge states, "Florida law is quite explicit regarding the rights of blood relatives over all other rights," and says that excessive exposure to Janine "would be confusing and potentially destructive." Janine's lawyer, when explaining the improbability of a positive outcome, states, "Florida law expressly forbids gays and lesbians from adopting." The Cataldis' lawyer makes a similar statement at the appeal.

The film then shows Janine working through the process of regaining her child by adhering to the rules set down by the judge. Demanding visitation from the Cataldis, she uses the courts that took Heather away from her as her own protector. For example, the police officer that escorts Janine to the Cataldis to ensure the visitation informs the Cataldis that any defiance of the order will be grounds for appeal. In the following appeal, the film attempts to discredit the homophobia implicit in the system; a psychiatrist rattles off statistics regarding the intelligence, sexual preference, and stability of children of gay parents. Like Maggie's questioning of straight parents' right to keep their children, Janine acknowledges the lack of a similar controversy over nonbiological heterosexual parents' rights regarding their children conceived by artificial insemination. Like *Two Mothers for Zachary*, *What Makes a Family?* ends with the intertitle "Janine's case is a landmark in child custody law. The judge overturned the Cataldis' adoption and returned Heather to the custody of Janine. Florida remains the only state that outlaws adoptions by gays and lesbians. Heather and Janine still live in Florida."

In these scenes of judicial triumph and calamity, the well-known faces of American actresses symbolically represent Every(wo)man's journey. Gitlin claims:"The triumphs of American TV naturalism, in fiction as in the news, is [*sic*] the revelation of familiar figures visibly coping with public troubles, right here in the living room" (192). These familiar personalities, already endeared to the viewing public, act out the injustices they render explicit regarding the American judicial system. The films attempt to use the actresses' recognizability to drive home the hypocrisy, homophobia, and personal ramifications of the actions represented in the films. I believe these films possess the ability to sway the audience because they have first drawn them in with familiar faces and personalized accounts. A notion of personal understanding and identification has a better chance of questioning bigotry and misunderstanding than facts and figures do. A preconceived bond with stars encourages this type of attachment. By using this manipulative tactic, coupled with the explicit problematizing of social givens, such as American justice and the idea of "real" family, the films attempt to inhibit the viewer's ability to simply dismiss the films' messages.

However...

Despite what I see as a more progressive approach to the MFTVM and perhaps a more effective means to present topics dealing with gay and lesbian issues, these films quickly slide into the trap of a heterocentric profit-driven television industry. In order to assure the greatest viewership, they compromise the message they promote by partaking in the false construction of an essentialized lesbian; they cast recognizable heterosexual actresses and legitimize the image of "*The* Lesbian" by means of physical and class construction. Using an actress with a bankable name and a nonthreatening image may aid in not alienating potentially threatened viewers. Through a combination of the reworking of true narratives, the choice of actresses to play the lead roles, and the visual portrayal in terms of beauty and class position, the films move to construct a safe lesbian. Furthermore, though scholars and producers often claim they have no responsibility to adhere to the facts, the label "based on a real story" immediately invokes a notion of authenticity. The visual representations imply a notion of the real and authentic.

The solidification of a legitimate lesbian occurs as thelesbian mothers shift from real-life lower middle-class and lower working-class (often butch) lesbians to glamorous middle-class-looking and middle-class-sounding lesbians, who are portrayed by attractive stars. These repeated and similar visual representations of *The* Lesbian in terms of beauty and class effectively aid in the construction of an essence. Judith Butler refers to this essential construction in *Gender Trouble*:

> Acts, gestures, and desire produce the effect of an internal core or substance, but produce this *on the surface* of the body, through the play of signifying absences that suggest but never reveal the organizing principle of identity as a cause…This also suggests that reality is fabricated as an interior essence, that very interiority is an effect and function of a decidedly public and social discourse.…(136).

The films' avoidance of the butch and the working-class, or their visual redefinitions thereof, and the repeated association of lesbianism with the feminized appearance of hetero stars help to reperform this interiority. Performing an acceptable notion of lesbianism (one that is contrary to that in the factual stories) encourages an acceptance of *The* Lesbian. Though the emotional nature of the films, along with their successful interweaving of political critique, may encourage the viewer to reconsider traditional notions of right and wrong or moral and immoral, s/he simultaneously is encouraged to do this with a set of qualifiers: middle-class, traditionally feminine, and therefore culturally assimilated and legitimized.

Though I have already argued that the use of established star personas may aid in the identification process with the lesbian protagonists, I believe the associated star personas create a catch 22, establishing a legitimate lesbianism when it adheres to the characteristics associated with the respective star personas. In the cases of both of these films, an actress who evolved publicly in terms of traditional notions of feminine beauty portrays the main lesbian, and reviewers repeatedly referred to the actresses in terms of their beauty. Various reviews commend the films for their ability to portray the nonstereotypical lesbian, with comments such as, "without resorting to the stereotype of a lesbian, Shields is impressive as the emotionally wrecked Janine" and "Colleen Flynn [holds her own] as the girlfriend, here called Maggie and neither stereotyped nor idealized" (Turegano TV6; Shales C01). Whereas these reviews attach the lack of stereotyping to a positive notion of representation, embedded in this avoidance of so-called stereotypical representations is the avoidance of a certain image of lesbianism. By legitimizing Bertinelli and Shields, the films devalue other types of lesbian presence (single, butch, nonmonogamous, poor, and so forth).

A comparison of the MFTVM images produced and the photos of the actual women on which the films base their stories highlights the politics of presenting *The* Lesbian in these films. The appearances of real-life parents Sharon Bottoms and April Wade diverge greatly from those of Jody and

Maggie. Throughout, *Two Mothers for Zachary* depicts Maggie as relatively feminine: her hair is in a neat, curly, shoulder-length bob; her clothes are less feminine than Jody's, but would likely not be described as butch; and she almost always inexplicably wears what looks like a silk scarf around her neck. Jody has a weakness for western wear, but often wears very stylish suits and a silk robe. Despite the occasional trite flannel shirt, the film fails in making Maggie and Jody look anything like their real-life counterparts; rather, it provides a feminized version thereof. Wade and Bottoms, who sport matching tattoos, have appeared in various magazines, Wade usually in some sort of traditionally masculine or "dykey" wear. In a photo of the two leaving the courthouse, Wade sports gray chinos, sunglasses, a plaid vest buttoned to the top, and she smokes a cigarette (Helber, 100). *Time* and *New York* both show Wade looking lanky and masculine (Henry 66; John Taylor 16). All of the photos depict Wade as significantly more butch than Bottoms, and she is consistently sporting the (supposedly) telltale lesbian mullet. Is it progressive to avoid depictions of a stereotype if the authentic source speaks to that convention?

What Makes a Family? made similar visual choices. In *The Advocate*, Neff Meron, one of the producers, refers to the real parents, Janine Ratcliffe and Joan Pearlman ("Sandra" in the film) as "a very middle-class couple." Director Maggie Greenwald states, "So we picked a wardrobe that was not glamorous. And Brooke was thrilled to be wearing the wardrobe. She has the willingness and joy to embrace this character in a deep way and not be treated like a glamour girl" (Stockwell). This statement works on the assumption that Shields can be totally removed from her glamorous star image, an assumption that clothing (that was not particularly unglamorous anyway) can construct the character against a preconceived notion of type. The real Janine and Joan were very plain, not traditionally beautiful women, and they had "non-ideal" body types and short, nondynamic hairdos. Shields and Jones each provide an image and aesthetic that adheres to traditional notions of beauty. Again, by avoiding a stereotype, the films render the butch invisible and thus delegitimized.

Likewise, the films transform real life middle-class and lower-class people into solidly middle- to upper-middle-class characters. Along with the transformation of their physical appearance, this shift of visible signifiers of class further assimilates the lesbian mother, with whom the audience is encouraged to identify, by placing her solidly within the false, generalized category of "middle-class American." This transformation of social class is most apparent in *Two Mothers for Zachary*. Though Jody is unemployed and on and off of welfare, her clothes are impeccable and are not recognizably attached to the class she claims to represent. Though Jody and Maggie joke about their white-trashness, their belongings and speech belie this. At least one reviewer recognized the contradiction between the film's intention regarding representation of class and its explicit representation of class: "The movie's first, insurmountable hurdle is making us believe that Redgrave is the mother of Valerie Bertinelli, and that they're both a step above Southern white trash" (Koehler F13). This misrepresentation of class directly relates to the erasure of the butch or lesbian visibility.

Scholars such as Christine Holmlund and Sue Ellen Case argue that rendering the butch, an image ingrained in lesbian culture, invisible aids in veiling the lesbian herself, as well as making implied statements regarding acceptable lesbian socioeconomic class. It was the working-class lesbian who often historically assumed the butch role. Case surveys the butch's disappearance or disavowal as the feminist movement dubbed the role "politically incorrect" or unsavvy. As the butch was deemed passé or oppressive, a major semiotic signpost that marked lesbianism was shelved (295–297). Holmlund addresses the proliferation of femme images in Hollywood-produced film, and states, "Admittedly the femme's lesbianism is visible most when she is in the arms of her lover...For most observers, the assumption of heterosexuality is so strong that the femme is easily seen as just another woman's friend" (148). Both of these films suffer from this type of butch invisibility. Implied in the representations of Maggie, Jody, Sandra, and Janine are a certain socioeconomic standing and the safety and assumed heterosexuality that go along with a femme in lieu of her butch lover. With the traditional feminization of all four characters (and actresses), the clear lesbian marking of the butch/femme pairing disappears. This neutralization of the social threat of lesbianism—through virtual invisibility— occurs when actresses so extradiegetically associated with heterosexuality and devoid of signifiers that would associate them with a recognizable lesbian community serve as the representation of the minority group.

Conclusion

Ultimately, these lesbian mother MFTVMs exist within a negotiated space of progressivity and restriction. Unlike the episodic situation comedy and the serial drama, the generic form of the MFTVM does not restrict narrative development (and possibilities) by either requiring these films to sustain a realistic lesbian relationship throughout a series or weekly or by needing to neatly resolve any controversial plotlines. Rather, MFTVMs have approximately two hours to tell a story that may or may not ultimately resolve in a pleasing or culture-confirming way. Allowing for and encouraging a troubling of social expectations, they hail the viewer through emotional means and simultaneously provide a critique of pervasive homophobia. However, like weekly series, the requirements of this heterocentric and profit-driven medium still constrain these MFTVM projects. Audience draw and maintenance of a legitimate vision of society encourage representations that lack breadth. Rewriting narratives and flattening the lesbian to a point of singularity, the mainstream MFTVM uses heterosexual stars to draw an audience, thereby attaching the notion of the sympathetic lesbian mother/character to socially sanctioned notions of beauty, gender, and class. As a result, they simultaneously dismiss and delegitimize lesbianism that differs in terms of socioeconomic background or visual gender adherence.

Although pay cable channels such as HBO and Showtime pushed the envelope further at this time by presenting more diverse images of lesbianism and lesbian eroticism in films such as *If These Walls Could Talk 2* (2000) and *Common Ground* (2000), network and basic cable MFTVMs found a more conservative means to introduce discourses surrounding lesbian issues into the mainstream, introducing and revealing some of the cultural trials faced by lesbians in our society. This step forward must not be dismissed because of feminized and pejorative cultural connotations or television scholars' negative framing of the genre, for the MFTVM shows signs of problemitizing representations that often turn to depoliticized caricatures in serial and episodic television programming.

The MFTVM's preoccupation with the lesbian mother (or with lesbians, for that matter) waned as the millennium turned. Since the airing of the aforementioned films, Showtime's *Bobbie's Girl* (2002) stands as one of the only lesbian-themed American MFTVMs to air on broadcast television or cable, either basic or premium. During this same period, however, American television has experienced shifts that have perhaps created spaces for similar nuanced looks at lesbian parenting. As I argue in *Cinema Journal*'s 2011 "In Focus" feature on writing and producing for television, the new millennium brought not only an increase in gay, lesbian, and bi (GLB) characters, but a creative environment where more ideologically and structurally complex narratives could flourish and a body of work where—across genres and networks—GLB characters appeared earlier, more often, and in more integral roles (Kessler). So, while this late 1990s/early 2000s prominence of the TV-movie-bound lesbian mom could be written off as a flash in the pan, or as just following the trends set by the series-bound lesbian moms on shows such as *Friends* (1994–2004) and *ER* (1994–2009), I prefer to see them as forerunners of the more fully developed and narratively complex— if still problematic—lesbian moms of Showtime's *The L Word* (2004–2009) or ABC's *Grey's Anatomy* (2005–). While such depictions lack the emotional ties of "based on true events" narratives and often eschew the legal battles inherent in such stories (which are still caused by the American state-by-state laws addressing gay and lesbian adoption), contemporary television's creators' and writers' willingness to delve more deeply into GLB characters allows for an increasing potential for well-developed images of lesbian parenting, warts and all.

Note

1. After Sharon Bottoms admitted to having oral sex with April Wade, a felonious crime in Virginia, Judge Buford M. Parsons ruled in favor of the grandmother, deeming Sharon "immoral" and an "unfit" mother who committed a "crime against nature."

CHAPTER 3

Complicating the Open Closet: The Visual Rhetoric of *Buffy the Vampire Slayer*'s Sapphic Lovers

Tanya R. Cochran

Buffy is neither homophobic, nor is it lesbian-
positive, and yet it is both... for it does not take up
a single portrayal, but instead develops slowly an
ever-evolving and complex vision...
> —Rebecca Beirne, "Queering the Slayer-text"

If words are always contextual and contested,...
static images, hot links, sound files, animation, and
video raises the stakes exponentially...
> —Helen Burgess, Jeanne Hamming, and
> Robert Markley,
> "The Dialogics of New Media"

From the earliest episodes of *Buffy the Vampire Slayer (Buffy)*, creator Joss Whedon was crafting landmark television. Foreshadowing in the third season's "Doppelg8Angland" (3.16) held particular promise for lesbian viewers. When a spell goes awry, Willow Rosenberg (Alyson Hannigan) meets her vampire doppelg8Anger, observing, "I'm so evil. And skanky. And I think I'm kinda gay!" A year later, Whedon introduced the subtext of a lesbian relationship between Willow and Tara Maclay (Amber Benson) in "Hush" (4.10). Before and after the episode aired, popular media responded with provocative headlines: "Kiss Each Other Girls, The Ratings Are Down"—*New York Post* (Kaplan 114), "Willow Gay?"—*Entertainment Weekly* (Rice), and *"Buffy* Creator Titillates the Audience"—*TV Guide* (Ausiello). But when Whedon proved he did not intend to exploit the relationship for ratings, mainstream attention waned. As the characters' interest grew from subtext to revelation in "New Moon Rising," the actors were cultivating their careers and becoming more visible by, among other decisions, accepting invitations to interview and pose for magazines. Particular photo shoots of Hannigan in *FHM* and Benson in *Stuff* created and continue to maintain a conversation that seems discordant with Whedon's self-proclaimed feminist agenda.

By drawing on sociology and media studies as well as theories of visual rhetoric and critical theory, I first examine primary sources: the television series and the magazines. Next, I demonstrate the significance of reading the television and magazine images, the dialogue and text in conversation. To reinforce my reading, I turn to theory to argue that neglecting the exchange of ideas among the dissonant images, text, and audiences denies the intricate interaction of cross-media images and text, ignores fans' blurring of actor/character identities, and dilutes Whedon's feminist intentions. The interaction of actors, characters, images, and text leads me to question and complicate, as an extension of Vito Russo's work, the idea of an open media closet or equitable opportunities for visual representation. Finally, I advocate for resistant readings of "questionable" content in addition to more critical readings that lead to new kinds of content altogether. The "vision" of *Buffy*—what is seen and what is understood—is complex, and because the series traverses media, it raises the stakes for writers and directors, actors, critics, and fans in that each group shapes the cultural productions of the other.

The Media Closet: New Moon Rising or Falling?

At the close of "New Moon Rising" (4.19) Willow enters Tara's dorm room carrying an "extra flamey" candle. The small light draws viewers' attention to the characters' faces as Willow declares her interest in Tara. Tara smiles and blows out the candle, closing the episode and leaving what follows to imagination. "New Moon Rising" supposedly marks the transition from subtext to text, of lesbian invisibility to visibility. Here, I challenge that idea, arguing that visual representations are always already slippery, constantly being reinterpreted by *Buffy*'s writers and directors, actors, critics, and fans. But first, the work of Vito Russo provides historical context for my contention.

In the first edition of *The Celluloid Closet* (1981), Russo outlines the roles and depictions of gays and lesbians in Hollywood film, an unkind history that produced flat characters excluded from "the American dream." Possibly Russo's most important observation and the reason for homosexuals' alienation can be summarized in one sentence: "When gays became real, they became threatening" (154). To circumvent the threat, the film industry adopted several strategies. Either by making gay men "sissies" and lesbians "bull dykes" and "vice queens" or by rendering both invisible in various ways (typically by murder or suicide), Hollywood denied the significance, even the existence, of intimate relationships among people of the same sex. Though by the book's second release in 1987 much had changed in American cinema, Russo still found its treatment of homosexuals and homosexuality hostile.

Traditionally, this hostility has been maintained in American film by the very visible celebration of the heterosexual male, one that has made any other orientation nearly if not completely *in*visible. Particularly, "the rendering invisible of all else has caused lesbianism to disappear behind a male vision of sex in general" (Russo 5). In Russo's estimation, then, no matter what a woman does or whom she does it with, she, as an object of sexual desire, embodies innocuousness. Because lesbians are female, their visual representations are prey to what I call "visual dilution," a particular form of (in)visibility that can blur and, as a result, weaken the intended meaning or full potential of an image or portrayal. Referring to Amber Benson and her character Tara, a fan—whose online pseudonym is "misterQ"—illustrates what I mean: "I have to say that I agree with Amber Benson being hot. Her innocence on the show makes her that way, [*sic*] plus, girl on girl, whew!" The exclamation brings into focus several key complexities posed by visibility. Q conflates Benson's identity with that of her character's. Also, misterQ normalizes and feminizes the character by emphasizing Benson's/Tara's innocence while simultaneously equating this innocence with physical attractiveness. Finally, the comment (though Q is not necessarily male or heterosexual) suggests the universally acknowledged and ignored or accepted assumption that straight men take pleasure in "girl on girl" g(r)azing—whether or not the female participants are, in fact, heterosexual. Thus, one way or another, "lesbianism is never allowed to become a threatening reality any more than female sexuality of other kinds" (Russo 5). In many ways, lesbian sex in particular is portrayed as being created by men for men, a portrayal that emphasizes sex over relationships.

Two decades after Russo's revised work appeared, one expects that TV and film representations of various sexual orientations have evolved. After all, some argue, television series such as *Xena: Warrior Princess, ER, Six Feet*

Under, Queer as Folk, and *The L Word* have favored and celebrated gay, lesbian, bisexual, transgendered, and queer (GLBTQ) characters and fans. What was once a closed or cracked media closet, then, has swung wide open—equal and fair visual representations for all. But as misterQ's post alone suggests, just saying or even believing so oversimplifies the situation. As a case study, *Buffy* illustrates the complicated relationships among media venues—film, TV, print, and the internet—and the portrayal of GLBTQ characters generally, lesbians specifically.

Many scholars and fans, for example, continue to debate whether Willow's admission of her interest in Tara in "New Moon Rising" (4.19) actually represents a lesbian coming out. In the passage that follows, of note is the obscurity with which Buffy and Willow dialogue. In their shared dorm room, the two discuss the sudden return of Oz, Willow's former boyfriend. Oz, who left earlier in the year to find a cure for his lycanthropy, has returned to Sunnydale and proposed that he and Willow rekindle their relationship:

Buffy: I wanna hear about you and Oz. You saw him, right?
Willow: I was with him all night.
Buffy: All night? [Grins.] Oh my god. Wait. Last night was a wolf moon, right?
Willow: Yup.
Buffy: Either you're about to tell me something incredibly kinky, or—
Willow: No kink. He didn't change, Buffy. He said he was gonna find a cure, and he did. In Tibet.
Buffy: [Smiling.] Oh my god. I can't believe it. [Pause] Okay, I'm all with the woo-hoo here, and you're not.
Willow: No, there's "woo" and, and "hoo." But there's "uh-oh" and "why now?" and...it's complicated.
Buffy: Why complicated?
Willow: It's complicated...because of Tara.
Buffy: You mean Tara has a crush on Oz? No. Oh! Oh. Um...well...that's great. You know, I mean, I think Tara's a, a really great girl, Will.
Willow: She is! And there's something between us. It, it wasn't something I was looking for. It's just powerful. And it's totally different from what Oz and I have....I was gonna tell him...but then we started hanging out, and...I could just feel everything coming back....He's Oz, you know?

Both Willow's confusion about what she actually feels and her inability, tentativeness, or refusal to name her relationship with Tara illustrate the obscurity of the scene. In fact, Rebecca Beirne insists that the entire episode is ambiguous, citing Steven Seidman's *Beyond the Closet* in which he argues that the "lesbian is imagined as a transitional status—an immature phase or a case of gender maladjustment" (143). Seidman contends that if their sexual preference is not denied, lesbians are often portrayed as standing on shifting sand; they may or may not actually be gay. Russo identifies such women in James Bond films (consider how 007 woos and "straightens out" Pussy Galore in *Goldfinger*) (154–156). According to Beirne, the ambiguity of Willow's revelation is one way to normalize her relationship with Tara. What remains for the audience is a "lack of any clear definition between the straight Willow and the lesbian Willow," an uncertainty that "lends a high level of inauthenticity to her sexuality" (Beirne). Ambiguity, then, is bound to inauthenticity. As Russo might note, Willow is just as disarming, or innocuous, after as before her declaration.

Even as late as the seventh and final season of *Buffy*, Willow's "gayness" remains somewhat unclear. When Kennedy questions Willow's sexuality in "The Killer in Me" (7.13), Willow explains that she has never loved women, only *a* woman—Tara. And though she eventually becomes intimately involved with Kennedy, Willow and her friends consistently avoid language that identifies Willow as gay. For instance, the word *lesbian* is only used once during the series. When the Watchers' Council comes to Sunnydale to interrogate Buffy and friends as well as offer unsolicited advice regarding the current "Big Bad," Willow describes her relationship with Tara to a Council member like this: "We're lesbian, gay-type lovers" ("Checkpoint" 5.12). A mostly British governing body, the Council trains and manages watchers who, in turn, train and manage slayers. It is portrayed as not only stuffy but also manipulative, so much so that Buffy leaves their auspices halfway through the series. The fact that Willow uses *lesbian* during the interrogation seems to suggest that a richer, more accurate definition would be difficult to articulate as well as lost on the bureaucratic audience. Consequently, Willow simplifies the relationship for them: *lesbian*, an adjective that suggests a definition only based on generalizations and stereotypes.

Dialogue alone does not support the indeterminate nature of Willow and Tara's relationship; they are also visually coded within "normal" boundaries for their gender, according to hair, dress, makeup, and behavior. More accurately, perhaps, their sexuality is visually unassuming: no stereotypically short, "butch" haircuts (Tara maintains long, silky locks throughout her tenure) and no conventionally masculine clothing (both are costumed in modest, nouveau hippy apparel—long, flowing skirts and long-sleeved, high-necked shirts often in geometric or floral prints). Yet they are not "lipstick lesbians," an identity likely incompatible with their practice of Wicca; rather, earth tones and natural makeup befit them. In collaboration with hair, wardrobe, and makeup, the traditionally feminized roles Tara assumes further dilutes the relationship, fortifying its normality and ambiguity. As Willow develops into a powerful, confident witch, for example, Tara is repeatedly cast as silent or at least as a quiet companion, moral center, and parent. In her shy and stuttering way, Tara encourages Willow's growing mastery of spells. But when Willow begins to use magic for her own convenience, Tara reprimands her, defining her actions as "wrong" ("Tabula Rasa" 6.8). Tara also assumes many of the caretaking responsibilities for Buffy's younger sister Dawn when Buffy's mother dies unexpectedly in the fifth season: she prepares meals, gets Dawn to school on time, and babysits when an apocalypse arises, a common occurrence in Sunnydale.

According to fan websites and discussion boards, the characters' inconspicuous wardrobe and traditional gender roles, though, are much less important to queer audiences than what they are chiefly denied: recurring visual depictions of Willow and Tara's physical relationship. While Buffy's intimate encounters—whether tender and loving with Angel or violent and sadomasochistic with Spike—are given detailed exploration and copious screentime, Willow and Tara are granted little more than hand-holding, cuddling, and occasional pecks on the lips. Kissing passionately and making love are rarely depicted. Curiously, as Beirne notes, the lovers' first sexualized scene occurs during Xander's dream sequence in "Restless" (4.22). Uncharacteristically bedecked in heavy, dark makeup and form-fitting, cleavage-revealing bodices (much like the actors who appear in *FHM* and *Stuff*), Willow and Tara perform like two straight women cast as lesbians in an adult film, a private (for the straight, male Xander) yet public (for the straight *and* queer audience) screening. Subsequent to Xander's fantasizing, Willow and Tara's lovemaking is presented mainly through the metaphor of magic—the casting of spells and body levitation. Their physical intimacy does visually crescendo, though, in "Seeing Red" (6.19). Extremely disturbing to most *Buffy* devotees is that Willow and Tara's most visceral expression of physical love and passion is immediately followed by Tara's accidental murder. Her death, lament some critics and fans, perpetuates the "lesbian sex = death" clich8E.[1] The couple's normality, their ambiguousness, does not prevent the seemingly inevitable.

Ultimately, Willow and Tara are (in)visible as well as (anti)stereotypical. In *Up From Invisibility*, Larry Gross argues that traditional views of femininity and masculinity and, thus, gender roles, continue to fuel the invisibility of GLBTQs on television where they appear "in roles that support the 'natural' order" (14); they are created to be anti-stereotypical and, therefore, unidentifiable. Unidentifiable queers are not the trouble, though. The trouble, Gross insists, is the double-edged result of normalizing GLBTQ characters: what is "normal" is unseen. And yet Gross finds this kind of invisibility rare, as the mass media much prefers the "weak and silly, or evil and corrupt" queer (16). The reason for such exaggerated, stereotypical characters, he suggests, is that "the visible presence of healthy, unapologetic lesbians and gay men [poses] a serious threat: it undermines the unquestioned normalcy of the status quo..." (16–17). Visibility, then, complicates, making Willow and Tara concurrently (in)visible and (anti)stereotypical. Visibility ramifies, compelling *Buffy* fans and scholars to question whether or not the "new moon" of accurate, objective, or equitable representation is actually rising (however gradually), falling, or simply standing still.

Regardless of perspective, the representation of Willow and Tara through image and dialogue is problematic. Even as Whedon created a feminist, cutting-edge text, he also created stereotypes. Whedon set in motion a never-ending cycle of creation and re-creation that occurs simultaneously within multiple spheres of cultural production: the team of writers and directors, the actors, the critics, and the fans. Each of these spheres contributes to the definition of what it means—what it looks like, sounds like, feels like—to be a lesbian. Such a definition is slippery and, therefore, resists discovery, a resistance complicated even more by considering the actors' personal and professional lives in light of the world's technologically networked culture.

For Him, the Stuff (In)Visibility Is Made of: Who Is that Woman in the Photo?

The cultural productions generated by the characters Willow and Tara cannot be read in isolation of those fostered by the actors Hannigan and Benson and their decisions to grant interviews and photo shoots to men's magazines *FHM* and *Stuff*, respectively. As Anne Wysocki notes in "Seriously Visible," "no technology is autonomous.... We use no technology outside the webs of its history, of its connections to other technologies, or of our motley and complex relations with others" (41). Just as intricately webbed are critics' and fans' readings of actors, the characters they play, and cross-media texts.[2] In the context of such readings and Wysocki's observation, the *FHM* and *Stuff* photographs are akin to the pornographic film or, more specifically, the stag film. "Distinctively primitive," according to Linda Williams, stag films boast "[a] male film spectator who is encouraged to talk to, and even to reach his hand into, the screen; a female film body who spreads her legs (and labia) for the eye and hand behind the camera" (76). With parted lips and engaged postures, Hannigan and Benson visually resound with their filmic relatives and are reminiscent of Roland Barthes's reflection on the desire that pictures can arouse: "This longing to inhabit, if I observe it clearly in myself,... is fantasmatic, deriving from a kind of second sight which seems to bear me forward to a utopian time..." (*Camera Lucida* 39–40).[3] He notes that the plethora of books about photography explains neither the pleasure nor the affect he experiences when looking at a particular photo. For him, composition or lighting do not matter. What matters is what is *there* in the picture: "Myself, I saw only the referent, the desired object, the beloved body" (*Camera Lucida* 7). That, too, is what is seen in the Hannigan and Benson photographs: referents, objects, bodies. In many senses, *who* is posing is of little or no consequence. The scantily clad figures and come-hither stares, by echoing an historical tradition of objectification, lack of agency, and patriarchy, mark the women in the pictures as ones with no identity at all.

And yet, simultaneously their identities as actors (both declaredly straight) *and* characters encourage viewers to read them not simply as bodies but specifically as lesbian bodies, ones intended for "the male gaze," specifically the straight male gaze of *FHM* and *Stuff* readers. In the magazines, words and images collaborate to accomplish such a blurring of identity and, in turn, create a "viseo-textual" invitation for readers to watch the series. As subtly—and even unintentionally—embedded as the invitation is, it is not without significance to the feminist movement, one Whedon sees himself a part of. As Annette Kuhn affirms, "feminism has regarded ideas, language and images as crucial in shaping women's (and men's) lives" (2). Some of those crucial words are found in Michael Olson's *Stuff* interview with Amber Benson. Olson euphemistically observes that Tara "doesn't care for 'riding the broom'" and wonders whether Benson is concerned about being "typecast as a lesbian Wiccan" (120). Benson responds, "Not really. If people are so stupid that they can't see beyond it, then that's *their* issue, not mine. I just do whatever comes my way" (120). Yet in other interviews, Benson has admitted she wishes not to market herself by exposing breasts and thighs but feels somewhat resigned to the "reality" of how Hollywood works. The articles on both actors contribute to the shape of straight and lesbian women's lives with these words: "You know her as Tara, the lesbian witch on *Buffy*. But there's more to Amber Benson than...sorcery. If only there were some way for you to find out more about her..." (Olson 118), and "*Buffy the Vampire Slayer*'s kindly witch flirts with her dark side" (Raub 132).

When text and images of the actors in lingerie, heavy makeup, and sexualized positions are juxtaposed—images that recall Xander's dream in "Restless" (4.22)—it is difficult to decide who is in the pictures. Is the woman Benson or her character Tara? Hannigan or Willow? Women with names and faces or nameless, faceless fantasy girls? All or none of the above? As Willow says, "It's complicated..." ("New Moon Rising" 4.19).

Presciently echoing Willow's confused yet clear understanding of her situation, Barthes illustrates the simplicity and complexity of an image, arguing that a photograph can never be separated from what it represents—at least not "*immediately* or *generally*": "By nature, the Photograph...has something tautological about it: a pipe, here, is always and intractably a pipe. It is as if the Photograph always carries its referent with itself...: they are glued together, limb by limb....The Photograph belongs to that class of laminated objects whose two leaves cannot be separated without destroying them both..." (*Camera Lucida* 5–6, emphasis in original). In respect to Willow and Tara, Hannigan and Benson, the logical extension of Barthes's statement suggests that both the characters and actors are referents of each other. In this visual age, the television and magazine images cannot be separated: "You know her as Tara, the lesbian witch on *Buffy*. But there's more to Amber Benson..." (Olson 118). Character and actor identity are amalgamated. Such words and images render the referents in the *Stuff* and *FHM* photos ambiguous: they could be the actors themselves, their characters, Everywoman, lesbians, or girl-on-girl action figures. But ostensibly all of them, because they imply each other, are woven into a web of (in)visibility; the referents are multiple "leaves" that cannot be separated.

Reading Images and Text in Conversation: A Win-Win Situation?

It is tempting to simplify, to say that the magazine and television images of Hannigan, Benson, and their *Buffy* characters are utterly different and, therefore, cannot be compared—separate audiences, exclusive mediums, literal versus fictional human beings. It is also tempting to dismiss the magazine photos as typical of the reading and viewing habits of straight men. The images, though, do not exist in vacuums or distant universes, a truth evident in a simple search of Internet message boards on the topic of Amber Benson's *Stuff* photo shoot. In a webbed culture, images talk, and what they say is not always easily deciphered. In fact, depending on when, where, how, and by whom they are read, some images may experience dilution as others are intensified; one set of images may lose or gain something over other images.

While Hannigan and Benson are certainly at liberty to pose in any position and in any magazine they choose, Benson herself, as noted earlier, has expressed a desire not to solicit notice by posing for the likes of *Stuff*. Still, the actors' actual choices make professional statements that cannot necessarily be separated from political or even commercial ones. Hannigan's and Benson's choices, the representations of themselves and their characters matter, especially to those invested in feminist ideals. Kuhn argues, "From the point of view of its politics...the women's movement has always been interested in images, meaning, representations—and especially in challenging representations which, while questionable or offensive from a feminist standpoint, are from other points of view—if they are noticed at all acceptable" (3). If *Buffy* challenges traditional representations of both heterosexual and lesbian women (and it certainly does), the challenge is still weakened by the actors' "questionable" photo shoots for *FHM* and *Stuff*. Particularly in question is reality.

According to Helen Burgess, Jeanne Hamming, and Robert Markley, "Rather than transcending technology, multimedia reinforces our sense of what [Michelle] Kendrick (1996) terms the 'technological real': the recognition, whether implicit or explicit, that *consciousness, identity*, and '*reality*' are and always have been mediated by technology and that this mediation is always dynamic (144)" (66, emphasis added). Similar to Burgess, Hamming, and Markley's understanding of Kendrick is Barthes's assertion that a photo or more precisely what is in the photo is often the center of a reader's attention, yet "a complex of concurrent messages" surround and supplement the image: the photo's caption, the article that it accompanies, the layout of the page, and even the name of the paper, magazine, website, or television show (*Image* 15). In regard to *Buffy*, intentional costuming, directed body language, scripted roles alongside extratextual images of the actors in suggestive positions accentuated by text that purposely blurs the actors' and characters' identities revises—in some ways weakening, in others neutralizing—the power of the series' feminist spirit. An even further complication occurs when pictures of the actors' day-to-day or "real" lives appear with captions such as the following: "Alyson Hannigan and Amber Benson play lovers on *Buffy*. In real life, they're just good friends. Very, very good friends."[4] Disregarded by many readers as witty, mock-innuendo, the text yet underscores that the imaginary is just as real as the real is imaginary—an always already dynamic mediation.

A film studies graduate of Wesleyan University, Whedon is no stranger to the mediated language of moving and still pictures. So while he did not deliberately construct *Buffy*'s Sapphic lovers to invite the gaze of *FHM* and *Stuff* readers or have control over which magazines, lingerie, or positions Hannigan and Benson posed in (as he should not have), he remains a collaborator in the visual dilution of his own purportedly feminist visual text. Whedon is caught in the web of Willow and Tara's (in)visibility. When read in dialogue, then, the magazine and television images suggest that a win-win situation may be possible for marketers and certain viewers of the series or readers of the magazines but is unlikely or impossible for many fans as well as scholars.

The Age-Old Dispute: Can Images Really Argue?

That the images of Hannigan, Benson, and their *Buffy* characters and the text that accompanies the images are in dialogue is neither a new nor an unfounded claim. To address any suspicion requires only a brief explanation of an ongoing dispute that usually ends in two contentions, however reductive: "there are those who think that the image is an extremely rudimentary system in comparison with language and those who think that signification cannot exhaust the images' ineffable richness" (Barthes, *Image* 32). Speaking for the former, Gross declares that, unlike text, the image—particularly the television image—"does not require literacy" (6). Are we, then, a society quickly becoming completely illiterate? After all, as Jay Bolter observes, our lives are "dominated by visual representation" (19). From food labels to magazine ads, from billboards to the Internet, we are daily and continuously bombarded with the rhetoric of images. It seems that J9Frgen Habermas and Paul Virilio agree that we, in fact, *are* becoming illiterate or, as Gross argues, that we do not need to be literate at all; rather than developing a discriminating palate, we simply consume what we see, swallow without savoring. Habermas in *The Structural Transformation of the Public Sphere* and Virilio in *The Vision Machine* contend that, whether transmitted via page or screen, images are predigested and standardizing; they render simplistic even the textual arguments they accompany. Thus, readers do not wrestle rigorously with ideas and then assume differing positions on issues, acts that Habermas and Virilio "believe necessary for the functioning of democratic societies" (Wysocki 43).

Though Habermas and Virilio maintain a firm position on the weakness of visual elements, Wysocki challenges them: "The assumption behind [their] critique of the visual is that we each take in what we see, automatically and immediately, in the exact same way as everyone else, so that the visual requires no interpretation and in fact functions as though we have no power before it" (43). Allegedly, the viewer is caught in what Wysocki describes as a Darwin-inspired, Schopenhauerian "imperative to reproduce," an infinite and inescapable cycle in which what is produced gives birth to re-production and what is "consumed is re-cycled" (48–49). In the face of such a position, Schopenhauer argues that the *only* possible response, in Wysocki's words, is "aesthetic resignation: We are to appreciate the beauty and to accept that we neither deny nor challenge our lack of independence" (49). In his own words, "Only knowledge remains; the will has vanished" (Schopenhauer 411). But Wysocki rejects such an argument, buttressing her position by demonstrating the intellectual rigor required to read—not simply view— two web projects: *Scrutiny in the Great Round* by Tennessee Rice Dixon, Jim Gasperini, and Charlie Morrow and *Throwing Apples at the Sun* by Elliot Earls. She concludes that reading images can be just as "pleasurably challenging" as reading print-only texts and stresses that in order to perform the reading, she "had to apply abilities and approaches and understanding from rhetoric and art and visual communication and philosophy and critical theory . . . " (56). No matter its object, reading is always already dynamic.

As the expression goes, "There are two sides to every story." But the story of image versus text has more. The world may be dominated by the visual, but many of us remain progeny of the word via books, magazines, newspapers, and websites. Significantly, in all of these mediums, pictures and text rarely exist in isolation; instead, they are in constant—sometimes complementary, sometimes contentious—conversation. For too long, as visual rhetoricians Mary Hocks and Michelle Kendrick note, academics have articulated the battle between image and word rather than "the dynamic interplay that *already exists* and has *always existed* between visual and verbal texts . . . " (1). And that dynamic interplay need not exist solely between the visual and the textual. Just as certainly, as I have argued in this chapter, images can argue between and among themselves.

Still, do *Buffy* fans read *FHM* and *Stuff*? Did the regular magazine readers actually begin to watch the series simply because they picked up their monthly copies? I cannot answer either question with certainty. I can, though, draw on personal experience as a *Buffy* scholar and fan to strongly suggest that what binds the magazines, the series, the readers, and the viewers is the Internet. Particular fans of *Buffy* hawkishly look for any article, image, video clip, or even single-sentence quote related to the series. They then alert other fans via chat rooms, message boards, and personal websites, a signal that sends them online or to local book stores in search of the source. Because of such notices, I—neither a straight man nor a gay woman—immediately went to buy *FHM* and *Stuff* when they hit newsstands. Since my purchase years ago, I have wrestled with the magazine and television images, questioning the reality of what I saw and grappling with the concept that these particular depictions of the actors and characters are at the same time historical and contemporary, stereotypical and normalizing. Not wanting to be caught in an "imperative to reproduce" or to experience "aesthetic resignation" (Wysocki 48–49), I have sought some way to "appreciate beauty" while not simply consuming it. My search for steady ground has led not so much to conclusions as to questions: "So what?" and "What now?"

To See through a Glass Darkly: Where Do We Go from Here?

As murky as the answers to the "so what" and "what now" questions may seem, answers *do* exist. Linda Williams suggests one of many. When she began writing about filmic bodies, Williams thought one of her books should contain a short chapter on pornography, short because pornographic films would "[illustrate] a *total* objectification of the female 'film body' as object of male desire" (xvi, emphasis in original). Williams found, though, that such a claim was far too simplistic. In *Hard Core*, she argues that the traditional positions of feminists—to celebrate or condemn pornography—has left little room for substantive debate; in fact, such positions have completely ignored the complexity of the genre, especially as it developed in the 1990s to reach more marginalized and "non-traditional" viewers such as GLBTQs and heterosexual women. Williams insists that we need to "come to terms with pornography" by not viewing it simply as misogynistic (though, much of it is) or denying that it is art (though, much of it is not) but by attempting to define what it is and why it continues to be so popular (5). Williams's assertion pertains to my argument in that, though *Buffy*'s message *is* "feminist," the images of Hannigan/Willow and Benson/Tara create a formidable affront to that message, one that scholars and fans continue to correctly but excessively praise rather than complicate.[5] As Beirne notes, the show is neither homophobic nor friendly to the GLBTQ perspective; it is also neither agonistic toward nor amicable to Whedon's feminist agenda. Instead, the series demonstrates the slippage of images. Just as letters and words, as signifiers, are not the objects they represent, so static or moving images slip, a deconstruction that makes impossible a fair or equitable representation of anyone. Where do we—writers and directors, critics, fans, and scholars—go from here, then?

First, we can continue to acknowledge what *Buffy* does well. In a review of *Buffy*'s seventh season, AfterEllen.com's Sarah Warn laments the passing of one of network television's most popular cult series and what the audience has lost: a lesbian couple they can identify with and celebrate ("DVD Release"). AfterEllen.com is one of few online media sources that has hailed *Buffy* for bringing about several important firsts for lesbians on TV, among which include one of the longest, most passionate kisses between two female lovers not "experimenting." Warn describes these firsts as giving lesbians much coveted and rarely granted visibility. She notes, "When the series ended in May, 2003, we knew lesbian visibility on TV would suffer[;]...it makes me long for the days when lesbian and bisexual women could watch [television]...and find an interesting, likeable, well-developed lesbian character like Willow..." ("DVD Release"). More than being personable or multifaceted characters, Willow and Tara hopefully altered the course of American television: "We *changed* the world," exclaims Willow in the last moments of the series finale "Chosen" (7.22). True. More than any other network series during its run, *Buffy* realized several milestones. It also did not conceal the flaws that come with being human. As Warn believes, the characters were humanized, normalized in ways so as to desensitize viewers to sexual attraction and love between women: "network television will never...be able to stuff the lesbian genie back into the bottle..." ("How *Buffy* Changed the World"). As the slippage of images implies, however, Warn's assertion is debatable.

The invisibility of normality constantly challenges lesbian visibility, so we must also acknowledge what *Buffy* in juxtaposition with such images and text as found in *FHM* and *Stuff* does *not* do: give each lesbian viewer the model she desires. Made too often are dismissive statements such as "It's *just* a TV show," "Boys will be boys," or "*FHM* and *Stuff* have really good articles!" I, like Todd Ramlow, neither understand nor believe the argument that what is popular is "'just' entertainment or ephemera." Popular culture accomplishes "real cultural work" that in too many cases upholds a dominant, closed-minded ideology: "The refusal to consider any social or political import to popular culture demonstrates how ideology functions through media to promote certain social and cultural values as 'natural,' and to make particular political investments and disseminations transparent" (Ramlow). *Buffy* does, in fact, do cultural work, work that is laudable. But *FHM* and *Stuff* do cultural work also.

Willow's words—"It's complicated..."—continue to echo ("New Moon Rising" 4.19). But the complex conversation of images and text is not so obfuscating that it is indecipherable and paralyzing. Problematizing opinions, hypotheses, and theories can lead to more resistant readings of "questionable" texts, readings that hopefully will prompt and even demand the production of new kinds of texts all together. As Bolter insists, "A new critical theory is needed that can make us aware of the cultural and historical contexts (and ideologies) without dismissing or downplaying the formal characteristics of new media" (34). The building of such a theory is what feminist scholars such as Laura Mulvey, Mary Ann Doane, and Jackie Stacey have been trying to accomplish from the very beginning of their work. They have advocated for media transformation—change in the form of more options, more choices for female actors and spectators. As media continues to evolve, scholars should look for ways, as Bolter suggests, that various media can become in themselves cultural and societal critiques, not per petuations of dominant norms (34). For "whatever it grants to vision and whatever its manner, a photograph is always invisible: it is not it that we see" (Barthes, *Camera Lucida* 6). So what is *there* in the photo, text, website, or new media project, what is leaf for leaf inseparable is what we all— producers, viewers, and scholars—are responsible for, what should drive us to question whether or not the closet of visual representation is indeed open, shut, or only standing ajar. We must note and understand that our cultural productions influence each other. We must defy any representation that attempts to define based solely on tokenism, stereotypes, or even archetypes. Ultimately, we must not merely consume but complicate the whole notion of an open media closet.

Notes

1. For a more detailed discussion of the clich8E, see, among other sources, Russo's *The Celluloid Closet* (156–174) and Andy Mangels's "Lesbian Sex = Death?" from *The Advocate* (70–71).
2. In his lecture "Searching for the Origami Unicorn: Media Convergence, Transmedia Storytelling, and the Matrix," Henry Jenkins presents his research on the growing phenomenon of "transmedia," or cross-media, consumption. For example, fans of the *Matrix* trilogy know a full understanding of the narrative is had only by viewing the films as well as reading the comic books, watching the *Animatrix*, and playing the video game.
3. Ironically, in this technologically advanced and webbed culture, it is still difficult, if not impossible, to acquire rights to reprint a photograph in a scholarly essay. Thus, the photos of Hannigan and Benson do not appear here; a description must suffice. In several of the *FHM* photos, Hannigan wears a black bra and panties. Her long, red hair is tousled, giving her a "bed head" look. Her makeup is heavier than what either she or Willow would normally apply. In other photos, Hannigan dons sheer, white, thigh-high hose with a baby blue garter that matches lacey bikinis and ribbed bustier. The bright lighting, cool colors of the set, and black and blue lingerie draws attention to Hannigan's porcelain skin. In nearly every photo, Hannigan gazes up, above the eye level of the camera with glossy, parted lips. In *Stuff*, Benson is placed against a backdrop of red curtains and red, carpeted stairs. She is clad in black, boy-short underwear and lacey bustier. The dim lighting complements Benson's rich, brown skin. Her hair is coifed like a lion's mane, and she poses kneeling or bending over at her hips, pouring her breasts toward the floor. She stares directly into the camera, straight-faced and bedroom-eyed.

4. The unattributed photo and caption of Hannigan and Benson at the celebration of *Buffy*'s one hundredth episode can currently be viewed on Majbritt's [pseud.] fan site at, http://www.alysonhannigan.dk/alypictures/alypub/idol/bp3.jpg..
5. See Mary Magoulick's "Frustrating Female Heroism: Mixed Messages in *Xena, Nikita*, and *Buffy*" for a recent and notable exception.

CHAPTER 4

Mapping Lesbian Sexuality on *Queer as Folk*

Rebecca Beirne

> Fundamental to Marilyn's enactment of patriarchal conceptions of femininity is the absence of female desire...Marilyn's absent desire, in particular, perpetuates the heterosexist notion that women are unable to define their desire. Heterosexual women have access to desire through men who define and contain that desire; lesbianism, which offers a site of female desire, is controlled in *Heartbeat* when it is rendered as nonsexuality.
>
> —Darlene Hantzis and Valerie Lehr, "Whose Desire? Lesbian (Non)Sexuality and Television's Perpetuation of Hetereo/Sexism," 112

The lesbian characters on Showtime's *Queer as Folk* (2000–2005) were remarkable in that, unlike almost all previous lesbian characters on television, they were not positioned in relation to a heterosexual environment. The television world of these characters is one that revolves around queerness, indeed, they exist in a homonormative environment rather than a heteronormative one. What exactly, however, does this homonormativity constitute? As I argued in "Embattled Sex," lesbians are excluded from the domain of "queer" that *Queer as Folk* privileges, and, by extension, from the realm of "sex." The series thereby enacts heteronormative patriarchal discourse even as it queers it, by maintaining gender distinctions that privilege male narratives and sexuality over female ones.

Like other television series that have presented lesbians, there are definite limitations to the presentation of lesbian desire and sex in *Queer as Folk*, particularly when compared with the presentation of gay male sexuality the series offers. In *Queer as Folk* lesbians and women in general are not, unlike men, figured as subjects consumed and driven by sexual desire. Lesbian characters Melanie (Michelle Clunie) and Lindsay (Thea Gill) are rarely involved in sexual activity in the series, and when they are, the manner in which these scenes unfold is temporally and representationally limited. While these factors in and of themselves would not be notable due to their ubiquity, here they are of particular significance since in *Queer as Folk* it is not heterosexuals who are the main protagonists, but rather gay men. Despite these limitations however, the lesbian characters on *Queer as Folk* are also of historical and representational significance, because they do indeed receive more screentime, have more on-screen sex, and certainly have more focus placed upon their lives *as lesbians* than in any previous television series.[1]

Melanie and Lindsay do at least take a step forward from the comforting arm pats or chaste kisses seen in *Heartbeat* or most of *Buffy the Vampire Slayer* or the tame titillation served up by sweeps week "lesbian" kisses.[2] At the beginning of the second season of *Queer as Folk*, the producers even appeared to be making an attempt to provide some degree of corrective to the lesbian sexual characterization of the first season, which was soundly critiqued by lesbian viewers. This is engendered both via showing the couple engaged in more sexual encounters and allowing them to respond to the frequent comments made by other characters about female, and particularly lesbian, sexuality. Take, for example, the following exchange:

Michael: . . . sex is different for men than it is for women, the need is more immediate, more intense. At least that's what I've read.
Lindsay: Where? In "Field and Stream?"
Melanie: Now, just for your information, Lindsay and I fuck like crazy, we pant and drool like a couple of bitches in heat. Our pussies soak the sheets.
Lindsay: And we go on a lot longer than the ten minute tumble you guys call sex.
Melanie: You don't wanna know how many times we get off in a night.
Michael: You're right I don't. Mom!! (2.8)

This interaction offsets the frequent comments made by Michael (Hal Sparks) and the others as to "the lesbians," as they are generally known in the series, perceived lack of sexual desire. It is perhaps further intended to imply that it is the characters themselves, rather than the writers of the series, who hold such views.

However, such progress is negated, both narratively, as will be discussed later, and by the representationally limited depiction of lesbian sexuality in the series. Perhaps the most marked feature of the lesbian sex visually depicted in *Queer as Folk* is the constant interruptions Melanie and Lindsay encounter—either within the narrative, through one or other of them losing interest in the activity, or by interruptions of phone calls and doorbells, or without, by cutting away to another scene during or immediately after initial foreplay. In a series that purports to be "all about sex" (1.1), we only very rarely see a woman at the height of pleasure, and only once do we see a woman achieve orgasm, rendering lesbian sex once again as mysterious and women's desires as unknowable and undepictable. This cannot be due to coyness or network restrictions, as not only are the male characters frequently depicted while orgasming, but orgasm is situated as central to many of the sex acts—whether by narratively focusing upon them (e.g., Justin's squirting scene in the first episode) or simply by presenting sex whose ultimate goal is orgasm. In fact, a "completed act of lesbian sex (with one of the women achieving orgasm on screen) does not occur until Episode 13's one-night stand, thus contextualising the act of female orgasm as an outlaw one" (Monteiro and Bowers). The de-prioritizing of orgasm in depictions of lesbian sex is not a new one. Even in a pornographic film made by and for lesbians discussed by Heather Butler "None of the scenes end with orgasm; in fact, orgasm does not seem to be a preoccupation in this film" (187). When placed in direct contrast to the male, goal-oriented sexuality in *Queer as Folk*, however, the presentation of only foreplay or frustrated sexual acts between the lesbian characters reinforces socially preconceived notions of lesbian sex *as* foreplay, inherently incomplete and lacking.

The more sexual characterization of lesbians in the early part of the second season, too, is directly undermined by the lesbian characters' narrative for the second portion of the second season, as they suddenly and inexplicably begin to wonder whether they have fallen prey to "lesbian bed death" (2.17). Such "bed death" is not an unusual plot device for the lesbian characters in *Queer as Folk*, having also previously been utilized in the first season. In the beginning of each of these seasons, the couple is shown happy and engaging in a traditional rite of passage (the birth of Gus in the first season and their wedding in the second); after which a period of "lesbian bed death" ensues, as do a variety of other conflicts; an act of extramarital sex occurs (Melanie's affair, the threesome with Leda); the couple is then reunified by someone else (Brian in season one and Leda in season two). After these seasons, the narrative pattern changes somewhat, and yet the depiction of the couple's sex life actually becomes worse. During season three, no sex is depicted between the two characters, aside from a rather lackluster and rushed insemination, the presentation of which would indicate that it should not be characterized as sex. Season four sees Melanie pregnant and amorous, but gaining little or no response from Lindsay, whose interest lies with Sam (Robin Thomas), while season five shows the couple estranged up until episode 5.9 where they share a passionately violent sexual reunion, perhaps inspired by a similar scene between Bette and Tina in *The L Word* (1.13). As can thus be seen, despite being a soap opera revolving around gay sex, the lesbian characters have little sex, and this further marginalizes them from the narrative. As Paul Robinson observes, "the women are no longer engaged in the dialectic of lust and love that is the leitmotif in the lives of the men" (156), a dialectic that is indeed, as Robinson sees it, "[t]he show's central theme" (152).

The only lesbian character in *Queer as Folk* who does seem to participate in this economy of desire is Leda (Nancy Anne Sakovich), the most markedly sexual and "queer" lesbian character in the series, who appears for a number of episodes in the second season. Leda seems to be an archetypal representative for the sex-positive lesbian: her relationships consist of one-night stands, she constantly refers to strap-ons, is dismissive of gay marriage, rides a motorbike, and organizes a stagette party for Melanie and Lindsay complete with lesbian strippers. She undermines homo/hetero boundaries and manages to surprise even Brian (Gale Harold) with her overt sexuality. This can be seen when she asks him whether he has "ever been fucked by a dyke with a dildo," thereby placing the quintessential gay male top into the recipient position (2.7). The manner in which this overt sexuality or empowerment takes place is an interesting one, as it appears that in *Queer as Folk* queer positionality is only available to women via entry into the phallic economy and identification with gay males over and above lesbians or straight women. Leda's frequent and vocal dissociation from and denigration of "the ladies who munch" (2.7), strangely shows her queerness as also constructed via opposition to "the lesbians," and even more curiously, cunnilingus. It seems that the only way the text is able to picture lesbians as queer or overtly sexual beings, is by figuring them as phallic women or "dildo dykes." This tendency can also be seen in the work of writers such as Michael Warner on whose list of "sexual outlaws" the only female outlaws consist of "dildo dykes" (32). And even the portrayal of Leda is returned to a normative understanding of female sexuality when she immediately latches onto Melanie and Lindsay after having a threesome with them, and she expresses a desire to "settle down" before riding off out of *Queer as Folk* (2.19).

While some male characters experience physical/psychological problems restraining them from having sex,[3] in Melanie and Lindsay's case their lack of sex is rather induced by a lack of desire, especially on the part of Lindsay. While these periods cause Melanie a significant amount of frustration and upset, as she discusses with Ted in the first season and expresses to Lindsay in the second, they do not appear to be an issue to Lindsay. In fact, Lindsay frequently yawns or otherwise expresses her lack of interest when Melanie does attempt to kiss or seduce her. In one of the few times we see Lindsay initiating what appears to be a seduction (at least of a woman), it soon becomes apparent that she is doing so in order to manipulate Melanie to "give Brian a chance" (1.5)—portraying feminine sexuality as a tool instead of an end in itself.

The suggestions of Lindsay's lesbianism as being somewhat unstable become more clearly textual in episode six of the fourth series, when a story line begins to develop that will see Lindsay having sex with a male character by episode ten. This begins via the introduction of the character of artist Sam, who is from the beginning characterized as a difficult and chauvinistic man. Lindsay, attempting to get Sam to show his artwork at her gallery, is initially horrified by both his rudeness and his clear objectification of women. Later Melanie, in a very uncharacteristic move, after listening to Lindsay's ranting that "the man is a pig . . . if I wasn't already a dyke he'd have me diving for the nearest muff"[4] advises her to use her feminine wiles to get his attention, and thereby his artwork.

The next time we see Lindsay, she is clad in over-the-knee black boots, flirting with and flattering Sam, who proceeds to repeatedly proposition and grope her. Their flirtation continues throughout Lindsay's curation of Sam's show, with several conversations occurring that use "art" as a barely veiled metaphor for Lindsay's desire for Sam, while her desire for Melanie is expressed in terms of filial connections and responsibilities, acting to rearticulate *Queer as Folk*'s association of creativity and cultural production within the phallic economy, regulating women's relationships and endeavors to the realms of hearth, home, and family.

Lindsay's desires are further indicated by a rare sex scene with Melanie (significantly, their first since episode 2.19) in 4.10. A very pregnant Melanie is performing cunnilingus on Lindsay, who quite extravagantly expresses her boredom with several sighs. Lindsay then requests that Melanie use a vibrator, which, as Sarah Warn remarks "we're clearly meant to understand is a phallic replacement" ("*Queer as Folk*"). Although the scene soon cuts away, their next conversation informs us that Lindsay was "wild" and "so turned on" (Melanie 4.10), although she has already turned back to avoidance of discussing anything sexual, and instead is deeply engrossed in the grocery list. Later in the same episode, after various displays of guilt-induced domesticity, including not attending the opening of the art show that she has curated, Lindsay has feverish sex with Sam (up against an original painting no less).

In a review of this series of rather unfortunate events, Warn asserts that the story line "does more damage than good":

> The lesbian-who-sleeps-with-a-man plot device has been used so frequently in entertainment that it dwarfs almost all other representations of lesbians on screen (except perhaps the equally frustrating lesbian-motherhood plot device, which *QAF* also employs regularly), and gives the impression that it occurs more frequently in real life than it actually does—that in fact, *most* lesbians want to sleep with men, rather than just a few. It also makes no distinction between lesbians and bisexual women, and continues to reinforce the notion that bisexual women will inevitably betray lesbians for a man, as if infidelity is the particular vice of one sexual orientation rather than cutting across all. (*"Queer as Folk"*)

While Warn's frustrations are completely justified, her later claims that *Queer as Folk*'s Lindsay is among the television characters that "momentarily switch sexual orientations" are somewhat inflated, since Lindsay has been depicted as latently bisexual throughout the series via her clear attraction to Brian.

The surrounding story lines do also act to somewhat contextualize, or at least add a degree of complexity to, this plot development. Such narrative contextualization can be seen in Michael and Ben's (Robert Gant) foster son Hunter (Harris Allen) being depicted dating a girl, having previously (with the exception of one comment) been presented as gay. In a highly comic series of scenes, Hunter is anxious about coming out to his gay parents as straight, eventually does so, and Michael expresses all the classic parental coming-out lines (e.g., questioning whether it is "just a phase?" and whether Hunter just needs to meet the right boy). Ben in contrast displays more understanding, albeit understanding that is underlaid by a polarized view of gay and straight. In answer to Michael's curiosity as to how this could be the case considering Hunter's previous sexual experience with men (within the context of sex work) and desire for Brian, Ben reveals that he himself had had sexual experiences with women prior to his coming out. The ongoing insinuations that Brian and Lindsay had sex when they were in college are even confirmed in this episode, showing that even Brian, the "ultimate homosexual" of the series, has had a heterosexual encounter.

Despite such narratives, the text refuses to name bisexuality. Sexual experiences with the opposite sex for "homosexuals," or same sex for "heterosexuals," are seen as aberrations to who one "really is" (Ben 4.11) and the *verbal* suggestion of bisexuality is never made. Even for Lindsay, who has had an ongoing struggle between her desires for Melanie and Brian, and in season four clearly is conflicted between her desires for Sam and her desires for Melanie, does not question whether or not she may be bisexual, or indeed simply "queer." During Lindsay's confession to Brian about her affair, he tells her "it's okay to like cock, and it's okay to like pussy, just not at the same time" (4.11). Lindsay herself also consistently expresses her sexuality in terms of an either/or choice. When Sam asks her "what about the part of you that secretly yearns for something else? The part of you that both of us know is there," Lindsay responds, "my house has many rooms, I occupy but a few, the rest go unvisited" (4.11). The emphasis placed upon "choosing a team" by both Melanie and Brian, appears to be one that the series as a whole espouses.

It is of definite significance that it is Melanie who is depicted as clearly lesbian while Lindsay displays attractions to men. From sexological discourse to pop-cultural representations and even within queer culture itself, there are often distinctions drawn between the real or authentic lesbian, who is almost always portrayed as masculine (or at least more masculine than her consort), and those whose sexual preference is depicted as more fluid, who are generally marked by their femininity. *Queer as Folk*'s Lindsay is portrayed as "less lesbian" and more identified with men than her partner Melanie precisely because she is coded as the femme. As such, the series activates a very traditional view of feminine lesbians—seeing them as latent heterosexuals. While "lesbian chic" may have already seen two blooms, little it seems has changed in the last two decades in regard to how feminine lesbians are represented in popular culture. This observation must be tempered by the fact that the vast majority of lesbians who appear in popular discourse at all *are* feminine in both appearance and narrative-identification. The point, however, remains that the sexualities of those characters *identified by the narrative with masculinity* (whether or not they actually *appear* to express female masculinity) are not similarly positioned as associated with fluidity of sexual-object-choice.

In *Queer as Folk* one cannot help but notice the curious practice of *encoding* Melanie as butch while not *presenting* her as such, much as characters were once coded as queer while not giving any definitive visible indication of their queerness (most famously discussed by Vito Russo in *The Celluloid Closet*). Melanie's appearance is less feminine than Lindsay's, with her fairly short, dark hair, less voluptuous physique and usual garb of pants and shirts.[5]

But she is certainly still visibly within acceptable codes of femininity—her hair is not *too* short, she is conventionally beautiful, wears makeup, and even occasionally wears frocks for work or social occasions. Her encoding as butch instead operates through contrast and on a verbal level. Such characterizations usually take place negatively, via jokes or insults at Melanie's expense on the part of the gay male characters (and at times Debbie [Sharon Gless]), though they are sometimes more positively framed by Melanie herself, or, on a couple of occasions, other characters. This need to encode rather than show is particularly peculiar in light of the portrayal of Emmett as a flamboyantly effeminate gay man, perhaps pointing to television reading female masculinity as more threatening than male femininity. One of the few times that a woman who is clearly physically expressive of female masculinity is given a foregrounded role (still of course a one-liner), she is characterized by the narrative as grotesque and fear-inspiring. Attending Gus's bris (1.3), Michael is greeted by a larger butch woman with a "hi Michael" and a hug. While this hug lasts for the briefest of moments, Michael displays an expression of extreme distaste and acts as if he is being squashed.

Whether or not Melanie actually performs "butch," the traditional associations directed at butch-femme relationships are present throughout the series, although these associations have been gradually undermined over the last two decades. The butch is seen as the authentic lesbian, who is figured as the desiring party with a higher sex drive than the femme, and the sexual top. Melanie also prioritizes her bond with and attachments to women, and is at times portrayed as anti-men. While *Queer as Folk* is willing to present a small spectrum of differently gendered presentations with its gay male characters (contrast, for example, the camp Emmett and the hypermasculine Brian)[6] without defining one as inherently more gay than the other, "true" lesbianism appears to only be accessible within the series to those in possession of (butch) lesbian signifiers.

While *Queer as Folk* has certainly been groundbreaking for its medium in its presentation of gay and lesbian characters in a gay world, in its candid sexuality and its willingness to engage with contemporary political issues that directly pertain to homosexuals, the manner in which its lesbian characters are represented has seen little change from earlier depictions of lesbianism. The distinctions between the manner in which the sexuality of heterosexual and homosexual characters are portrayed in televisual texts with one or two gay characters, are, in *Queer as Folk*, displaced onto gender—with lesbians taking up the desexualized role. Perhaps the clearest lesson coming out of *Queer as Folk* is that even when operating within a queer framework, attention still needs to be paid to the specificities and privileges of gender.

Notes

The author's monograph *Lesbians in Television and Text after the Millennium* (Palgrave Macmillan) contains a longer discussion of the lesbian characters in *Queer as Folk*.

1. While such characters as *Buffy the Vampire Slayer*'s Willow, e.g., may have received proportionately more screentime, little attention was paid to her lesbianism.

2. U.S. television has a long tradition of broadcasting same-sex kisses between women during "sweeps week" in order to boost their ratings to entice advertisers. See Virginia Heffernan's *New York Times* article "It's February; Pucker Up, TV Actresses."

3. For example, in episode 2.9, Ted (Scott Lowell) is unable to achieve an erection due to an overload of sexual imagery, while Brian experiences a similar problem shortly after completing treatment for testicular cancer (4.9).

4. Reinforcing the popular notion that lesbians "turn to muff" not because they like it, but because of male chauvinism.

5. Traditional coding in both mainstream and subcultural sources of many kinds still almost always presents the femm(er) character as blond and the butch(er) character as dark-haired. The butch character is also generally of a lower socioeconomic status. An exception to this rule can be seen in *The Incredibly True Adventures of Two Girls in Love* (1995), which depicts a femme African American character dating a butch Caucasian girl (though the socioeconomic code still holds).

6. The spectrum is certainly not large. We see a few drag queens as one-off characters and there are a few references to transgenderism, but generally speaking, *Queer as Folk* is limited in its presentation of gender diversity.

CHAPTER 5

"Going Native on Wonder Woman's Island": The Exoticization of Lesbian Sexuality in *Sex and the City*

Melissa M. M. Hidalgo

The increasing visibility of lesbians on mainstream television in the post-*Ellen* era points to a gradual cultural acceptance of lesbian sexuality and of female sexual agency in general. One show in particular, HBO's *Sex and the City*,[1] figures prominently as a cultural phenomenon that brought visibility and viability to the idea of a liberatory female sexuality. As Samantha, the show's vixen, says early on in the season, this is the "first time in history" that "women have as much money and power as men do." Samantha, constructed throughout the show's six-season run as a sort of "honorary" male, a masculinized female who sees not "color but conquest" in her sexual exploits and adventures, celebrates what she sees as women's sexual freedom to have sex "like men." Of course, this sexual "freedom" is granted to those women who are privileged racially, economically, and it favors those women who maintain and perpetuate heteronormativity.

But is visibility enough? What are the implications of valuing sex "like men"? Perhaps the question should be, What is the value of having sex like lesbians? In shows like *Sex and the City* and *The L Word*, the body of the lesbian woman of color becomes the site of sexual exploration and affirmation for the privileged white heterosexual woman. Now that lesbianism and its representations have arguably become more mainstream, there remains a tendency in certain shows, particularly *Sex and the City*, to construct it as subversive or even threatening to the heterosexual order upon which the logic of the television show and the two *Sex and the City* films rests.

Sex and the City premiered on the premium cable channel HBO in June of 1998. Over its six-season run through 2004, the show garnered much praise from the television and entertainment industry, earning Emmys, Golden Globes, and other honors for its stars and producers. A year later, in September of 2005, *Sex and the City* premiered on US television in syndication, debuting on the WB on 19 September 2005, effectively widening its audience and mass appeal and building a larger fan base for the pair of movies in 2008 and 2010.

Unlike the television show, which enjoyed steady praise and critical acclaim, the two theatrical releases, *Sex and the City: The Movie* (2008) and *Sex and the City 2* (2010) were received less favorably. In fact, *Sex and the City 2* was uniformly panned by film critics from the *New York Times* to the *Village Voice*. Critics decried the film's exhibitionism and the "unexamined privilege" (Scott) of the four women's extravagant travels to "the New Middle East," or Abu Dhabi (filmed in Morocco).[2] Nevertheless, the tired marketing machine that is the *Sex and the City* franchise clearly occupies an important space in the popular cultural landscape, both for viewers and now for academics. In 2004, the year the television series ended, a volume of academic essays devoted entirely to the HBO hit show was published.[3] It is this volume that interests me most, because while a few of the contributors do well to address the show's "freakish" treatment of non-normative sexuality (Greven) and the commodification of lesbians for consumption (Zieger 100), the issue of race *and* lesbianism is never fully engaged critically.

Given this oversight, it is important to consider the show's treatment of not only lesbians, but of lesbians of color. Certainly, Charlotte's "Power Lesbians" and Samantha's Maria need to be considered as representations of a racialized non-normative femininity. Accordingly, this paper will address these current manifestations of the straight-white-woman-meets-exotic-lesbian-of-color themes on popular shows like *Sex and the City,* which position the body of the queer woman of color as the site upon which the anxiety of white female heterosexuality gets played out throughout the series and in *Sex and the City 2*.

On the show, lesbians and lesbian women of color become mere tools to deliver white women out of the closet just long enough to reaffirm and secure their heterosexuality and whiteness. When lesbian sexuality appears to threaten the heterosexual order of the four characters' lives, it must otherwise be contained in order to restore that order or keep it intact. Throughout the course of the HBO show, each character has her own brush with lesbianism, or in Carrie's case, with a bisexual female, played by Canadian rocker Alanis Morissette. For two of the show's characters, Samantha and Charlotte, lesbian spheres and spaces become what Kelly Hankin would call "site[s] of heterosexual tourism" (18), safe spaces for the straight girls to visit and play with the (lesbian) natives for a night or three before heading back to the safe confines of heterosexuality.

As such, the representations of lesbianism in these episodes and over the course of *Sex and the City*'s six-season run operate as reminders to viewers of the exoticism and non-normative nature of racialized lesbian sexuality, including that of Charlotte's Irish nanny, Erin, in *Sex and the City 2*. In the show, Samantha and Charlotte risk nothing by visiting "Wonder Woman's island,"[4] because their whiteness and heterosexuality grants them that privilege. Therefore, these representations of lesbians—white and nonwhite—vis-à-vis their white heterosexual counterparts ultimately serve to remarginalize lesbianism, reinstating its status as an exotic and taboo sexuality, while eliding the political, historical, and cultural consequences that actual lesbians face because of their sexuality in the United States and elsewhere. Ultimately, *Sex and the City*'s racial coding of lesbians serves to recenter normative white hetero female sexuality, while positing lesbian sexuality as temporary and disposable, a label that only suits those who don it out of their heterosexual privilege.

"Poof! You're a Lesbian!"
Designer Lesbianism

In this section, I will discuss two episodes of *Sex and the City* to argue that queer[5] female sexuality is commodified within the heterosexual matrix; as a commodity, lesbianism carries an exchange value for white hetero women, allowing them the possibility of advancing socially or economically, which ultimately positions lesbians as disposable and void of value once they have been "used" by straight women. Episode 3, season 1, called "Bay of Married Pigs," which aired on June 21, 1998, features plot lines that shape and inform the show's future treatment of lesbians in representing Miranda as a "pseudo-lesbian," eager to please her law firm's senior partner. This episode also establishes Miranda's queer potential for, as a successful, career-oriented lawyer, Miranda is the pessimist of the show, eschewing anything "girly" and viewing with cynicism the cultural dictates that tell single women in their thirties that if they are not married (or partnered) with children by that age milestone, they are worthless.

The show sets the stage at Miranda's firm's annual softball game. Miranda's colleagues, frustrated that they cannot "figure her out," assume she's gay and set her up with Syd, a lesbian lawyer at the firm. Syd's androgynous name goes well with her androgynous appearance; her short hair, lack of makeup, and softball athleticism; she is coded as lesbian and therefore must be an ideal match for Miranda. Given this episode's preoccupation with the anxiety surrounding single women and the "discrimination" they face from their married friends, Miranda already is frustrated that her single status renders her practically invisible by her firm's partners. Her male colleague responsible for setting her up with Syd prides himself on his ability to "pick 'em," as Syd is a "real find," even though Miranda has to break the news to him that she's not gay, despite the fact that she has not been seen with a man in the eight months she has been at her firm. As Carrie's voice-over tells us, the "pseudo-lesbian couple got the attention of Charles, the firm's senior partner," and he proceeds to invite the couple to his house for dinner. Later, an exasperated Miranda tells Carrie that he only invited her because he thinks she's part of a couple. She tells Carrie, "he seemed so relieved to finally figure me out." Miranda, coded as lesbian by wearing a dark suit and tie, slicked-down hair, and little makeup, arrives at the dinner party with Syd, coded femme in this scene. After what seemed like a successful date, Miranda confesses to Charles that she's not with Syd and only came with her to "bend [his] ear about [her] work at the firm."

Disappointed, he tells Miranda that his wife "will be disappointed" because "she was looking to add a lesbian couple to our circle," suggesting that Miranda is only valuable as a lesbian. Her butchness is what grants her access, albeit temporary, to her boss, and to the potential of a higher income. But what about Syd, who is represented as the actual lesbian? She holds no currency on her own but suddenly acquires value to both Miranda and Charles.

For Miranda in this episode, lesbianism's value as a commodity works for her so she can get the attention of her firm's lead partner. Syd, the lesbian in this context, is "trafficked," assigned a value within a system of heterosexual exchange because of her potential "usefulness" to Samantha, Charles, and his wife. (Rubin 164).[6] The "traffic in lesbians" within the television economy of *Sex and the City* renders lesbianism an object—"a find"—to be used and consumed for a greater purpose: in the service of Miranda's job security and social status to the hetero couple. As a commodified lesbian, Syd adds value to previously single Miranda in the eyes of her employer. Miranda is "determined to make partner even if it's as a lesbian." In this context, "lesbian" is not a sexual or political identity, but a label of convenience tried on by heterosexuals like Miranda to advance herself in her field. As Mandy Merck notes, "The idea of homosexuality as erotically in fashion, but wrong for Miranda, is rammed home by Carrie's comparison" therof to a DKNY dress: a fashionable, temporary thing to "try on" (53). However, Miranda attempts to fashion for herself an identity that could turn profitable for her, albeit at no risk to her.

Miranda's heterosexual privilege is invoked here, which allows her to "negotiate and rejuvenate" her chances at making partner as a heterosexual single woman, only to "discard" the lesbian and the label of lesbian (Hankin 35). Furthermore, while being gay could have stabilized Miranda professionally, her faux lesbianism and partnership with Syd are reified into a spectacle, an object to be collected and added to an already existing circle of friends. However, the heterosexuals are the ones that get to make that choice; their privilege allows them to coopt the lesbians and assume that they would even want to be a part of their circle. Furthermore, heterosexual privilege produces another social irony. The politics of being "out of the closet" at the workplace frame this part of the episode, but being out only works for her because Miranda is not gay.

In a later episode, Miranda runs into a gay colleague at a club who asks that she not "out" him, for fear of losing his job at the firm and getting harassed by the older, more conservative partners. Clearly, there are consequences for gay people that accompany being out at work, as this later episode acknowledges. For Miranda, coming out as a lesbian with a partner enables her to sell herself as a worthy prospect for partner at her law firm. Economic privilege trumps sexual orientation, and the threat of coming out at work is rendered nonexistent. Instead, the lesbian label becomes a useful tool for straight people, worn by Miranda to maintain economic security at her prestigious job. In effect, this particular episode elides the very real consequences for many gay men and lesbians, who literally cannot afford to come out at work or show themselves with partners at functions as such.

In another episode, "lesbian chic" is tried on by Charlotte in an attempt to escape a life "complicated by men," which leads her to the "safe[ty] and warmth" of her new circle of lesbian friends. Episode 6 of season 2, "The Cheating Curve" (July 11, 1999) features "power lesbians." Charlotte's gallery hosts an opening for a lesbian artist from Brooklyn. The point that she's from Brooklyn, an already racially coded, "other" place, is significant. Recall that in the show's final season, Miranda very reluctantly moves to Brooklyn, which she considers to be an outpost of backward, unfashionable living when compared with Manhattan. As Carrie's voice-over trumpets, the power lesbians are defined as "lesbian chic meets art-world cool, a fabulous combustion that no one saw coming. They were the latest group to flaunt their disposable income." The power lesbians in Charlotte's gallery "seemed to have everything—great shoes, killer eyewear, and the secrets to invisible make up." Of course, their "power" comes only from their economic privilege and their affluence; their income is as disposable as they are in this world.

Susan Zieger writes, "the episode represents [the power lesbians'] sexual difference through their specific high-end consumption" (100). I would also add that this episode enables a reading of lesbians of color as not only disposable, but as exotic, framing Samantha's foray into lesbianism with Maria in later episodes.

As Carrie speaks, the camera catches a group of these power lesbians striding around Charlotte's gallery, "apparently the only venue in which the principals can possibly encounter homosexual women" (Merck 56). The power lesbians hold champagne and look like they own the place, moving with confidence in the space designated just for them. We see an interracial lesbian couple, but in this world, black and white women are equalized by their earning power and high socioeconomic status. The white lesbian is a VP at Warner music, while her ex, a black woman, works on Wall Street. These power lesbians represent commodified lesbianism, one in which racial difference is erased by money, and lots of it. Capitalism here promotes the transcendence of race and sexuality issues that would otherwise stifle and repress the mobility of actual lesbians in the world. Money also "whitens" blackness within this framework, and along with it, renders lesbianism a safe, desexualized space that Charlotte comfortably fits into.

This episode is also important for locating the lesbian sphere in a marginal space that exists outside the realm of heteronormative female sexuality, one that gets constructed as "an exotic tourist locale" (Hankin 19). In this episode, the power lesbians take Charlotte on a tour of their "homeland," as Carrie explains in a voice-over: "Drinks at G-spot, dinner and scintillating conversation at Luke's, the hot new French fusion restaurant with its equally hot Sapphic chef, followed by late-night dancing at the Love Tunnel." The evening "left Charlotte as exhilarated and happy as she had been in ages" in the relaxing and liberating atmosphere. Here, food is equated with consumption of lesbian chic, a temporary stay on the island, itself an "alternate universe that contained no thought of men." The camera's slow-motion captures Charlotte swaying, eyes closed, body writhing in a sexless sex act, in the throes of passion among many hot (mostly femme) women. Charlotte is constructed as a tourist flanked by racially diverse lesbian "natives" of the island. Because Charlotte thinks "her" lesbians and their embrace of her as their "new friend" must be attributed to her (mis)conception that "sex is not an issue," she sees no danger in associating with them.

Yet, when sex is enunciated and becomes the "question on everybody's mind," it has to be coded racially so as to maintain its taboo marginalized status. When Charlotte meets up with Lydia and the lesbians, it is clear that

Lydia likes Charlotte and later, she takes her to a gathering at Patty Aston's house (Aston is played by Jodi Long). As Carrie explains, "Patty Aston was the ex-wife of a Hollywood movie producer" who's now a lesbian, "the queen bee of the power lesbian social hive." Implicit here is that Patty was a straight woman who has "gone native," but more significantly, situated within the cultural moment of the time, this scene resonates with other references of such women.[7]

Placed in this cultural context, the message of the episode reads as a warning to straight women who might be "converted" by lesbian society. But the conversion never happens, as lesbianism is drained of its sexuality. Patty asks Charlotte something "everybody wants to know," which is whether or not Charlotte is gay. Charlotte says no, although she "connects to the female spirit," "sexually, [Charlotte] feel[s] that [she is] straight." Patty, a woman of Asian descent, retorts: "sweetheart, that's all very nice, but if you're not going to eat pussy, you're not a dyke." She walks away, leaving Charlotte stunned and rejected. Essentially, Charlotte has just been dumped, and her vacation to "Wonder Woman's island" is over. Patty sexualizes and racializes lesbianism; by speaking explicitly about "eating pussy," she reorients lesbianism within a sexual realm that is also delineated by racial difference. Becoming/being a dyke becomes an exclusive thing, a club to which the "real lesbians" belong. Here, however, lesbianism becomes exoticized. As a woman of color, Patty (and later, Maria) represents an extreme version of marginality; race is the marker of the other, and in this case, of the exotic.

As Patty reminds the viewer, being a lesbian is first and foremost about sex, but in the show, it is also about being a racialized other. Contrary to Charlotte's claim, being a lesbian *is* an issue, not the "non-issue" she wants it to be. Within the context of "cheating," the episode's thematic vehicle, Charlotte was trying to cheat and she got caught. A narrative of "I came, I saw, I conquered" frames the show's dialogue and plot: lesbianism is coded as a "discovery," an "island," an "alternate universe," just waiting to be discovered by Charlotte. The Asian woman is the "authentic dyke" who eats pussy and basically casts Charlotte off her island. Charlotte cannot go native here. The sex act of "eating pussy" authenticates the lesbian experience and identity, defining it as primarily a sexual identity, one that Charlotte is unable to claim for herself because she does not engage in lesbian sex acts.

In rejecting Charlotte from the "lesbian club," Patty ejects her back into Heteroland, and the world of lesbians remains intact, although as a faraway place, an exotic locale contained within itself. The world of lesbians remains a site of "heterosexual tourism;" it is a fixed space where power lesbians wear Prada, buy art, dance at clubs called the G-spot, and eat pussy. Once the sexual act is articulated, the Asian dyke woman seals off "the club" for

Charlotte, but in doing so, she services the hetero norm. The episode ends with a shot of Big and Carrie dancing, their rekindled relationship on display. The power lesbian subplot generates a reading that positions lesbians as a diversion, a detraction from the hetero subplots, even though it momentarily renders heterosexuality as an unstable construction. Lesbianism is more assured and stable as it destabilizes heteronormativity, but it in order to do so, it must exist in its own realm, as a faraway alternative universe, a safe distance away from ever encroaching on the heteronormative spaces inhabited by Charlotte and her friends.

"The Glorious Boceta:" Racializing Lesbian Sexuality and "Eating the Other"

During Season 4, three episodes ("Defining Moments," "What's Sex Got to Do with It?" and "Ghost Town") featured the lesbian relationship between Samantha and Maria, played by "Brazilian bombshell" Sonia Braga. Significantly, the producers cast Braga to play the part of the exotic Brazilian artist because they had to overmatch the usual sultry sexiness exuded constantly by Samantha's character. It seems that the only way to accomplish this was to cast a Latina, who, according to stereotypes, is already a sexualized, alluring, seductive figure by virtue of her brown skin and accent-inflected English.[8] Sonia Braga "others" the character of Maria, who is "explored" and eventually discarded by Samantha. These three episodes showcase a colonial fantasy narrative of "eating the other."

Samantha meets Maria at Charlotte's gallery which (again) is hosting the opening of a lesbian art show. This time, Maria is the artist and is already figured in terms of commodity exchange. Charlotte owns Maria; the Brazilian is a hot lesbian artist, a commodity to be shared and exchanged within the space of her gallery. When Samantha announces that she and Maria are dating, Charlotte stutters, "Mm-mm-*my* Maria? From the gallery?" Samantha replies, "Well she's *my* Maria now." This dialogue exchange signifies their ownership of the other, "the traffic in Maria" being exchanged among white hetero women. However, Maria is assigned a different value according to her use. For Charlotte, it's about the success of her gallery; for Samantha, it's about an exciting new sexual foray, always valued by Samantha. Maria represents the sexual frontier that Samantha has yet to "explore" and conquer. Maria is exoticized not only as a racialized other, but as a sexual other; her race is necessary to mark her as other, apart from the white hetero woman framework. Marked as such, Maria becomes something—a body—to be exchanged, owned, conquered, and disposed when her use value is spent.

Maria's racialized sexual agency is apparent from the beginning to the end of these three episodes. In almost every frame she's in, Maria's race and Brazilianness are emphasized and made visible. She wears bright colors—lipstick red or cobalt blue—or all black. Her long black hair is either tied up in chopsticks or left long and hanging, as if out of control. She speaks Portuguese to an ex-girlfriend and struggles constantly with English colloquialisms that are not translatable to Portuguese. In the breakup scene in the last of this set of episodes, Maria is reduced to a flat stereotype. Merck writes this about the Maria character: "And true to form, the 'real' lesbian of the couple is the darker of the two women, ethnically marked in colouring, dress and accent" (56). In an echo of the earlier episode in which Patty, the Asian woman, is marked as the "authentic dyke," Maria's race makes visible her "sexualised difference" (56).

Maria shows a frustrated and bored Samantha the "fireworks" she longs for; as salsa music plays in the background, Maria throws dishes to the floor, breaking them. She is violently animated, and the scene turns her into a caricature of a stereotypical fiery Latina woman with exaggerated movements, her behavior highly racialized and coded as irrational and uncontrollable. Here, Maria is coded as the "libidinally excessive and sexually uncontrolled" non-European woman (Loomba 155), a reading that carries more meaning if we read this relationship as another example of Samantha's colonial sexual fantasy. Effectively, Maria has been reduced to a "savage" brown body by the end of the relationship. As she begins her seduction of Samantha, Maria explains to her that helping her with her art "is a Brazilian thing." Maria, ever the smooth lesbian who knows how to "work it," seduces Samantha as Brazilian samba music plays in the background, her cleavage showing, her body sexualized next to an unusually modestly clad Samantha. Visibly and linguistically, Maria is cast as an outsider, a foreign presence in the white-washed, heterocentric world of *Sex and the City*.

Yet once she has seduced Samantha, Maria becomes the teacher of proper sex between women. The second episode that features Maria and Samantha posits Maria as kind of native informant, an "authentic insider"[9] of lesbian sex, teaching Samantha about the "glorious *boceta*," while continuing the theme of a disposable, commodified lesbianism. Although for Samantha, "lesbian" is a label, "like Gucci or Versace," it is a reality for Maria, with risk involved. Yet economic and heterosexual privilege allow Samantha to claim lesbianism like a designer fashion, something she's wearing for the moment until it goes out of style.

Additionally, lesbianism is figured in this episode as a pedagogical spectacle to be appropriated by Samantha in the service of and as "inspiration" to help her straight friends consummate their hetero relationships. Carrie's voice-over informs the viewer that "inspired by Samantha's willingness to explore new territory, Charlotte felt it was time to conquer some old territory: The bed, where she and Trey had so much trouble as man and wife." The rhetoric of colonization and conquest shapes Samantha's encounter and involvement with the other. Consider bell hooks's articulation of the politics and economy of interracial sexual encounters in her essay, "Eating the Other:"

> Exploring how desire for the Other is expressed, manipulated, and transformed by encounters with difference is a critical terrain that can indicate whether...potentially revolutionary longings are ever fulfilled....To make oneself vulnerable to the seduction of difference, to seek an encounter with the Other, does not require that one relinquish forever one's mainstream positionality. When race and ethnicity become commodified as resources for pleasure, the culture of specific groups, as well as the bodies of individuals, can be seen as constituting an alternative playground where members of dominating races, genders, and sexual practices affirm their power-over in intimate relations with the Other. (22–23)

I cite this passage at length because of its bearing on my analysis of Maria and Samantha's relationship, as well as the other lesbian figures in the show; it is through hooks that we can come to understand how *Sex and the City* others a lesbianism that ultimately reinforces the status quo. The episode draws out the connections between Samantha's "willingness" to engage in lesbian sex and the consummation of the marriage bed for Trey and Charlotte. As members of dominating races, genders, and sexual practices, Samantha, Trey, and Charlotte affirm their power-over in intimate relations, ultimately tied to the conquest of the other.

The transitional voice-over cues us to the next scene, in which Maria instructs Samantha how to make love to her liking. Carrie's "Meanwhile, at Casa de Lesbo..." exemplifies racialized and homophobic language inflected with sarcasm, devaluing the relationship. In this scene, Samantha initially assumes the role of the man. As she dives right in between Maria's legs, Maria has to stop her, explaining that "it's not really working for me." Samantha tells her that she's "never gotten any complaints from the men." Here, heteronormative sex practices inform Samantha's understanding of what women want, but Maria knows the difference: "I'm not a man. This is love making. It's not a porno flick." As she lies down, she tells Samantha "to look at [her] *boceta*...that's a Portuguese word for pussy." Maria's *boceta* becomes a visual aid in a pedagogical moment, and she also exoticizes it by calling it by its Portuguese name.

Samantha has much to learn about women's sexuality, but she proves to be an eager student. Samantha excitedly tells the girls about the "fascinating education" she's getting from Maria. Now, *she's* the one teaching Charlotte and the girls all about lesbian sex, explaining what an engorged vagina looks like, and downplaying the importance of a dick: "Maria has 10 dicks," Samantha gushes, as she holds up her fingers, wiggling them. She continues, "Well, I can tell you right now that this [*she jabs her finger violently into the air as if mimicking what a dick does*] is not the same as . . . this [*swirls a finger into the air and pretends to lick it*]." As she describes her newfound knowledge about the joys of lesbian sex, Samantha's face moves as if she is savoring a sweet dessert, or engaging in what hooks would call "eating the other."

Sex with Maria is conflated with eating, as food (such as strawberries) becomes the primary tool of seduction. Furthermore, this scene represents cultural appropriation by the dominant members of society. Samantha's linguistic appropriation of the *boceta* is used to educate her straight friends about their own sexual habits and anatomy. Later, we see that Samantha successfully arouses Maria, so much that Maria's orgasm results in "female ejaculation." Obviously, Samantha is a deft student who's learning quickly, although in the end, the other has been "eaten, consumed, and forgotten" (hooks, "Eating the Other" 39).

Conclusion

Considered within the narrative arc of the show's six-season run, most of the lesbian action occurs within the first four seasons; the last two seasons are dedicated to tying up any loose ends, culminating in the closure that sees Carrie, Miranda, Samantha, and Charlotte in stable heterosexual relationships. Two of them—Miranda and Charlotte—are married with children or with kids on the way. The two *Sex and the City* movies that followed the series end promulgate the heteronormative lives lived out by Charlotte and Harry and their two girls, as well as Miranda's happily domesticated life in Brooklyn with husband Steve; their son, Brady; Magda, the Ukrainian nanny; and Maggie, Steve's mother. Happily-ever-after married life even touches Big and Carrie, whose wedding and subsequent lives as newlyweds serve as the primary narrative frameworks of both films.

An interesting twist to the representation of racialized lesbian sexuality in both the series and in *Sex and the City 2* is the character of Erin, the "hot Irish nanny" who works for Charlotte and Harry in the second film.

Erin is a minor character whose voluptuous, unbridled breasts become the point of anxiety for Charlotte, who fears that Harry will cheat with the hot nanny while Charlotte is away in Abu Dhabi with the girls. Erin does not wear a bra, and every time she appears on screen, the camera captures her in slow motion while an Irish jig befitting an Irish Spring or Lucky Charms commercial plays in the background. The Irish flute and jig music is one way the film marks Erin as "other" and "exotic," a young lass with bouncing, bountiful breasts that prompts a gaping-mouthed Samantha to dub her "Erin Go Bra-less."[10]

It is significant that Erin is cast as an Irish nanny, a character that falls in line with the show's trend of racialized lesbian sexuality that I have traced throughout the series and that also speaks to the larger history of the Irish as racialized "others." As Bronwen Walter notes in her article, "Gender, 'Race,' and Diaspora: Racialized Identities of Emigrant Irish Women:"

> [T]he Irish have historically been marginalized from hegemonic "White" British society through processes of representation that have cast them as a racial "other." The British still wield considerable representational authority over the Irish as derived from their historical position as colonizer." (339)

This latter point is driven home with the fact that Alice Eve, a London-born UK actress, plays the role of the Irish nanny, who, we find out, rather "prefers the company of other hot nannies." Yes, we find out Erin is a lesbian, thus quelling Charlotte's fear that she would seduce her husband and underscoring lesbianism's service in preserving heterosexual unions. In the film's closing shot of Charlotte, Harry, and the gang at their daughter's birthday party, we see Erin coupled with another feminine-presenting "hot" brunette alongside the other "normal" families, happily ever after and safely contained within heteronormative marriage standards.

Such affirmation of heterosexual women's roles as primarily mothers and wives is a politically regressive, retrograde construction of female sexuality, and the lesbians have faded from sight, not part of this particular hetero equation or somehow folded into it, as is the case with Erin and her "hot nanny." As David Greven writes of the series, "[It] reinforces the notion that gay sex is transitory, fleeting, intangible, but that heterosexual sex is forever" (42). I suggest a similar argument be made for lesbian sex or any other non-normative sexual practices as they are represented in the show. Throughout *Sex and the City*, lesbianism is coded in racialized terms in order to exoticize it; for Maria, Patty, and Eileen (the black partner of Lydia), their race is aligned with a taboo, an other-than-white, other-than-norm characterization that maintains distinct spheres of existence. In the show, the lesbians of color are the "authentic" lesbians who play the gatekeepers, like bouncers for the straight white women who want admission to the club. While *Sex and the City* celebrates female friendships as long as they are maintained and contained within a heternormative framework, sexual relationships between women become a commodity to be used and discarded, excluded altogether. *Sex in the City* conflates queer/lesbian female sexuality with art and food, as something to be consumed and later expelled, or just bought on a whim with no thinking, no strings attached, and no real consequences for the consumer. Queer female sexuality gets folded into a discourse of temporary erotic adventure-seeking, or as just another fashionable accessory to be added to or appropriately incorporated within a heteronormative sexual morality. To echo Judith Butler's words, though *Sex and the City* is "surely important to read as [a] cultural text in which homophobia and homosexual panic are negotiated, I would be reticent to call [it] subversive" (*Bodies That Matter* 126).

Notes

1. *Sex and the City* aired from January 1998 to September 2004. In 2008, New Line Cinemas and HBO released *Sex and the City: The Movie*, and two years later, its sequel, *Sex and the City 2* (2010).
2. Although it is beyond the scope of this essay to elaborate on *Sex and the City 2*'s problematic engagement with "the New Middle East," it is worth considering the film's setting in the current climate of US military involvement in the Middle East. The foursome's dallying in Abu Dhabi can be best captured by thinking about their excursion as what Melani McAlister would term an "epic encounter." She writes, "I argue that cultural products such as films or novels contributed to thinking about both values and history in two ways. First, they helped to make the Middle East an acceptable area for the exercise of American power. Second, they played a role in representing the Middle East as a stage for the production of American identities" (3). See Melani McAlister, *Epic Encounters: Culture, Media, and U.S. Interests in the Middle East, 1945–2000* (Berkeley: University of California Press, 2001).
3. I refer to *Reading Sex and the City,* edited by Kim Akass and Janet McCabe (London: IB Tauris, 2004).
4. Quoted material in reference to *Sex and the City* and any of its characters, unless otherwise indicated, refers specifically to dialogue taken directly from the show.
5. For the purposes of my discussion, I will use "queer" interchangeably with "lesbian," as both point to the non-heternormative ways in which women express their sexuality or are coded themselves as non-normative, either in terms of race and/or gender.

6. I thank Meg Wesling for pointing out the usefulness of Rubin's essay in this discussion.
7. For example, Melissa Etheridge's former partner, Julie Cypher, who apparently left Lou Diamond Phillips for Etheridge; Anne Heche's well-publicized, notorious disowning of her former gay self when she was dating Ellen DeGeneres; *Sex and the City*'s own Cynthia Nixon announcing that she is now with a woman after being with her (male) high school sweetheart and the father of her two children for fifteen years.
8. The stereotype of the exotic Latina temptress returns in *Sex and the City 2* (2010) in the form of Spanish actress, Penélope Cruz. Cruz portrays Carmen García Carrión, vice president of the Bank of Madrid, and a "sultry temptress" (*Daily Mail*, UK) who flirts mildly with Big at a party, much to Carrie's discomfort.
9. Eileen Julien's term (*African Novels and the Question of Orality*).
10. A pun on "Erin go Bragh," an anglicization of the Gaelic phrase, Éirinn go Brách, which roughly translates into 'Ireland Forever.' (www.irish-sayings.com)

CHAPTER 6

There's Something Queer Going On in Orange County: The Representation of Queer Women's Sexuality in *The O.C*

Allison Burgess[1]

The media hype around the introduction of a lesbian story line into the second season of the television show *The O.C.* in 2004–2005 suggested that this would be yet another overlysimplistic and unrealistic representation of queer identity in mainstream media and a stunt for a ratings boost during February sweeps week. The lesbian story line began in episode 2.9 ("The Ex-Factor"), which aired in North America on January 20, 2005, and it ran through to the end of episode 2.16 ("The Blaze of Glory") on March 17, 2005. I expected that this story line would be caught up in the teen drama series' usual overly dramatic sagas, its extra-heightened moments of teenaged sexual tension, and the exploitation of newly "chic" queer characters. To my surprise, however, the representation of queer women's sexuality on *The O.C.* was much more realistic and was more respectfully portrayed than the media hype at its outset intimated. The first five episodes of the eight-episode plotline depicted a genuine story line that was potentially "one of network TV's best portrayal[s] of a lesbian relationship in several years" (Warn, "A Disappointing End" para 3). Indeed, I argue that this lesbian relationship began as something new and exciting, representing a nuanced and fluid understanding of women's sexuality on prime-time television. Disappointingly, in the last three of the eight episodes, the writers of *The O.C.* negated the earlier promising portrayals, and by episode 2.16, the creators of *The O.C.* reified the dominance of homophobic and heteronormative discourses in popular culture.

This is distinct from more recent televised examples of queer women's sexualities, which I will point to in the conclusion of the paper.

Queer Visibility on Television

Queer visibility in mainstream media has increased significantly in recent years. Gay and lesbian characters, who were once virtually invisible in popular culture, are beginning to make more appearances in film and television. Often these appearances have consisted of unidimensional stereotypes or comic relief, and the number of gay characters in mainstream media, particularly the number of queer women characters, has been so minimal that a short list of their appearances can quickly be accumulated. The website www.afterellen.com, which keeps a comprehensive database of all of the appearances of lesbians and bisexual women on US television, lists only five lesbian or bisexual characters who appeared in at least three episodes of a show between 1976 and 1991, and indicates that there were an additional six appearances in movies on television (www.afterellen.com, "Timeline of Lesbian and Bisexual Regular and Recurring Characters...").

Since then, lesbian and bisexual television moments include *L.A. Law* (1991), *Roseanne* (1992–1997), the subtextual lesbianism in *Xena: Warrior Princess* (1995–2001), and perhaps the most famous of all lesbian moments on television, when Ellen DeGeneres' character Ellen Morgan came out on her network sitcom *Ellen* in 1997. Many lesbian characters since the 1990s have become fuller and more realistic representations that go beyond the usual tragic stereotypes to represent much more genuine understandings of lesbian sexuality, including Willow Rosenberg (Alyson Hannigan) and Tara Maclay (Amber Benson) on *Buffy the Vampire Slayer*, and the characters portrayed on *The L Word*.

Gays and lesbians share a common history of having been rendered invisible in popular culture. Larry Gross (*Up from Invisibility*) argues that "our vulnerability to media stereotyping and political attack derives in large part from our isolation and pervasive invisibility" (15). Gay and lesbian visibility are often referred to simultaneously, but their representations in mainstream media are also significantly different. Gay men's representation in the media began primarily with the popularity of "camp," a gay male strategy of subversion (Gross 18), which functioned to suggest queer interpretations of mainstream straight culture (Creekmur and Doty 23). Lesbians have had a far less visible or active role in the history of popular culture. Creekmur and Doty suggest that

> lesbians seemed less invested than gay men in popular culture production and criticism before the 1970s, perhaps because achieving positions of power and control within popular culture industries has always been difficult for women (whether lesbian or not), whereas closeted gay men…often achieved prominence and power in the popular culture mainstream. (5)

Thus Creekmur and Doty recognize that, beyond the homophobic repression experienced by lesbians and gays, lesbians are further subjected to sexism. They argue that closeted men still have access to the same kinds of power that (presumably white) heterosexual men have access to, whereas lesbians are othered by both their gender and their sexuality (along with other interlocking systems of oppression).

Gay and lesbian characters are no longer invisible in mainstream media. While there was and is still much to be critical of in the representations of many of the queer characters and queer sexualities on television, invisibility of queer sexualities is no longer the core critique made of popular culture by queer scholars and activists.

With the quick change in visible representations of diverse sexualities in mainstream media, it becomes important to consider the kinds of implications this change has on queer politics in popular culture. Joshua Gamson asks pointedly, "if the invisibility party is over, new questions are still circulating about the new visibility party that has taken its place: who is invited, and by whom, and at what price, and with what political and social consequences" (340). There are certainly some representations of queer sexualities that are much more popular than others—for example, gay white men Will Truman (Eric McCormack) and Jack McFarland (Sean Hayes) on *Will and Grace* (1998–2006). It is also clear that simply increasing the visibility of queer sexualities does not necessarily equate with decreasing discrimination or oppression. Critiques arise, particularly around the increased acceptance of gays and lesbians who are more interested in becoming a part of the heteronormative mainstream than they are in challenging assimilation. Gamson questions whether or not this new queer visibility in mainstream media should be celebrated, arguing that it has "reproduced once again the political tension between those advocating assimilation and normalization as routes to social progress and those pursuing a 'queer' challenge to norms as a social change strategy" (349).

So no longer is the queer critique of mainstream media only about invisibility. Suzanna Danuta Walters (*All the Rage*) asks us to consider how

> this new visibility creates new forms of homophobia…and lends itself to a false and dangerous substitution of cultural visibility for inclusive citizenship. In many ways, this moment provides us with a picture of a society readily embracing the *images* of gay life but still all too reluctant to embrace the *realities* of gay identities and practices in all their messy and challenging confusion. (10)

If there is something commercial about gay or queer, it is the heteronormalizing and mainstreaming of these identities and sexualities. Thus, anyone who exists beyond this heteronormative definition of sexuality has, until recently, been denied representation and visibility and is subjected to continued marginalization.

The O.C.

As explained on the Fox Broadcasting Company's homepage for the show, *The O.C.* "is a story of fathers and sons, husbands and wives and the relationships between a group of teens in Southern California" ("The O.C."). Ryan Atwood (Benjamin McKenzie) is from Chino, the "tough" working-class neighborhood on the "wrong" side of the tracks, but he is adopted by the Cohen family in rich and elite Newport Beach in Orange County, California. The Cohens' son, Seth (Adam Brody), and Ryan, now brothers, are best friends and a dynamic duo as the "geeky misfit" and the tough and brooding outsider. Ryan's constant love interest is Marissa Cooper (Mischa Barton), while Seth's is Summer Roberts (Rachel Bilson), and each couple is repeatedly in and out of love throughout the series. Summer and Marissa are also best friends. While other teen characters are introduced periodically throughout, Ryan, Seth, Marissa, and Summer are a tight-knit foursome around which the majority of the show's teen drama is focused. It is during season 2, between episodes 2.9 and 2.16 that a queer plotline is introduced for Marissa, who begins to explore her sexuality and enters into a relationship with another woman.

While *The O.C.* is certainly not a realistic representation of teenaged life (nor does it claim to be), a cultural critique is certainly still significant. bell hooks (in *bell hooks,* dir. Sut Jhally 1997) reminds us that it is important to be critically engaged in the world in which we live, including being critically engaged in popular culture. Thus, it is important to consider how queer sexualities are represented and embodied in mainstream media, because of their inevitable connections and relations to circulating discourses of sexuality.

Queering *The O.C.*

During the second season of *The O.C.*, Seth dates Alex Kelly (Olivia Wilde). In episode 2.9 ("The Ex-Factor"), Alex announces to Seth that her ex is coming to town and that she needs some space from him while she deals with her ex, with whom she has not yet broken up. Seth gets jealous, and it is Ryan who first "discovers" that Alex's ex is a woman named Jodie (Emmanuelle Chriqui), and, after much pestering from Seth, Ryan reveals Alex's ex's gender to him.

As the male characters support Seth while he is consumed with his girlfriend's other relationship, a separate plot develops in which Marissa independently finds herself attracted to Alex. The developing relationship between Marissa and Alex is overly dramatic and somewhat predictable. The first major hint that Marissa is romantically interested in Alex (aside from the mass media hype surrounding the relationship) is at the end of episode 2.9, when Marissa sleeps over at Alex's place and the two share a longing look.

The two characters quickly begin spending all of their time together. Marissa skips school to spend her days with Alex, and Alex's nights are filled working as a bartender at The Bait Shop, the local club. The tension builds when Marissa wants to spend yet another day with Alex, who asks her "Aren't you sick of me yet? We've hung out every day this week!" "The Accomplice"). Before Alex and Marissa hook up, the sexual tension between the two mounts quickly, and after a number of cues, Marissa begins to flirt more directly with Alex. In both episodes 2.10 ("The Accomplice") and 2.11 ("The Second Chance"), Marissa casually pulls her shirt off in front of Alex, both times catching Alex's attention. Marissa is attracted to Alex, and her coy flirtation with Alex is also a coy flirtation with queer sexuality.

There are three particularly formative moments in the relationship between Alex and Marissa, which are both sexually progressive and queer-positive, and which suggest that *The O.C.* attempted to create one of the better representations of queer women on television. The first of these moments occurs at the end of episode 2.11. The mutual attraction between Marissa and Alex has become obvious to them both, but Marissa is nervous and uncertain. At the end of the episode, Marissa enters The Bait Shop, walks over, and slips her hand into Alex's. Surprised, Alex looks to Marissa, and they share a smile and squeeze their hands tighter. This is significant because in this moment, Marissa has boldly made a physical connection to show her emotional willingness toward Alex. Rather than suffering through internalized homophobia and hatred towards herself and her flirtation with queer sexuality, Marissa is instead open and receptive to exploring her sexuality and to a relationship with Alex. The show's creator Josh Schwartz explains that

> Marissa is at a point in her life where she's trying to find herself and her true identity. There's another character who she really connects with. It's a girl, which is not something Marissa may have anticipated. But she's willing and game to explore and experiment with that. (quoted in Warn, "Marissa Gets a Girlfriend" para 6)

This moment is both honest and nervous, and importantly, it is public. Despite the fact that Marissa is still closeted and has not told her friends about her interest in Alex, she also performs this gesture in the public space of The Bait Shop, which is regularly frequented by all of her friends and peers. While none of the other main characters is there that night, she has no way of ensuring that this moment will happen in secret.

The second formative queer-positive moment occurs at the end of episode 2.12 ("The Lonely Hearts Club"), in which Alex and Marissa have an unplanned date on the beach at the end of the night on Valentine's Day. The two characters sit on the beach, waiting for the tide to turn, and when it does, Alex leans in and kisses Marissa. The kiss is romantic and the camera pans away while a slow ballad plays in the background, and the viewer watches the two women kissing on the beach from a distance. Rather than creating an exploitative or oversexed moment, the writers of *The O.C.* instead present a romantic and tender moment between the two characters. Writing just after episode 2.12 aired, Malinda Lo suggests that "so far, [the show's creator] Schwartz is actually following through on his promise to deliver a 'resonant' relationship...Despite the fact that all of this is conveniently occurring during February sweeps...the Alex-Marissa relationship is the best representation of lesbianism on network television since *Buffy*" (Lo, "Taking Stock" para 2–3). It is worth noting again that this moment occurs in public. While the beach is empty for this first kiss and the two seem to be alone together, the same beach is often the site where characters assume the privacy of the beach but are "caught" or "spotted" in the open public space by others from the pier. These two formative moments were an early suggestion that *The O.C.* would treat the lesbian queer subjectivity respectfully and positively.

A third important queer-positive moment in the development of the Marissa and Alex relationship is at the end of episode 2.13 ("The Father

Knows Best"), during which Marissa confesses that her anxiety and reluctance to come out to Summer was partly rooted in her own anxieties about not being ready for her relationship with Alex. Alex assumes Marissa's hesitation means that they will break up, but Marissa decides to come out to Summer and consequently feels happier about being with Alex. As coming-out stories are often full of anxiety and stress, it was a relief to watch a variation on the standard coming-out story: one that realistically considered the difficulties of coming out, but which portrayed an alternative to a painfully belabored process.[2]

Discourses of Heterosexual Masculinity

There are simultaneous discourses of masculinity that are competing throughout this story arc. In just a few conversations, Seth, Ryan, and their friend Zach Stevens (Michael Cassidy) reveal these discourses of heterosexual masculinity in response to queer women's sexuality. In episode 2.09, the three are in a car, driving to the Bait Shop so that Seth can confront Alex about her relationship with Jodie. This reveals three discourses therein:

Ryan: So Alex hooked up with a girl. It's not a big deal, Seth.
Seth: Ryan. My girlfriend dated a girl. It's a very big deal. There's only one thing I can do to make it okay.
Zach: You're going to hook up with a guy?

[*Awkward silence and shifty eyes between Ryan and Seth.*]

Seth: I repeat. There's only one thing I can do to make it okay. I need to see this girl. Because right now, my imagination is just running wild.
Zach: Dude, so's mine. [*To Ryan*] She's hot, right?
Seth: Listen. I know I'm supposed to be attracted, okay? And I'm supposed to be turned on. I've read *Maxim*, I've read *Stuff*, but you know what? All it's making me feel is that Alex is even more out of my league.
Ryan: Maybe you should just wait to talk to her until you calm down a little bit.
Seth: Nope. I've got a lot of testosterone pumping right now, Ryan. Testosterone being the key ingredient that's missing from Alex's last relationship. I just need to remind her of that.

First and most obvious is Zach's embodiment of the stereotypical heterosexual male's response to lesbian sexuality. In this scene and in future ones, he jokes about the lesbian fantasies he's having, inspired by Alex and Marissa.

Never are his reactions to their relationship any more complex than the homophobic eroticization of the two women together.

Ryan's reaction, however, contrasts significantly with Zach's. Throughout the series, Ryan's character embodies the ultimate macho masculinity. Although he is sensitive and caring, he is known to get into physical fights and is overly protective of the people in his life. Throughout the queer story line, Ryan is the most open-minded about the lesbian relationship. In this scene, he is not concerned with the topic of lesbianism, nor does he seem to have a problem with lesbian relationships; instead, he looks out for Seth's well-being and tries to convince him to avoid confrontation.

Seth's reactions to queer women's relationships, however, are particularly interesting. In this scene, he is jealous and insecure about the fact that his girlfriend is dating someone else while she is dating him, and his feelings are heightened by the fact that his girlfriend's other relationship is with a woman. He admits that while he knows that he is supposed to be turned on and recognizes how society has socialized him in a particular way as a heterosexual male to react to lesbians by fantasizing about them, instead he feels like Alex is out of his league because she is more experienced than he is. Here, queer is the new chic, and Seth can't keep up. As Suzanna Danuta Walters (*All the Rage*) writes about the development of gays and lesbians on television, by the mid-1990s, "gayness wasn't just a verboten titillation anymore. Suddenly, gayness was cool" (96). This is clearly evidenced by Seth's intimidation by his "chic" queer girlfriend. Seth also relies on homophobic discourses of "the problem with lesbian sexuality" to prove that he is Alex's rightful (heterosexual) partner, by explaining that what's missing from Alex and Jodie's relationship is testosterone. This falls directly in line with homophobic discourses in response to lesbianism, in which a lesbian just needs to have sex with a man to confirm her heterosexuality and to realize "what she really wants."

In another scene between these three male characters, Ryan, Seth, and Zach are walking on the boardwalk in the opening of episode 2.10, discussing the situation between Seth and Alex:

Seth: What do I do?
Zach: What do you want to do?
Seth: What I want to do is just drive over to her apartment and ask her flat out: are we in a relationship or are we not?
Zach: Good, man, you should do it.
Ryan: He's not doing it.
Seth: Ryan, it's been almost a week, okay? And I still don't know where Alex stands. Is she back together with her lesbian ex? And if so, are

they open to some sort of ménage three-way, as in the film *Summer Loves*?

Zach: Ohhhh…I didn't even think of that!

Seth: Yeah, well I did. Quite a bit, actually.

Ryan: If you have to wonder about it, it's probably not going to happen.

Seth: Which part? The threesome or the relationship?

Here, again, Zach expresses homophobic eroticism by fantasizing about a three-way relationship with two women. Ryan once again is not concerned with Alex's queer identity, but is instead focused on Seth's well-being, and he discourages Seth from confronting Alex about their relationship status. He also shuts down Seth's and Zach's fantasies about the three-way by suggesting that they are not grounded in reality.

It is Seth's character who makes the most interesting change at this point. Initially, Seth claimed to not be excited about the prospect of Alex's queer sexuality and he was revealed as being anxious and vulnerable. However, in this scene, he has had more time to think about it and to regain some control. He relies on the available and accessible homophobic discourses of heterosexual male sexuality and wonders about a three-way. Although his initial inquiry at the beginning of the conversation leads the viewer to think that he wants to get back together with Alex, later he only suggests that either Alex will be with her girlfriend or that the three of them will be in a relationship together; he does not present the possibility that he and Alex will get back together. Although in the earlier scene Seth suggested that all that Alex needed was his testosterone to make her see what was missing from her relationship with Jodie, here he seems resigned to the fact that Alex's queer sexuality is going to take precedence. Thus, the creators of *The O.C.* simultaneously tackle three stereotypical reactions to queerness through the representation of these discourses of masculinity: homophobic eroticization (Zach), acceptance through heterosexual male approval (Ryan), and vulnerability, which turns into a homophobic eroticization (Seth).

Coming Out in Orange County

Marissa experiences the angst of coming out when, in episode 2.13, after twice avoiding it, she confides in her best friend, Summer. She interrupts their conversation and announces:

Marissa: I've been dating Alex.

Summer: What?

Marissa: I mean, Alex and I. We've been dating.

Summer: W-W-W-What? [*Confused head shake.*]
Marissa: Just for a couple of weeks.
Summer: Alex. Seth's Alex?
Marissa: Mm hmm.
Summer: Girl Alex?
Marissa: Yeah.
Summer: Huh. Well, who knows?
Marissa: Uh, just you.
Summer: Uh huh. So, are you...are you like a...
Marissa: No! No, I don't know. I just...I really like her.
Summer: Well, she is pretty hot. [*Confused head shake.*]
Marissa: Hey look, you don't have to say anything. I just, I really needed to tell you. [*Summer nods.*] We're still friends, right?
Summer: Of course we are. Come here. [*Hug.*] Ohhhh. This isn't turning you on, right?
[*Both giggle, Marissa playfully pushes Summer away.*]

This conversation between Marissa and Summer is particularly interesting for two main reasons. First, it is important to note that while Summer is surprised to hear that Marissa is in a relationship with another woman, she is not disgusted or mad. Although Marissa is worried that this new relationship with Alex will have a negative effect on her friendship with Summer, Summer reassures her that this is not the case. Second, this scene simultaneously exemplifies contemporary open-mindedness towards queer sexualities as well as contemporary forms of subtle homophobia as Summer "jokes" that Marissa might be turned on by their hug. This is a common reaction embedded in homophobic discourse, in which it is assumed that queer people are overly sexual and are attracted to all members of the same sex. Marissa generally has the support of Summer in her relationship with Alex, but this scene is an example of how subtle forms of homophobia are acceptable and are intricately embedded in cultural representations of queer sexuality.

"It's Just a Phase:" Lesbianism as Teenage Rebellion

As argued earlier, visibility is no longer the only focus of queer representation on television. However, although there are more lesbian, bisexual, and queer women characters, many queer coming-out stories on television do not end well (Lo, "Taking Stock"). For example, Ellen DeGeneres's character came out on *Ellen* in 1997 and her show was canceled after the next season. Bianca is raped and her lover leaves the country after she comes out on *All My*

Children in 2000; and in Dr. Kerry Weaver's coming-out story on *ER*, her girlfriend is killed in the line of duty (in 2004) and Kerry suffers through a vicious custody battle for their child (Heller, "States of Emergency"). On *The O.C.*, the relationship between Marissa and Alex begins as a queer-positive one, but ends in such a way that confirms homophobic discourses in popular culture. The undoing of their relationship begins in "The Rainy Day Women" (2.14), when it becomes clear that Marissa's involvement with Alex is mostly a form of rebellion against her mother.

Unlike the queer-positive representations previously portrayed, Marissa's sexuality in episodes 2.14–2.16 becomes less about her attraction to Alex and more about her teenage rebellion. At Marissa's house in episode 2.14, Marissa's mother, Julie Cooper-Nickel (Melinda Clarke), is in the kitchen making breakfast. Marissa and Alex enter, and Alex is introduced to Julie. When Julie's back is turned, the two begin making out. As she turns back, they stop before they are seen, and Alex leaves.

> *Julie*: She seems nice! And you know, I have no problem if you want to have a friend stay over, it's just if you could let me know beforehand.
> *Marissa*: [*sarcastically*] Oh, you didn't get the memo?
> *Julie*: Ha-ha. You know, Marissa, I don't think it's too much to ask to know what's going on underneath my roof. That's all.
> *Marissa*: Oh, you want to know what's going on with me? I'm here to tell you the truth. No screaming, no crying, just the truth.
> *Julie*: You have no idea how happy it makes me to hear that.
> *Marissa*: Hold that thought. Alex is my girlfriend.
> *Julie*: I know, and I'm so happy that you've made a new friend, although I hope you keep seeing Summer.
> *Marissa*: No, mom, not my friend who's a girl. My girlfriend. [*Julie stares, stunned.*] Yeah.

Later, Marissa arrives at Alex's apartment:

> *Marissa*: I can't believe it, but I did it!
> *Alex*: You, uh…you told her.
> *Marissa*: Woah. I thought you'd be happy.
> *Alex*: No, I…uh. It just depends. Did you tell her to piss her off?
> *Marissa*: Hey, look, I told her so this could be real. For us.
> *Alex*: Wow! So, what happens now?
> *Marissa*: She's probably having a meltdown as we speak, so I can't go home.
> *Alex*: So stay here.

Marissa: Are you sure?
Alex: Yeah! [*They kiss.*] But first, let's get you out of these wet clothes.

Sarah Warn ("A Disappointing End") suggests that when Marissa comes out to her mother, she is not doing it to upset her mother, but also believes Marissa when she suggests that it is about making her relationship with Alex more real. However, in contrast to her coming-out experience with Summer, Marissa's coming-out experience with her mother is about rebelling against her. Alex's tentative response to Marissa is rooted in her speculation that Marissa is really just trying to make her mother angry. Marissa assumes that her mother will be upset with her when she comes out to her, but this does not happen. Although she invokes homophobia in a later reaction (she writes Marissa's relationship off to the common "it's just a phase" discourse), her mother's first concern for Marissa is for her well-being.

At the end of episode 2.14, there is more evidence that Marissa's involvement with Alex is a form of rebellion, rather than curiosity or queer sexuality. Marissa has now moved in with Alex (which echoes the discourse perpetuated through the "joke" that a lesbian brings a U-Haul to her second date), and Alex reminds her that the garbage needs to go out and that rent is due. Marissa looks unimpressed, and in this moment she realizes how her immediate reality involves bills and chores. At this point, she begins to reject Alex and her queer sexuality. This is reechoed at the beginning of the following episode (2.15, "The Mallpisode"), when Marissa fails at doing the laundry by turning all of their clothes pink. She tells Alex that she just wants to have fun, but Alex reminds her that she has to go to work. The realities of living on her own beyond the comforts of her home, her parents, and her rich way of life have set in.

The early signs that Marissa is beginning to reject Alex and queer sexuality seem to simultaneously be about her return to heterosexuality. In a conversation with Summer in episode 2.16, after Alex and Marissa have had a fight, Summer says:

Summer: I don't know, Coop. Sounds like a pretty bad fight. I mean, maybe you should just move home.
Marissa: I can't.
Summer: Because you love Alex, and wherever she is, that's your home?
Marissa: Because it would make my mom too happy.

So if it has not yet already been confirmed, here Marissa has had a total personality change in which she is no longer interested in Alex, but is instead more interested in rebelling against her mother.

That Marissa is "really heterosexual after all" is also couched in the homophobia expressed by Kirsten Cohen, Seth's mother, who is friends with Julie. Julie and Kirsten are comparing notes about the sordid details of their lives. When Julie tells Kirsten that Marissa is a lesbian, Kirsten replies,

Kirsten: Marissa? Well, I'm sure it's just a phase!
Julie: It was for me!

Thus, they rearticulate the notion that teenaged lesbian experiences can be nothing more than a phase of sexual exploration. The overtones in this scene deny the possibility that Marissa is queer (or lesbian or bisexual), and the interaction is deeply couched in homophobic rhetoric, thus denying the possibility for fluid sexuality.

Reconfirming Heterosexuality: Queer Might Be Chic, But It Does Not Seem to Last

In episode 2.15, Ryan overhears a conversation between Summer and Marissa. Summer says that for better or for worse, she's really happy to be with Seth, indicating the stability of her own heterosexual relationship. Summer then asks if Marissa's feelings towards Alex are the same as her own towards Seth (and here Ryan is referred to as "him"):

Marissa: Well, truthfully, I think the only person I've felt that way with is...
Summer: Yeah. I mean, is it weird being here with him? I mean, me, Cohen...
Marissa: No, it's fine.
Summer: Good. Because I know you're like, into chicks now and everything, but do you ever think about getting back together with him? I mean, Lyndsay's [Ryan's ex-girlfriend] gone now...
Marissa: Yeah, Lyndsay's gone. And he's heartbroken.
Summer: Do you miss him?
Marissa: Every day. [*Shrugs shoulders.*]

What is implied here is that Marissa is just waiting to get back together with Ryan. What is stopping her is not her relationship with Alex, but Ryan's emotional unavailability because of his own recent breakup. Ultimately, then, Marissa reiterates the notion that her lesbianism is just a phase. Although she never says this explicitly, and her actions could be interpreted as an embrace of fluid sexuality in which the gender of her sexual attractions is unimportant, it seems unlikely, given that she does not spend any further time exploring this possibility; nor is the demise of her relationship with Alex connected to any discussions about the implications of the relationship for Marissa's sexual identity. Marissa's character instead embodied Suzanna Walters' critique of queer visibility in popular culture: that images of queer lives are *available*, but there is still a reluctance to embrace the *realities* of queer identities and practices (9–10).

Although Marissa never speaks of regretting her relationship with Alex, once the two characters break up, there are never references to Alex on the show, and only once in season 3 is there a reference to Marissa's queer relationship. It was predictable that Marissa and Ryan would end up back together, as their relationship is one of the television series' main premises and story lines. In her article on January 17, 2005, "*The O.C.*'s Alex Boosts Bisexual Visibility on TV," Sarah Warn predicted,

> Given Marissa's predominantly heterosexual past, the huge fan support for the Marissa and Ryan pairing, and the controversy *The O.C.* would court by making one of its principal characters bisexual, it's likely that her "real feelings" for Alex will only last a few episodes. (para 12)

Although the creators of *The O.C.* began this story line by suggesting a discourse of fluid sexuality, they rejected this with its conclusion. Lo ("Taking Stock") writes that "if Marissa quickly forgets about Alex and starts dating boys right away, all of Schwartz's gay-positive press will be revealed as merely spin" (para 14). She argues that Alex's departure should have serious consequences for Marissa. At the very least, the relationship would likely have some kind of an effect on friends and family. Instead, after the breakup, Marissa literally returns to Ryan's embrace and happily rejoins her life at school. When Alex and Marissa break up at the end of episode 2.16, they have the following conversation:

> *Marissa*: Well this is my life. [*Points at the bonfire pep rally which she has organized.*] Okay? That's it. So what do you think?
> *Alex*: I think...I think this is your life and I don't fit in. Pep rallies, cheerleaders, boys...
> *Marissa*: Nothing happened with Ryan.
> *Alex*: Yeah, not yet, but what do you give it? A week? A month?
> *Marissa*: [*Looks down. Both are crying.*] I really wanted this to work between us.

Alex here confirms that Marissa is really only interested in a relationship with Ryan and a rich, upper-class, white, Newport Beach teen lifestyle. This is not a denial of her potential to have a fluid sexuality, but the constant refrain that Marissa and Ryan are meant for each other reconfirms that for Marissa, queer is just a phase. Immediately after Alex leaves, Ryan is Marissa's comfort. With his arm around her, he offers to take her home. In this moment, he is taking her home to her mother, but metaphorically also returning her to her heterosexuality.

It is unfortunately the assessment made by Marissa's mother, Julie Cooper-Nickel, which ends up being the most accurate summary of Marissa's relationship with Alex. Julie says to Alex: "You are this week's yard guy.[3] Marissa's latest drama weapon of torture to inflict upon me…Marissa's only been in love once, and he looked a whole lot different in a wife beater."

Conclusion

Burston and Richardson (2) ask, "Can we identify a particular 'lesbian' or 'gay' way of self-representation which is fundamentally different from the ways in which homosexuality and homosexuals are imagined by heterosexuals?" Burston and Richardson are seeking to uncover whether there is a way in which queer sexualities might be represented beyond both the imaginations of heterosexual people, but also beyond the heteronormative constraints of sexual relationships and the relations of capital they support. *The O.C.* failed to do this. By couching Marissa's character in inevitable heterosexuality, the show only continues to reconfirm heteronormative and homophobic discourses of sexuality.

Walters is critical of the oversimplistic way that queer people are often portrayed on television. She writes:

> Far too often, gay access to cultural visibility seems predicated on an acceptance of two possible modes of representation: the exotic but ultimately unthreatening "other"…or gays as really straights after all, the "aren't we all just human beings" position that reduces cultural specificity to a bland sameness that ends up assuming and asserting the desirability of the mainstream. (15)

Here, Walters is critical of the continued homonormativity espoused by some conservative gays and often shown in media representations of gays and lesbians. What is particularly upsetting about the queer portrayal of Marissa on *The O.C.* is that the first half of the story line refuses to fall within these parameters. Marissa is indeed interested in Alex, and the two begin an exciting romance in which Marissa's exploration of her sexuality is nuanced. However, the plotline takes an unexpected turn and Marissa ends up using her relationship with Alex to get back at her mother. Her attraction to Alex is overshadowed by her rebellion. As soon as her relationship with Alex becomes somewhat domesticated and exists in any kind of reality in which there are bills and laundry, Marissa panics and returns to her carefree and fun-loving life with her friends Summer, Seth, and Ryan.

The end of Marissa and Alex's relationship is marked by the immediate return to her relationship with Ryan. While this is not in itself a justification for the denial of a queer sexuality, and certainly it remains the possibility that Marissa might identify as queer or bisexual, the writing on the show denies this opportunity and instead reasserts the domination of heteronormativity in Marissa's life in a way that ignores and erases her history with Alex. Instead of offering the potential for Marissa to continue to embrace a fluid sexuality, the writers of *The O.C.* reconfirm the dominance of heterosexuality, indicative of the homophobia and heteronormativity at work in so many discourses of popular culture.

Since the conclusion of *The O.C.*, more recent explorations of queer sexualities on television have continued to emerge. Indeed, the representation of queer sexualities on television has continued to become increasingly popular. While many fall prey to predictable and disappointing portrayals similar to those on *The O.C.*, others offer alternative representations.

Particularly notable is the examination of young women's sexuality on *South of Nowhere*, a television program that aired for three seasons between 2005 and 2008. Remarkably, the show's central relationship is between teens Spencer Carlin (Gabrielle Christian) and Ashley Davies (Mandy Musgrave). Set in Los Angeles, the program sensitively examines Spencer's personal life as she navigates the usual televised teen dramas alongside questioning her sexuality, coming out, and demanding the acceptance and respect of her friends, family, and community. Though the third season falls prey to overly dramatic and ridiculous portrayals of the rich and spoiled, the relationship between Spencer and Ashley remains the driving story line, around which other friends and family members revolve. The show interrogates issues such as conversion therapy, male titillation, and lesbian sexuality alongside breakups, family dysfunctions, and homework. The series concludes with a cheesy Webisode set five years in the future in which Spencer and Ashley are still together and Ashley is pregnant. While the series resists falling prey to homophobic representations in which queer women return to heterosexuality, are criminalized, or are killed, it is arguable that the show instead concludes with a "we're just like heterosexuals" narrative. However, with the exception of the concluding episodes, the relationship between Spencer and Ashley over the course of the series is complex enough to avoid being read as simply one mode of representation or another. These more complex representations of sexuality, which allow for multiple interpretations and possibilities, are the most interesting. It will, however, be much more exciting when representations of queer women on television can offer new narratives, new complexities, and new possibilities that surprise and challenge dominant narratives, rather than continuing to reaffirm them.

Notes

1. I would like to thank Dr. Roger Simon for his feedback on an earlier version of this paper, and Amy Gullage and Marie Vander Kloet for their insightful comments, edits, and suggestions. Thanks to Rebecca Beirne for her editorial comments. My thanks also to Caitlin Burgess for our early talks about this paper and for her help with the Pause and Rewind buttons needed for the collection of transcript materials.

2. The portrayal of Alex on *The O.C.* is also considered one of the better representations of bisexuality on television. Sarah Warn argues that Alex is one of the most realistic bisexual characters on prime-time TV: "Beyond the initial surprise factor, her bisexuality and her (past) relationships with women are for the most part treated fairly matter-of-factly by the writers. So far, at least, the writers have avoided saddling her with the usual promiscuous and non-monogamous stereotypes that afflict most bisexual women on TV" (Warn, "*The O.C.*'s Alex" para 11). Like the lesbian story line, this remains true until the last few episodes, in which Alex's character has a total personality change, becomes jealous, and warns Ryan to stay away from Marissa by physically threatening him.

3. "This week's yard guy" references an ex-boyfriend of Marissa's in a relationship that involved class transgression, which was yet another example of a relationship that Marissa used to rebel against her mother.

CHAPTER 7

Reconfigurations of *The L Word*

M. Catherine Jonet and Laura Anh Williams

When we originally wrote this essay in 2006, Jenny Schecter was alive, Dana Fairbanks was healthy, and Moira Sweeney had just endured the most uncomfortable dinner party ever. Jane Lynch's Sue Sylvester was not yet menacing the kids at McKinley High on *Glee* and Jules and Nic, the characters from the Oscar-nominated *The Kids Are All Right,* probably hadn't even started looking for a sperm donor. Television characters may come and go, but for the lesbian community, they are about as ever-present as the names on Alice Pieszecki's board, with lines connecting actor to character and character to show. Because of the rarity of popular cultural representations produced by and for women (let alone queer women), *The L Word* stands, for better or worse, as a milestone for lesbian representation. Reaching beyond a sweeps-week same-sex kiss, or even a story line in a primarily heterosexual drama, the series did center its focus on the lives and loves of a group of queer women and their immediate families and circle of friends.

But how did the focus appear? From avant-garde aspirations stemming from the vision and indie "street cred" of New Queer Cinema creators such as Rose Troche, Guinevere Turner, Kimberly Peirce, and Moisés Kaufman to multiple-storied soap operatic drama, to "whodunit" murder mystery with even more pitfalls, *The L Word* delivered less of a coherent narrative to its audience than it created a very bumpy ride without seatbelts. Each season seemed to begin with a different generic approach, and even the final season's neo-noir central theme, "Who Killed Jenny Schecter?" was left unsolved by the finale. The series' interest in representing multiple queer and women's issues took on an exhaustive array of topics. As Nicholas Fonseca writes ("*The L Word* Series Finale" on *Pop Watch*):

> But years from now, will it even matter how the show went out in its final hour? It was really the other 69 episodes that made *The L Word* a TV milestone. As the retrospective that aired beforehand reminded us, its impact expands far beyond its barrier-busting stories: TV's first deaf lesbian, its first regularly occurring transsexual character, bisexuals of both genders, drag kings, the US military's don't-ask-don't-tell policy, biracial identity, gay parenting, sex/drug/alcohol/gambling addiction, sexual abuse, midlife sexual awakenings, breast cancer... this show took on *a lot*.

The series was peppered with guest appearances appealing to different generations of lesbian fandom and feminists alike. From Gloria Steinem and Kate Clinton to Helen Shaver (star of *Desert Hearts*) and Lucy Lawless (star of *Xena: Warrior Princess*) to Tegan & Sara and Peaches, *The L Word* cast a wide net. For us, looking back on the series, it is a kind of queer fossil—an artifact of something now extinct that has left us with many questions, an archeological trace loaded with representational potential.

Just as it had initially, this essay argues that *The L Word* is a "restive" text. Barbara Page, in her 1996 essay, "Women Writers and the Restive Text: Feminism, Experimental Writing and Hypertext," maintains that the restive text is the product of contemporary experimental feminist writers, such as Carole Maso, whose "restiveness" is more than a struggle with established forms or even conventions (par. 2). Restiveness is that sense of anxiety and unease brought about by restriction, by a feeling of impatience in the face of external coercion. Restiveness is produced by the work of feminist writers who engage in normalized notions of theme, plot, literary form, and even language itself in order to rearrange them and relate to them differently from the gendered, racist, heterosexist, and classist norms of their society. Such writers, Page contends

> as a rule, take for granted that language itself and much of canonical literature encode hierarchies of value that denigrate and subordinate women, and therefore they incorporate into their work a strategically critical or oppositional posture, as well as a search for alternative forms of composition. They do not accept the notion, however, that language is hopelessly inimical or alien to their interests, and so move beyond the call for some future reform of language to an intervention—exuberant or wary—in present discourses. (par. 2)

The L Word, too does not accept the notion that visual media are necessarily inimical to queer women, women of color, and/or working-class women. It searches for alternatives to the extant body of lesbian representation, while interrogating that representation. Page states that the aim of writers she terms restive is "to rend the surface of language and to reshape it into forms more hospitable to the historical lives of women and to an esthetic of the will and desire of a self-apprehended female body that is an end unto itself and not simply instrumental" (par. 2). *The L Word* attempts to rend the surface of lesbian representation to reshape it to a form that is more hospitable to queer women, and it seeks to dislodge the usage of female same-sex sexuality as instrumental to heterosexuality in visual culture.

Judith Roof's *A Lure of Knowledge* (1991) provides a useful framework for approaching lesbian representation like *The L Word*. Roof employs the concept of "configurations" to describe how "lesbian sexuality occupies certain specific locations or positions" in discourses as wide-ranging as cultural narrative, cinema, literature, and psychoanalysis (4). Roof conceives of configurations as "different from an analysis of lesbian images, a study of lesbian portrayal, or making any claims for lesbian women or lesbian sexuality *per se* (5–6). She notes:

Across these discourses, lesbian sexuality tends to be represented in the same range of configurations in similar rhetorical or argumentative positions. As titillating foreplay, simulated heterosexuality, exotic excess, knowing center, joking inauthenticity, artful compromise, and masculine mask, configurations of lesbian sexuality embody the conflicting impetuses of representational insufficiency and recuperation. (4–5)

The conflicting impetuses of representational insufficiency and recuperation are part and parcel of *The L Word*'s restiveness. Its representation of lesbians and queer women will always be insufficient. It will never achieve the "truth," authenticity, or even the "inside glimpse" described by *The L Word* producer Rose Lam when she suggested, "But now with this show [*The L Word*] and some of the others, people who wouldn't normally go out of their way to find out more about gay or lesbian family members can have an inside glimpse" (Bennett, "Producers Like Telling the Truth").[1] Its restiveness can upset the "phallocentric terms" in which lesbian representation is most often configured (Roof 74). In the end, as Roof argues about Diane Kurys's film *Entre Nous* (1983; French title, *Coup de Foudre*), the series is not about the voyeuristic pleasure of consuming queer female sexuality. The series becomes "a play on voyeurism that nonetheless exceeds that play and does become something else" (Roof 82). The "something else" that *The L Word* becomes is a productive rather than prohibitive site to interrogate and possibly even repudiate the heterosexual matrix of power by decentering its privileging of itself in discourse.

The L Word's very first representation of lesbian sexuality works to directly confront the voyeuristic tradition of lesbian representation in straight male pornography. Early in the pilot episode, Jenny (Mia Kirshner) is shown spying on two women having sex in the swimming pool next door. Jenny crouches behind the fence to observe the scene, and the voyeuristic quality of her viewing and the camera's gaze is reinforced by the partial visual barrier of the fence. There are two fleeting aerial shots of the women's activities in the pool, but the focus of the scene is on Jenny's view through the fence and on her intrigued reaction. Even though this first representation of lesbian desire in the series could be described as voyeuristic, as it entails superfluous sex acts being witnessed by Jenny, the titillated third party, her fascination transforms into desire. The female spectator's sexual identification, then, functions to dislodge the centrality of a heterosexualizing gaze. Jenny's gaze is not merely for the sake of titillation, but rather it serves as an early step toward her self-recognition of her desire for women.

In fact, shortly thereafter, Jenny describes what she has witnessed to boyfriend Tim (Eric Mabius) during the couple's foreplay. While this, at first sight, appears to be the standard stuff of heterosexual male pornography, the show instead turns that kind of convention on its head in order to make this scene one of Jenny's first experiences of lesbian sexuality. This moment constructs the heterosexual couple's desire as contingent on the lesbians' lovemaking. It is, as Judith Halberstam says of James Bond's masculinity in *Female Masculinity*, "prosthetic," in that it has "little if anything to do with biological maleness and signifies more often as a technical special effect" (3). Jenny and Tim's heterosexual desire has little to do with "natural" heterosexuality, but signifies a prosthetic effect. As the straight couple's foreplay is built upon Jenny's detailed description of the lesbian sex, they, as Lauren Berlant and Michael Warner argue, become displaced and are "no longer the referent or the privileged example of sexual culture" (355). Unlike the pornographic heteronormative configuration of lesbian sexuality as preliminary to legitimate heterosexuality (the opening act to the main event), the centrality of straight sex is destabilized when Jenny says "and then she begins to fuck her," and Tim, referring to his own sex acts asks, "Like this?" In this moment, lesbian sexuality, rather than serving as erotic foreplay for the heterosexual couple, becomes a central model to emulate. Tim virtually offers himself to Jenny as a lesbian. His ultimate obliviousness to Jenny's lesbian desire, captured here, is repeated several times, before Tim walks in on Jenny acting upon this sexual desire with Marina (Karina Lombard) in episode 1.5, "Lawfully."

This capacity for lesbian desire to displace heterosexuality continues in "Let's Do It" (1.2), when, after Marina leaves Tim and Jenny's dinner party, their remaining guests continue to discuss her appeal. Tim's co-worker Randy (Kwesi Ameyaw) states, "Wow. Just one question, who is in love with that woman?" Randy's wife Carol (Jennifer Copping) immediately responds, "Count me in," before asking Jenny, "Don't you have just a little crush on her?" Carol, Randy, and Tim are again, as Tim was earlier, repositioned as lesbians, and, while Jenny firmly replies after pausing, "No," she does so in order to shield her feelings for Marina, with whom she is already having an affair.

Lesbian desire also reconfigures heteronormative spaces, such as public restrooms. Jenny and Marina's first encounter takes place in Bette (Jennifer Beals) and Tina's (Laurel Holloman) restroom during a party. Another intimate encounter in the same episode takes place in a restaurant bathroom. And an early sexual encounter occurs in a bathroom stall at The Planet (1.4, "Lies, Lies, Lies"). In later episodes, the restroom becomes the setting for covert sexual liaisons between Alice (Leisha Hailey) and Dana (Erin Daniels) (2.1, "Life, Loss, Leaving"), as well as between Jenny and Carmen (Sarah Shahi) (2.9, "Late, Later, Latent"); and in the series' opening titles from season 2 onward, Shane (Kate Moennig) is featured pulling a woman into a men's restroom to make out. The women's restroom, as well as women's locker rooms for both Dana (with Lara) and Tina (with her spinning instructor) and their equestrian counterpart, the stable (for Dana's mother as seen in 1.8, "Listen Up"), and tennis summer camp (for Dana in 1.11, "Looking Back" and 3.11, "Last Dance," are unfixed as sites of homosocial primping or bonding. They are revealed to be sites where homosexual desire may emerge. Lesbian desire works to disorganize and disorient heteronormative space, privilege, and centrality.

Beyond the series' deployment of lesbian sexuality to destabilize heterosexuality, the show also seems to overtly complicate narrative desires to discover what lesbians are really like. This critique occurs significantly in the second season story line, which centers on the male filmmaker's project to chronicle his lesbian roommates' lives via cameras hidden throughout the house. From the outset of the attempts by Mark (Eric Lively) at voyeuristically consuming his lesbian roommates (Jenny and Shane) by secretly installing nine "strategically and respectfully placed" cameras throughout their house, he overtly acknowledges the gap between straight male fantasy and reality and articulates a desire to bridge that gap. During a take for the introduction of the video he wants to produce about Jenny and Shane, which purports to be a documentary exploration of lesbians and not simply pornography, he tells the camera: "My name is Mark Wayland and I live

in a house with two lesbians. Now, I know what you're probably thinking. You're wondering if I've hit it yet. Well, the thing is they're two real
lesbians. Or else I would have. But don't worry, I'm still going to try" (2.5,
"Labyrinth").

In the project's initial stages, he pitches his idea to his roommates in a
way that emphasizes his own centrality, "I'm about to show the girls that
this is mainly about me." Describing his videos to them as a "journal of my
life with the two of you guys," he establishes this centrality in terms of their
financial dependence on him. He states, "If I could just get some footage,
which [...] I know that I could get this [project] financed and then we can
all get paid, which is something I know *you both need*" (emphasis added).
When he is met with resistance, he attempts to appeal earnestly in terms
of value. He elaborates on the edifying quality of their involvement, "Plus,
honestly, think about how educational this is going to be for people who
don't know anything about people like you," and "Think about how much
you're going to be helping out some poor, little lonely lez...stuck out in the
Midwest without a role model in sight."

The potential danger of the intrusive pornographic gaze is established,
not only in Mark's own introductory statement, but also at the outset of the
episode, when Mark's filmmaking partner Gomey (Sam Easton) is shown
at work as a security guard, using surveillance cameras in a stairwell to
zoom in on a sexual tryst. From its conception, Mark's film project teeters
between his stated intention to document the lives of his lesbian roommates and Gomey's blatantly exploitative attitude toward the women. In
fact, in "Lynch Pin" (2.4), the episode when Mark is first introduced and
moves in with Jenny and Shane, he and Gomey observe Shane making out
with another woman and then skinny dipping with a group of women in
Bette and Tina's pool next door, and Gomey states, "Man, you so fucking
scored." This voyeuristic and intrusive pornographic gaze is presumably
what inspires Mark's documentary project. It is not only Gomey's influence
that persuades Mark to install the hidden cameras, but also the women's
refusal to comply or to satisfactorily answer his desire to know what lesbians do in bed.

Mark's increasingly bewildered and obsessive gaze, gradually directed at
Shane, is connected to Tim's gaze in season 1. In two particular instances
when Tim accidentally witnesses Jenny having sex with another woman,
he appears astounded, as if the act he observes in no way coalesces with
cultural fantasies of same-sex sexual relationships between women, which
he has internalized to be under his male jurisdiction in one sense, and to
be unthreatening, even impossible in another. Moreover, he does not find
himself as a straight white man being addressed by this act. He is not hailed

to dominate or even enjoy it, as the cultural fantasy of lesbian sexuality addressing straight men would suggest. In the first instance, peering through a door window, Tim views Marina performing cunnilingus on Jenny (1.5, "Lawfully"). He appears to be more startled by Jenny's reception of the pleasure than by her infidelity. In "Losing It" (1.6), he confronts Marina and demands, "What is it you do? You girls? Should I even care? Does it even count?" Marina's reply, "You were there. You saw how much it counts," enrages Tim.

In the second instance, after his breakup with Jenny, he views her and another woman through the same door window, and is once again startled by the two women having sex (1.13, "Limb from Limb"). In a sense, Tim and Mark are both horrified by the women's lack of lack. They are both horrified and filled with a sense of dread that the male presence is not missed or wished for in the women's lovemaking. In the case of Mark, the fact that lesbians do not need him to legitimize, define, or to produce knowledge about them through filmic representation is confounding.

In "Luminous" (2.7), Jenny confronts a male classmate in her creative writing class after he reads a Henry Miller-esque short story that includes such sentences as: "Watch my cock, Madeleine. Watch me beat it again while Miss Jasmine fathoms your pussy for the twenty-seventh time this morning." This story exemplifies the locating of female same-sex sexuality as subordinate to male heterosexuality. However, Jenny retorts:

> Your main character, Jasmine, she opens up Madeleine's world by giving her the best fucking orgasm she's ever had, which I don't know if you know this, is the primary sex act that two women can actually have, and then you go ahead and you belittle it by turning it into pornography and I think that the reason why you're doing this is because men can't handle the fact these women can have this amazing, fucking, beautiful, mind-blowing orgasm without a fucking cock!

This speech hearkens back to Mark's initial on-camera interview with Jenny and Shane, in which he inquires about the "primary lesbian sex act" that would approximate "that one, ultimate, foregone conclusion" for heterosexual couples—"fucking"—referring exclusively to vaginal penetration by a penis, and the climaxing of the sex act brought about through male orgasm. Just as in Jenny's response to her classmate, the series does not locate or assume "one act," but instead places value on female orgasms. For example, in a conversation between Lara (Lauren Lee Smith) and Dana during the second season, Lara asks Dana, "What do you think counts as sex?" (1.7, "L'Ennui"). Dana responds, "Having an orgasm." Lara categorically states,

"Well, if that was the case, that would mean thousands of women who are married with children have never had sex."

As the series progresses, the camera remains a central motif for many of the main characters. The focus is broader than the pornographic gaze, however. In the third season, Helena Peabody (Rachel Shelley) falls for documentary filmmaker Dylan Moreland (Alex Hedison). A major sexual encounter occurs, in fact, during a private screening of Dylan's documentary. In a later episode, Dylan films Helena as she seduces Dylan. This tape, however, is used as evidence against Helena in a set-up sexual harassment case pursued by Dylan and her partner to get money from Helena's fortune. In season 4, Tina becomes an executive producer for Helena's film studio, where Jenny subsequently becomes a director of the film adaptation of her own memoir in season 5. In season 5, Alice becomes a cohost of a daytime talk show, "The Look."

The series' fixation on the role of film, visual representation, and women as creators behind and victims in front of the camera come together at the end of the fifth season, when the series' great champion of the art world, Bette, finds herself the subject of her former lover's vengeful video installation piece. As Tavia Nyong'o puts it, "art moves and wounds Bette" (103). This wounding of her character moves beyond the Stendhal Syndrome Nyong'o describes from season 1, to literally wounding her by creating a purposely exploitative and hurtful video piece. Moving beyond familiar tropes such as Mark's pornographic surveillance camera or even Dylan's videotaped entrapment, Jodie Lerner (Marlee Matlin) pushes the harm created by video images into the realm of fine art. In the fourth season finale, "Long Time Coming," Jodie introduces her installation, explaining that its title, "Core," is "because it's about core values: love, loyalty, honesty, commitment." The installation piece, projected onto the walls of the gallery, consists of non-naturalistic, segmented images of Bette's face, her mouth, her eye, while the disjointed soundtrack cycles through a series of phrases Bette utters, including, "I love you," "please just stop," "go without me," "leave me alone," and "fuck me." The series' interest in the exploitative power of filmic representation comes to a crescendo in this instance. It seems to be offered as restorative in the series finale, as virtually all characters are featured in joyful farewell video clips at Bette and Tina's going-away party. These clips play on, however, to an empty room, as Jenny's lifeless body is discovered in their swimming pool. This juxtaposition undermines the reparative potential of filmic representation in this series.

The "bonus" scenes offered several weeks after the series ended featured the "Interrogation Tapes" of the characters supposedly being interviewed by police about Jenny's death. These clips reveal nothing about Jenny's death, but rather center more on character development of each interviewee. Broadly speaking, the clips simultaneously offer up new avenues for narrative development, even as these avenues are foreclosed as the result of the ending of the series. The possibility for narrative closure is hinted at and disrupted by the multiple modes of visual representation employed throughout the series.

Decentering, for example, continues as a strategy in the third season. However, it now extends itself to the main characters, and the class and seemingly normative gender privilege they inhabit. Even though Shane comes from a working-class background and is androgynously gendered to the extent that her own gender identity is at times indeterminate, her free-spiritedness as well as her trendsetting ways somehow insulate her from occupying a space of inscrutable difference. But Jenny's love interest Moira (Daniela Sea), a masculine, working-class woman from Skokie who transitions from female to male (FTM), stands in contrast to the hyper-feminine main characters in such a way that she becomes an object of scrutiny, ridicule, embarrassment, and shame.

With the exception of Moira, female genderqueer masculinity has been limited to the androgyny of Shane and to the transgendered leanings of Ivan the drag king (Kelly Lynch), as well as various masculine women, who appear as extras in the series' backgrounds in what Marga Gomez refers to as "dyke feng shui"(quoted in Halberstam's "I Love *The L Word* Not" 41). Lesbian and queer masculinity have been a hot topic since the show's debut. Halberstam, the theorist most associated with the concept, regards the limited representation of masculine queer women on the series as one of its greatest weaknesses. Halberstam argues in "The I Word: 'I' for Invisible, as in Real-World Lesbians on TV" that the show adheres to "the unwritten rules for lesbian TV," which include that none of the characters be "too butch" (18). Halberstam has stated, "I am really irritated by the show's deliberate erasure of genderqueer sex and genderqueer characters" ("I Love *The L Word* Not" 41). Moira's arrival within *The L Word* universe seemed to address this criticism directly; however, her female genderqueer masculinity was almost immediately supplanted by her transition to become male. Lucas Cassidy Crawford details why Moira's butchness does not linger:

> When the ruggedly boyish character Moira debuted in season three of Showtime's (in)famous program *The L Word*, many of us working-class, rural, or butch dykes finally undid the collective knot in our boxers. Moira's impromptu move from Skokie to Los Angeles coincided with hir transsexual awakening, however, and s/he transitions to become "Max" in subsequent episodes. Relocating from Illinois to California puts Moira

not only literally but also figuratively in different states: of mind, of identity, and of desire. The queer pilgrimage to the city is a far from innovative motif, and even in theories that are attuned to the role of place in queer life, the role of the rural is presumed to be inconsequential. (127)

As soon as Moira is introduced in the series, the character undergoes many transformations. And the transformations do not seem to end. In season 6, Max, Moira's chosen name, is pregnant with a child. It is as if the series' creators understand transgenderism to be a constant succession of changes. As Crawford's quote points out, the show does not linger on Moira's working-class, rural butchness. The series also does not linger on other changes it puts Moira/Max through, from FTM transitioning, to having a sexual relationship with a gay man, to dating and having a child with a different gay man. Later in the series, Max is also considering surgically changing his body and has throughout struggled with the effects of different levels of testosterone. He attends a Lamaze childbirth education class sporting a full beard, visually challenging other parents' idea of giving birth and parenthood.

Moira's transition to become Max seems to be initiated after a failed job interview at a tech company, InTechMode (3.5, "Lifeline"). At the interview, she is dressed in a smart dark suit with a white shirt. Moira answers in a way that is not defensive or embarrassed, "Yeah, I'm a girl," when her interviewer struggles to reconcile her female name with her gender-ambiguous appearance. "I wasn't saying I didn't know if you were a girl, I was just asking about the name," the interviewer replies. However, as the interview progresses, her computer programming skills and impeccable letters of recommendation are upstaged by her gender ambiguity. Inquiring about her previous workplace experience, the interviewer asks if Moira's former co-workers had any "problems with you being…you know…hard to peg? You're kind of neither fish nor fowl, if you know what I mean."

The camera shots reflect the interviewer's scrutinizing gaze as he scans from Moira's sturdy black dress shoes up to her hands resting on her knees. Insisting that the company does not discriminate against anyone, he suggests they are merely looking for someone who is "a team player." Moira smiles and responds, "Yeah, I'm a team player." The closeup shot captures Moira at the left half of the screen, and it remains tightly focused on the emotional shift as the interviewer then asks, "What side do you bat for Moira?" The camera zooms in to an extreme closeup of Moira's face as her smile withers. It lingers for several seconds, focused on the side of Moira's head as she turns her face to the left, out of the frame. Moira's gender ambiguity and the interviewer's demand for her to identify herself either as fish or fowl literally push the character out of the picture.

This job interview scene, like the dinner party scene in which Moira is introduced to the main cast, places pressure on Moira to occupy a space that seemingly reestablishes gender norms. Moira's working-class masculinity unsettles everyone else's entitlement. When Moira excuses herself from the table, the group discusses Moira's gender performance. Although Bette says, "She comes from a place where you have to define yourself as either/or. It's probably just the only language she has," Moira has not appeared to need to define herself as either/or *until* her arrival in Los Angeles (3.3, "Lobster"). Her previous life in a rural area has not seemed to require the kind of singular alignment demanded by the tech interviewer or by her new group of friends. Although Moira does not land a position at InTechMode, her male counterpart, Max, not only gets hired (by the same interviewer), but ends up dating the boss's straight daughter.

It is interesting that, in the fourth-season finale, the imposition of singular gender performance occurs when the gender-androgynous character Shane and her single-mother girlfriend, Paige (Kristanna Loken) are presented through a multilayered filmic device. When discussing the possibility of renting a home together, along with Paige's son and Shane's younger brother, Shane and Paige are presented in a fantasy space as the perfect 1950s style heterosexual nuclear family (4.12, "Long Time Coming"). Are they a butch/femme couple? Or is this gender crossing—has Shane become a man in this fantasy? The sequence cuts between Shane and Paige having sex, removing each other's clothes, and getting dressed again, and stylized idyllic domestic set pieces of nuclear family life: making breakfast, mowing the lawn, etc. This fantasy space of potential happiness is never offered to Moira/Max. Moreover, Shane's androgyny is literally rewarded, when she becomes an underwear model for Hugo Boss. The episode "Layup" ends with Shane's photo shoot, which features the character posing for the camera wearing nothing but a pair of white men's briefs and covering her breasts with her hands. Her performance of androgyny does not threaten other people, and it can be eroticized and given a potential freedom that Moira/Max's initial gender ambiguity and subsequent trans status never does.

The show has received much criticism for the ultimate failure of Moira/Max's characterization.[2] And, to be sure, Max is a negative representation of a transgender character. As soon as Moira begins transitioning to Max, the character's supposedly testosterone-induced tantrums, his desire to pass as a "real man" to gain access to male privilege, and his increasing investment in and assimilation to heteronormativity could certainly be read as a negative stereotypical representation of a transgender character. The character's transition opens a space for the other major characters to work through conversations about gender and transgenderism. Max's desire to remove his breasts gets juxtaposed with another major character's breast cancer. Through this juxtaposition and the series' consistent focus on his struggles, Max's gender identity is validated as a matter of life and death for him.

Another way to view the show's handling of Max is that, as Malinda Lo states in an early critique of the series, the show is not about gender but sexuality ("Does *The L Word* Represent?"). More specifically, the show is about queer female sexuality. From this perspective, it is possible to argue that the show is not trans-phobic as much as it is critical of heteronormativity. In the final episode of the third season, Jenny begins an affair with another woman, Claude (Élodie Bouchez), with Max's full knowledge. In one scene, Max attempts to prevent Jenny and Claude from slow dancing in a ballroom filled with straight couples. When Max suggests their presence would make others feel uncomfortable, Claude critiques Max's normative aspirations:

Claude: Then they deserve to feel uncomfortable, don't you think?
Max: No. I don't think anyone deserves to feel uncomfortable.
Claude: Max, I don't understand why you want to be like these people. You seem so much more interesting as who you are.

Claude's critique of Max, echoing Jenny's comments throughout the season, does not focus on his transgender status, but on his desire to assimilate, to join the heteronormative majority of the ballroom, who would exclude the queer female couple in order to feel more "comfortable." Moreover, it is also quite possible that this series, which has invested a great deal of its narrative energies into threatening and troubling male privilege, is threatened and troubled by the prospect of a FTM trans subject possibly gaining or having access to male privilege.

Following Page's theory, the restive text offers a way to make sense of our ultimate frustration by, disappointment in, and simultaneous embrace of *The L Word*. The series' proliferating web of story lines and unresolved questions generate both a sense of desire and impatience. The show's configurations challenge, succumb to, and even create new locations for lesbians to occupy in the cultural imaginary. Perhaps, as Fonseca suggests, the series' significance lies not in the unresolved central narrative of its sixth season ("Who Killed Jenny Schecter?"), but rather in its collective, messy entirety. Like Alice's diagram of characters' sexual interrelationships that eventually increases exponentially in both numbers of relationships charted and in complexity, goes beyond a whiteboard, and gets uploaded to the Internet, the series' shortcomings suggest the impossibility for lesbian representation to be contained by a single television show. The online version of Alice's chart invited visitors to input their relationships, and it became not a two-dimensional diagram, but a multidimensional constellation.[3]

The series suggests to viewers that female same-sex sexuality is a constellation, rather than a sweeps-week same-sex kiss, or something to be relegated to a show's subtext or secondary text. It's something big enough that even a show ostensibly dedicated to female same-sex desire couldn't begin to manage it. Neither representational demand nor the restrictions of conventional narrative is responsible for the show's inability to coherently structure its representations of queer women and trans-masculinities. These realities are far more complex than limited representations are able to allow. As Travis Wimberly states:

> [T]he unfortunate reality is that *no* shows seem to be taking on the challenge of portraying a different kind of gay individual...the *only* representation[s] available of gay and lesbian culture on television are those that are rich, beautiful and professional. What is harmful then, is not the existence of this particular representation, but the fact that no alternate representations are available. ("Diversity")

Perhaps an argument could be made that *The L Word* did try, in its own way, to offer itself as containing alternate representations among its repertoire. Art curator Bette Porter offered an opportunity to broadcast Catherine Opie's photography among other visual artists, the ownership by Kit (Pam Grier) of The Planet allowed artists such as Peaches, Sleater-Kinney, and the B-52's to perform. The series' focus on the ejection of Tasha (Rose Rollins) from the army offered a dialogue on Don't Ask, Don't Tell that was absent elsewhere on prime-time television, although we realize that even listing these details from the show can initiate a further dialogue over what the series never addressed.

The L Word's failures suggest the reasons it remains a milestone and also its legacy. Even a show jam-packed with lesbian characters, lesbian love stories and sex scenes, lesbian musicians, and popular culture references and icons cannot begin to represent, or indeed even satisfy, its target audience. The impatience and dissatisfaction that its restiveness produces is also a prompt to never accept television as it was before *The L Word*.

Notes

1. Lam's full statement suggests her focus on mainstream audiences: "It's a series that addresses mainstream culture more so than people realize [...] We all know somebody in the family or a friend who is gay or lesbian. A few years ago,

that fact was never discussed. But now with this show [*The L Word*] and some of the others, people who wouldn't normally go out of their way to find out more about gay or lesbian family members can have an inside glimpse."

2. These criticisms are most succinctly articulated in a January 2009 entry of a blog called Midwest Gender Queer, written by transgender activist and performance artist JAC Stringer. Stringer writes, "Max isn't so much a transguy as he is a compilation of every negative trans-masculine stereotype imaginable. He's an insecure, hyper-masculine, misogynistic, homophobic asshole. And it just so happens that the character only turned into an asshole after he came out as trans." Rebecca Beirne critiques this characterization in "Dirty Lesbian Pictures: Art and Pornography in *The L Word*," for *Critical Studies in Television* (2007). Jennifer Reed also discusses the character's arc in "Reading Gender Politics in *The L Word*: The Max/Moira Transitions" in *The Journal of Popular Film & Television* (2009).

3. In January 2007, Alice's chart was spun off into OurChart.com, a social networking site for lesbians that included a blog by Ilene Chaiken and also invited fans of the series to contribute their names to a constellation of names. By January 2009, OurChart was shut down and redirected users to the official *L Word* page on Showtime's website, sho.com.

CHAPTER 8

Gray Matters: Bisexual (In)visibility in *The L Word*

Jennifer Moorman

A perusal of the history of American television reveals only a handful of regular or recurring characters whose behavior could be described as bisexual. Rarer still are those enabled to give this behavior a name. As Wayne M. Bryant suggests in regard to world cinema:

> The invisibility of bisexual characters in film is compounded by the dearth of writing on the topic. While there are a number of books on homosexuality in the cinema, there has never been anything written—until now—about bisexual characters in film (xi).

In this regard, not much has changed since his book was published in 1997. In their seminal books on queerness in television, Steven Capsuto (*Alternate Channels: The Uncensored Story of Gay and Lesbian Images on Radio and Television*), Steve Tropiano (*The Prime Time Closet: A History of Gays and Lesbians on TV*), and Larry Gross (*Up from Invisibility*) all mention bisexuality in a cursory fashion; only in Gross's book is the word "bisexuality" in the index, and only then with the qualifier: "on talk shows" (187). These omissions occur with good reason. The latest of these books was published in 2003. The Showtime network's hour-long drama, *The L Word*, which premiered in 2004, provided the first instance of an American fictional television program to depict multiple characters who exhibit bisexual behavior *and* had one character, Alice (Leisha Hailey), who openly identifies as bisexual beginning with the pilot episode, and who explores and elaborates on her sexual identity throughout the show's run.

Much of the debate that has surrounded *The L Word* since its inception has focused either on its (in)ability to represent an underrepresented community, or on the nature of its intended audience. Some argue that, with its high concentration of "girl-on-girl action," it appeals mainly to a straight male audience, with the inference that this constitutes a betrayal of and an exploitation of the lesbian community. Others claim that the show offers a sympathetic representation of a lesbian community, and as such appeals to a lesbian audience seeking an articulation of their own experiences. But what of a bisexual female audience? Bisexual characters can play a unique role in helping to fulfill the creator's stated intent of demystifying queerness for a general (read: heterosexual) audience (Ilene Chaiken, quoted in Brown-Bowers D05), even as they open up a space for the questioning of and sub-version of dominant conceptions of the nature of sexual identification. The extent to which the characters[1] of Alice, Tina (Laurel Holloman), Jenny (Mia Kirshner), Marina (Karina Lombard), Moira/Max (Daniela Sea), Paige (Kristanna Loken), Niki (Kate French), Molly (Clementine Ford), and Dylan (Alexandra Hedison)—all of whom exhibit what could be described as bisexual behavior—actually do fill this role is, however, compromised by the show's overall ambivalence in regard to bisexual representation.

Toward a Theory of Bisexual Representation

As suggested above, the issue of bisexual representation has occasionally been addressed by film theorists, but prior to the 2008 publication of the previous version of this essay, it had yet to be taken up in any depth in the context of television studies. In the history of American cinema, a fair number of characters have had intimate relations with both men and women, but the tendency among critics and viewers is to define any given character's sexual orientation according to the partner that the character pairs off with at the end of the film (and, yes, they are almost always paired off in the end).

As Esterberg argues, "Bisexuality has been variously defined as behavior, as identity, and as anti-identity. It has been seen as essential and, at the same time, as socially constructed" ("The Bisexual Menace" 216). In response to centuries of heterosexist oppression, the gay liberation movement adopted a predominantly essentialist mode of representation in the early 1970s and into the 1980s, for specific political motivations. If sexual orientation is not a "choice," but rather is an inherent trait like ethnicity, then one cannot be condemned as sinful simply for being oriented in a certain way. Bisexuality was, in this context, considered alternately nonexistent or irrelevant. From the perspective of lesbian feminism, however, sexuality was reconfigured as a choice. This did not improve matters, however, as "bisexuals [were] seen as trading on heterosexual privilege and selling out the lesbian movement. In a sex-obsessed world, lesbians alone (and primarily lesbian feminists) [were] seen as standing firm against patriarchy" (216).

Meanwhile, even among those who identify as bisexual, there is no consensus as to how the term should be defined. The anthology *Bi Any Other Name: Bisexual People Speak Out,* edited by Loraine Hutchins and Lani Kaahumanu, for instance, includes people who acknowledge desire for both men and women, but who do not intend to act on all of these desires; men and women who consider themselves to be gender-blind; and conversely, those for whom being with a man is quantifiably different from being with a woman, and they simply enjoy both.

Bisexuals have been discussed at different times and in different circles variously as traitors, as a menace, as a myth, as sexually indiscriminate and irresponsible, as hopelessly confused, as bottomless pits of desire with a lust unsated by man or woman alone, and perhaps most commonly, not discussed at all. It is therefore no surprise that bisexual characters appear so infrequently in American cinema, and even less often in the explicitly commercial-driven medium of television. The greatest barrier to increased bisexual visibility seems to be that of the crisis of signification. Patrick Califia's observation that "It is very odd that sexual orientation is defined solely in terms of the sex of one's partners" (195), applies equally well to the realm of representation, if not more so: practically speaking, if a character is in a monogamous relationship, his or her sexual orientation is conventionally determined according to the sex of his or her partner—unless explicitly stated otherwise.

Maria Pramaggiore argues that: "temporal and narrative conventions are critical to a bisexual reading practice," and says that "narratives which reinforce notions of coupling and closure," whether the final coupling be heterosexual or gay or lesbian, may make a bisexual reading difficult or impossible" (278). Certainly, the notion of temporality is central to any discussion of bisexual representation based on behavior. In order for a character to exhibit bisexual behavior, s/he must appear long enough to have relations with or express desires for both a man and a woman. Triangle situations allow for a compression of such temporality. Pramaggiore focuses her argument on a discussion of films involving romantic triangles, as "such triangles can remain unresolved when the films' conclusions offer open-ended possibilities for erotic desires" (279).

Although a character need not be involved in a romantic triangle to be described as bisexual, the issue of ultimate coupling, a narrative tradition that remains particularly strong in Hollywood narrative cinema, certainly complicates any attempt to identify a character as bisexual. The tendency of viewers and critics to designate a character's sexual orientation according to the gender of whomever that character is coupled with by the film's end is reinforced by widely held stereotypes about bisexuality; the most prominent among them is the idea that bisexuality is not a sexual identity in its own right, but merely a "phase" along the way to the adoption of either a heterosexual or homosexual identity. It would seem that, in order to ensure that a character is truly represented as bisexual, the character must either explicitly identify as such (and, ideally, continue to reiterate this identification even after the final coupling) and/or continue to have intimate relations with both men and women—to "oscillate" between the two, as Pramaggiore suggests—and/or not be engaged in a monogamous relationship at the film's end.

A Brief History of Representations of Bisexual Women on Television

Due to the primary role of temporality or duration in theories of bisexuality, one could argue that the episodic nature of serial television programming is ideally suited for both the representation of bisexual characters and for the practice of bisexual spectatorship. For practical reasons, serial television programming can allow for greater focus on character development, as opposed to the more plot-driven storytelling typical of narrative cinema. This is not to exaggerate differences between film and television based on essentialist terms opposing "the drama of character to the drama of plot" (Boddy 84). In *The L Word*, for example, viewers were able to watch various characters developing relationships with both men and women over the course of the series' run. The show simply had significantly more time to devote to the depiction of these relationships and the development of the characters than would a feature-length film on the same subject.

Nonetheless, despite the rise in queer representations on American television in the last few decades, bisexual characters have remained all but nonexistent. The general consensus among historians of queer TV posits C. J. Lamb of CBS's *L.A. Law* in 1991 as the first regular or recurring female character to be portrayed as bisexual on a fictional television show (Capsuto 273). Despite the uproar created by the "first lesbian kiss on network television," which was in fact a kiss between a bisexual woman, C. J., and a straight woman, Abby (Michele Green), the character was not allowed to develop a meaningful relationship with a woman during her time on the show. "The bisexual C. J. was given a lesbian former lover in one fall 1991 episode, but at the end of the spring season she was embarking on an affair with a straight man. After the season ended, she too left the show" (Gross 87–88).

The only regular or recurring bisexual female character to appear on American television between 1992 and 2002 was Nancy on *Roseanne*. According to Sarah Warn, writing on AfterEllen.com, " it wasn't until 2000 that we saw another bisexual woman on network TV—Sophie (Brittany Daniels) on the Fox sitcom *That 80s Show*—but her bisexuality was mostly used as a running gag, and the series didn't last long" ("*The O.C.*'s Alex Boosts Bisexual Visibility"). During this time period, HBO's *Sex and the City* occasionally referred to the concept of bisexuality in a flippant, ironic sort of way. In episode 3.4, for instance, Carrie (Sarah Jessica Parker) dates a bisexual man (Donovan Leitch), but suggests that she's "not even sure bisexuality exists." Samantha (Kim Cattrall) suggests that bisexuality is merely a fad: "That generation is all about experimentation. All the kids are going bi." In the same episode, Carrie attends a "bisexual party," during which she kisses another woman (Alanis Morissette). Her voice-over narration indicates that in this moment she "was in Alice in Confused-Sexual-Orientation-Land."

Beginning in 2002, a handful of shows included at least one regular or recurring bisexual female character: *All My Children* (ABC, 2002), *Two and a Half Men* (CBS, 2003), and *Coupling* (NBC, 2003). After or concurrent with *The L Word*, the following shows also introduced bisexual female characters in 2004: *Six Feet Under* (HBO), *North Shore* (FOX), *Rescue Me* (FX), *The O.C.*, *One Tree Hill* (WB), and *Starved* (FX).[2] As is discussed elsewhere in this volume, a bisexual character, Alex (Olivia Wilde), also appeared on *The O.C.* (FOX, 2004). Typically, however, her relationship with primary character Marissa (Mischa Barton) endures only through a few episodes, at the end of which time Marissa has seemingly reunited with her ex-boyfriend and Alex leaves the show in a jealous rage. Most recently, the Canadian series *Lost Girl* (Showcase, 2010) has become the first television program to feature a bisexual female lead, Bo (Anna Silk), but Bo perhaps epitomizes the oversexed bisexual stereotype in that she is in fact a succubus, who uses her sexuality to kill or control both men and women.

Unlike *The L Word*, none of these shows also includes regular lesbian characters; apparently, one type of queer woman is as much as any one show can handle. These lists, however, must be problematized, as their industrial and production contexts vary widely, and a concept that would be condemned as too radical on network television could be capitalized on, overtly and vocally, as cutting-edge in the context of a premium cable channel. Furthermore, the barrier to any attempt to identify all of the American television shows to have featured bisexual characters is the perpetual question of how to define "bisexual."

As mentioned above, bisexuality has typically been defined either according to a behavioral model or through explicit identification. This issue has been addressed in psychological studies and in the social sciences, but it poses particular problems for representation. Should all characters who have desires for or sexual contact with both men and women be defined as bisexual? If so, then how would one describe, say, a character who had been in a heterosexual marriage, and left her husband for another woman, at which point she describes herself as lesbian? Should her behavior take precedence over her explicit sexual identification?

In the case of *Buffy the Vampire Slayer* (WB), Willow (Alyson Hannigan) has meaningful sexual and romantic relations with a man and subsequently also women, but her character is depicted as progressing from heterosexual to lesbian.[3] Joss Whedon, the show's creator, has argued that "it would be disingenuous for us to make her bisexual...and that would be a real betrayal to the gay community, particularly since we killed off her lover. So yes, she's gay to stay; she's here, she's queer; get used to it" (Naughton, "*Buffy:* Here to Slay?" 28). Thus a relationship that spanned more than two seasons—that between Willow and her boyfriend Oz (Seth Green)—becomes invalidated. While his dedication to serving the interests of queer fans of the show is admirable, for Whedon, bisexuality apparently is not queer enough; he feels that it would constitute a betrayal to the "gay community" for him to allow Willow to identify as bisexual, despite the fact that her behavior certainly could be described as such, and despite bisexuals' well-established place in LGBTIQ communities. Many of the characters on *The L Word* manifest a similar disconnect between behavior and identification: Marina, who is revealed to have a husband in Italy, despite her polyamorous relationships with women; Tina, who was in a relationship with a man before meeting and subsequently entering into a domestic partnership with Bette, and who later dates another man before returning to Bette; and Jenny, who was engaged to Tim even as she had an adulterous affair with Marina, and would later date both men and women, all ultimately identify as lesbian.

The B Word? Bisexuality in *The L Word*

While each of the characters mentioned above on *The L Word* exhibits what could be termed bisexual behavior, only Alice and occasionally Tina explicitly identify as bisexual, and in later seasons even Alice refers to herself as a lesbian as often as she describes herself as bisexual. Jenny initially resists defining her sexual orientation and ultimately identifies as lesbian, despite the fact that both her behavior and her (rather vague) initial articulations of her desires suggest that she too could be described as "genuinely" bisexual, that is, in more than a purely behavioral sense. Both Alice's and Jenny's dialogue, character development, and interactions with other characters allow for a continuing discussion about the nature of sexual identity, even as they—in their dualistic desires—embody a mainstream-palatable segue into the lesbian world of the show by (theoretically) appealing to both lesbian and straight male audiences. In later seasons, other characters would also begin to question and deconstruct their identities, but in the first two seasons, it is Alice and Jenny who repeatedly rearticulate and/or rework their sexual identities—sometimes agonizingly or uncomfortably—and as such their sexualities stand in contrast to the monosexual identities of the other characters on *The L Word*, and indeed also to mainstream conceptions of sexual identity in American society at large. Even so, the show remains strangely resistant to the label and to the very concept of "bisexual" throughout its run.

Alice's sexuality is initially constructed through responses to other characters' questioning of and occasional hostility toward her sexual orientation. The antagonism Alice endures from her lesbian friends—most notably Dana—has some basis in reality. As Kristin G. Esterberg puts it, "Some of the sharpest debates about bisexuality have occurred within lesbian communities" ("The Bisexual Menace" 222–223). In the context of the second season, in which Alice and Dana become a couple, it appears that Dana has been criticizing Alice out of a combination of jealousy and insecurity, both in regard to Alice's confident self-identification and her (un)availability to Dana. Esterberg suggests that

> Bisexuality raises the issue of sexual jealousy among straights and gays alike. Even if a bisexual is involved in a monogamous relationship with a nonbisexual, holding bisexual identity continually brings to the fore the lover's potential inadequacy. (224)

Indeed, once Dana and Alice become a couple, Dana continues to question Alice's identity. When, for instance, Alice suggests that they use a strap-on dildo (2.9), Dana quips, "Is this a bisexual thing?" Dana will not agree to try strap-on sex until Alice has convinced her that "many bona-fide lesbians do it." In this case, Dana seems to be reacting to the fear that she is not "enough" for a bisexual woman or that a bisexual woman's relationship with her could constitute "just a phase," and that Alice could therefore leave her for a man.

Significantly, the only man we see Alice become involved with for any length of time is Lisa, a "lesbian-identified man."[4] Lisa and Alice consummate their relationship (1.8) in a scene that works to contain notions of sexual difference. The sequence begins in a cabin on a lesbian cruise ship, during a party attended by all of Alice's friends, with a medium shot of Alice sitting on a bed, Lisa kneeling behind her, holding his hands beside her temples. Her eyes are closed, until he says, "I'm working telepathically on your glutes"—at which point Alice opens her eyes and begins to look every which way, as if searching for what on earth he could be talking about. This exemplifies the primary way in which *The L Word* ultimately depicts Lisa, and by extension the whole concept of a "lesbian-identified man"—as ridiculous. The viewer is encouraged, along with Alice, to read Lisa not as a gender nonconformist, but as a confused, New Age-y weirdo. As he begins to move his hands along her body, however, she closes her eyes once again and her face takes on an expression of sexual desire.

Alice and Lisa then begin to kiss passionately, removing most of their clothing. From a close shot of their faces, the camera pans across the length of their bodies to show Alice's hand reaching into Lisa's boxer briefs. Lisa grabs Alice's hand and says, "Wait," as the camera pans back up to their faces. He pulls out a dildo and runs it along her body, until the camera cuts to Alice's exasperated face as she asks, "You're kidding, right?" This exchange follows:

Alice: You're a man! You've got the real thing.
Lisa: That's not how I want to make love to you.
Alice That's how I want you to, okay?
Lisa: It goes against who I am.
Alice: You're a man. You're a man named Lisa, but you're definitely a man.
Lisa: I'm a lesbian...man.

As Lisa speaks this last line, the camera pans to follow Alice as she moves down the length of his body to perform oral sex. A cut to Lisa's face shows him opening his mouth and sighing in ecstasy, despite his protestations. The implication follows that she coerces him into performing a sex act he is uncomfortable with: heterosexual vaginal intercourse. Her unwillingness to accept his sexual identity on his terms naturally raises questions about her own identity; all the more so when one considers the ways in which her desires change throughout the series (in this case, she has chosen to become involved with Lisa after swearing off women for a while), and the fact that she must repeatedly defend her identity to her lesbian friends, who frequently question and/or tease her about being bisexual, and urge her, essentially, to choose a "side."

The actions in this scene are exclusively tightly framed. When they speak, we can see their faces; otherwise, we see body parts. This compartmentalizing camerawork is fairly typical of sex scenes in Hollywood narrative film and, to perhaps a lesser extent, in American fictional television, but in this case, it works to a particular effect. In the cabin, we have a woman (Alice) embodying desires for both men and women—but, as she reveals in this scene, not for both in the same person—and a man (Lisa) embodying both masculinity and femininity. Two phalluses in one room proves one too many for Alice; a shorthand indicating too much sex and gender subversion for one TV show. The tight framing of the scene suggests the need to contain the breaking down of boundaries within the walls of the tiny cabin, lest it undermine the normative frameworks through which American television has articulated sexual identification and gender roles since its inception.

The final scene of Lisa and Alice's interaction on the boat firmly establishes their sexual encounter as a violation. In a tightly framed shot of their heads and shoulders, they stand outside the door to the cabin in which they had sex. When Alice leans in to kiss Lisa. Lisa turns his head in disgust. His face passes through a series of anguished expressions, and as he storms off, Alice throws up her hands in exasperation and cries out, "But you had a good time!" In this way, the story line is framed as sexual assault; her dialogue resonates uncomfortably with the rapist's all-too-familiar line, "she wanted it." Through Alice's coercion of Lisa into using his penis, an old trope is revisited: the containment of sexual difference through sexual violence. And yet, the viewer's sympathies are clearly intended to lie with Alice, who remains a central, increasingly well-developed character, whereas Lisa's story line soon ends. Indeed, Lisa exists on the show only through his interactions with Alice. This works to define Alice against Lisa; her bisexuality can be read as less strange or threatening, by comparison with the supposed absurdity of a "lesbian-identified man."

Ultimately, Alice insists that when she wants to be with a man, she wants a lover who is 100% male. While some bisexual individuals insist that gender is irrelevant, that, as Alice puts it (1.1), they "look for the same things in a man as [they] do in a woman," others feel that there "are things [that are] fundamentally different with men and women" (Karen Klassen, quoted in Hutchins and Kaahumanu 332). Despite Alice's initial claim to be gender-blind, before meeting Lisa she has insisted on wanting to be exclusively with men for a while. As Shane explains to Lisa in season 1, episode 5, "She doesn't want to be a lesbian anymore." Shane's use of the word "lesbian" here provides the first, but not the last, instance of a character referring to Alice as "lesbian" or "gay," despite her explicit identification as bisexual. In this context, it means that Alice is entering a phase during which she does not want to be with women. After Lisa, Alice briefly feels even more vehement in this regard. She seems to be rejecting her bisexuality. In episode 10 of the first season, Alice rescues Dana from a blind date with a man by approaching him and questioning him about his sexual preferences. When he insists that he is completely straight, she says dreamily, "So, no shades of grey or anything?... Wow."

Soon after all of this, Alice begins dating women once again. In the first episode of season 2, Alice again claims that "There is no difference between men and women." If that were so, then why is she happy to use a dildo with Dana, but not with Lisa? This statement of course also calls into question her earlier desire to be exclusively with men. Perhaps she has merely changed her mind; but this depiction does little to challenge common stereotypes about bisexuality: "Bisexuals are seen as hopelessly confused: as fence sitters, unable to make up their mind about what they 'really' are," Esterberg comments ("The Bisexual Menace" 216). In the absence of different representations of bisexuality, and alongside Jenny, who remains overwhelmingly confused about her sexuality throughout most of the first two seasons, Alice's confusion in fact seems to perpetuate these stereotypes. The show, via Alice's dialogue, keeps telling us that bisexuality is normal and valid, but the show's actual depiction of bisexuality remains unstable and conflicted.

Ilene Chaiken, the show's creator, acknowledged the need for a multiplicity of representations of queerness, and implicitly acknowledged the limitations that any one show invariably encounters in attempting to depict a queer community. With "so many stories to tell," she noted, "*The L Word* cannot hope to portray them all" (quoted in Kelly-Saxenmeyer, "Articulating '*The L Word*'"). These considerations certainly influence the depiction of bisexuality on a show that was created, first and foremost, for lesbians. That we do not see Alice in the course of six seasons date a "real" man—that is, one who does not call himself a lesbian—for any significant length of time is perhaps indicative of a desire on the part of the show's creators not to alienate the queer community by depicting too much straight sex. As one viewer complained of season 1, episode 4, in which Jenny has sex with both Tim (Eric Mabius) and Marina, "There was more straight sex in that episode than gay sex" (Brown-Bowers D05).

At the start of the series, Jenny is introduced as the girlfriend of Tim, who lives next door to Bette (Jennifer Beals) and Tina (Laurel Holloman). Jenny has just moved in with Tim, and on her first day in Los Angeles, she sees Shane making love to a woman in Bette and Tina's pool. She is aroused by this, and tells Tim about it later. As she describes the scene, Tim takes off her clothes and they too have sex. In later scenes, after having met and developed a strong attraction to Marina, Jenny will again fantasize about

lesbian sex while having sex with Tim. After Jenny and Marina have sur-
reptitiously indulged in sexual encounters, Jenny repeatedly envisions her
female lover, Marina, while engaging in heterosexual intercourse with her
boyfriend, Tim.

In one such instance, when she actually sees Marina's face superimposed
over Tim's; she is in effect participating in a *ménage-a-trois*. Indeed, it is the
triangularity of Jenny's desires that indicate her potential bisexuality; however, unlike Alice, throughout her personal odyssey of sexual identity, Jenny
only once uses the word "bisexual" to describe herself (1.9).

After the affair with Marina has destroyed Jenny's relationship with
Tim, she discovers that Marina is in an open but committed relationship
with another woman. To Jenny's shock and pain, Marina responds: "You'll
find that your life is richer, more full of possibilities and choices...I opened
up your world." This seemingly optimistic articulation of her seduction of
Jenny in fact embodies one of the classic fears at the root of homophobia: the
idea that a lesbian or gay man can "turn" a straight person gay. One almost
expects Melissa Etheridge to show up, bearing a toaster oven.[5] Viewed from
this angle, Marina's words become sinister, pathologized. In a sense, it dele-
gitimizes Jenny's (bi)sexual identity, by suggesting that it was manipulated
into being by an outside agent (namely, Marina); yet, at the same time, it
functions to affirm the fluidity of sexuality.

This becomes clearer still within the context of the next triangle in which
Jenny involves herself. After Marina, she briefly dates a man, Gene (Tygh
Runyan), and a woman, Robin (Anne Ramsey), concurrently. In season 1,
episode 13, she brings Gene home, only to find Robin waiting for her. As the
three listen to a message from Marina left on Jenny's answering machine, her
dates become uncomfortable, and each offers to leave. Jenny replies, "No,
no...I don't want either of you to leave." This constitutes the most explicit
articulation of Jenny's bisexuality of any point during the first two seasons.
As the episode ends, we watch through the window as the three play a board
game, and later, Jenny sits awake, seemingly pondering her sexual identity,
as the other two lay asleep on separate beds. Both of these triangles in which
Jenny participates function to illustrate the fluidity of Jenny's sexuality. At
the start of the show, she identifies as heterosexual; and she is initially surprised and disturbed by Marina's attempt to seduce her. By the end of season
1, she clearly feels confused, but also intrigued by the idea of exploring her
options. At the start of season 2, she refuses a lesbian identity (2.1), but soon
thereafter adopts the term and uses it more or less consistently throughout
the rest of the show's run.

In episode 5 of the second season, Mark (Eric Lively) asks his new roommates, Shane (Katherine Moennig) and Jenny, if he can conduct a video

interview with them for a "project" that he's working on. It turns out that this "project" involves candidly filming the two women in their most personal moments…Mark encourages the women: "Just think about how you're helping some lonely little lez out in the Midwest without a role model in sight." At this point, they are unaware of his ulterior motives and reluctantly agree to being interviewed. He immediately begins to interrogate them about lesbian sexuality. He refers to Jenny always as lesbian, and she does not contradict him—despite her attractions to men.

In a scene from season 2, episode 9, the series acknowledges the difficulties inherent in any attempt to represent a marginalized group. The porn producer to whom Mark attempts to sell his (at this point, rather tame) tapes of Jenny and Shane insists: "We want hot, lesbian sex and we want it now." Mark responds, "This isn't just about sex." This line could be speaking directly to the supposed 62% of the show's audience comprised of straight males, ironically both warning them that the sex scenes should not be read as gratuitous and that the show's intent is not to sensationalize, and acknowledging the impossibility of avoiding sensationalized receptions of the show (Brown-Bowers D02).

Characters like Jenny and Alice can be read as intermediaries between the presumably disparate worlds of straight male viewers and lesbian viewers. Just as in mainstream pornography marketed to straight males, Jenny and Alice love women, but they love men too—and are thus presumably less threatening to the fragile collective straight-male pride. This idea caters to yet another stereotype accorded to bisexual women: that they are in effect consorting with the enemy. If both Jenny and Alice move toward being romantically involved exclusively with women, it could arguably be for this reason—to ward off accusations that they exist to cater to straight male fantasies.

Similarly, when Tina begins to date Henry in season 3, most of her friends view it as disloyalty to her community: she is supposedly "cleav[ing] to the heterosexual paradigm" (3.12). Perhaps most tellingly, Alice, the show's resident bisexual, accuses Tina of being "stuck in the far reaches of heteroville" (4.2). When Tina replies that she seems to recall Alice "lurking around there" herself, Alice says, "Yeah, but I came to my senses." She seems to be joking, but not entirely. Alice later tells Papi that Tina "went straight. Feels like a betrayal" (4.8). In seasons 4 through 6, Alice seems to adopt and then cast off both bisexual and lesbian identities, sometimes for political reasons, as when she identifies as lesbian during Tasha's trial (5.9). Significantly, Alice is not shown to struggle with or examine her sexual identification; rather, she flippantly refers to herself as bi in one episode and as a lesbian in the next. This could perhaps be read as a depiction of bisexuality as a fluid identity, but it seems more likely to represent the show's unwillingness to allow for bisexuality—or queerness as a broad term for fluid sexuality—as a coherent identity.

As for Tina, she initially fights back against these accusations, but ultimately seems to internalize and accept them. At one point in season 3, Tina actually slips up and begins to refer to straight people as "we," before correcting herself (3.6). While still dating Henry in season 4, Tina insists, "I still identify as a lesbian." Alice demands, "Why don't you just be a bisexual," to which Tina responds that she thinks of "lesbian" as a political identity (4.4). Once Tina breaks up with Henry, she fully readopts a lesbian identity. As Rebecca Beirne puts it, "Although Tina's 'return to men' is explained away by the character in the fourth season as being accounted for by her 'humiliation at finding out that her lover was cheating on her' (4.9), this does not narratively make sense in light of both her relationship with Helena that directly followed Bette's affair or the intensity of her desires for men as they were portrayed in the third season" ("Lesbian Pulp Television"). Tina eventually describes Henry as boring, and the show depicts the entire affair as unfulfilling and in every way inferior to the lesbian partnerships: again and again we see that Henry simply does not "get" Tina the way Bette and her friends do. Once they break up, Tina once again adopts a lesbian identity, and viewers presumably breathe a sigh of relief.

There is something to be said for that, however. The show clearly wants to resist any narrative in which a character can be perceived as becoming straight or in which a character's queerness could be viewed as just a phase. Beirne writes that mainstream society finds the idea of the feminine lesbian particularly threatening, so "portraying these lesbians as always potentially bisexual undermines the challenge of depicting such characters, assuages the discomfort of potentially homophobic viewers, and allows male viewers to feel that they 'have a chance' with such women" ("Lesbian Pulp Television"). Perhaps it is more than that. Bisexual behavior per se does not prove particularly threatening to the binary oppositions required by dominant conceptions of sexuality. Regarding a bisexual female character, sex with a man can be described as heterosexual, and sex with a woman as lesbian sex. Bisexual identification, however, does undermine these mainstream behavioral frameworks of sexual representation. That which is not named—a character's oscillation between male and female lovers, ultimately coupling with one or the other—allows for the perception that such behavior constitutes a phase, in line with liberal models of "progress." Alice's insistence, however, that she is bisexual even when she is in love with Dana, in the final episode of season 2, constitutes a radical act, one that is practically unheard of in the history of American fictional television programming.

At the close of season 2, Alice goes so far as to romanticize her bisexuality, "I follow the heart and not the anatomy" (2.13). At this point, it seems as though the serial nature of the show and the writers' willingness to explore issues of sexual identity in depth allow for Alice's sexuality to be depicted ultimately not as confused, but rather as fluid. Like many people, she has moments of self-doubt, and like many bisexuals, she has moments of feeling more attracted to one gender than to another. Her character emerges from the first two seasons as complex and well-rounded, rather than simply (and stereotypically) confused. So why does the show insist upon undermining this complexity in the seasons that follow?

Much like Mark's documentary from season 2, Tina and Jenny's film, *Lez Girls* reflexively acknowledges the challenges inherent in trying to depict bisexuality. In season 5, the producers decide that Jesse (the character based on Jenny) should go back to her boyfriend at the end of the movie (5.12). Tina argues that *Lez Girls* was meant to be a movie by, for, and about lesbians, and furthermore was supposed to be the movie that "changed all that"—"all that" being "the guy gets the girl, the end." The producer replies that the film is still "chock full of lesbians," and adds that "Elise [nee Alice], the bisexual, she's not interested in men."

Chaiken seems to be reflexively acknowledging her own fear that, even in a show "chock full of lesbians," having even one character return to the straight world (in the show's terms) undermines the depiction of lesbian sexuality. By calling attention to the importance of closure—of who a character ends up with—the show is in effect imposing a cinematic paradigm on a TV show. In six seasons of programming, with dozens of queer and lesbian characters, would it really undermine the show's depiction of lesbian sexuality to allow just one character to maintain a bisexual (or queer/fluid) identity throughout, or to allow a female character who identifies as bi to be in a fulfilling relationship with a man at some point?

Those characters who do exhibit bisexual or fluid behavior on the show refuse to consistently identify as such. Paige initially balks at Shane's characterization of her as straight, insisting that she'd "rather not be called anything. I'm sexually fluid" (4.9), and she doesn't so much revoke that description of herself as not deny it when she is described as "gay" in a later episode (4.11); soon thereafter she disappears from the show. Max becomes interested in men after transitioning, but the possibility for bisexuality appears to be dismissed when he explains that he's read that what is genetically encoded in us is not attraction to men or to women, but same-sex attraction (5.9). This statement is problematic in that Max is saying it to Grace, with whom he has just had an affair, so we might not take it at face value, except that it constitutes the show's last depiction of Max's articulation of his sexual identification. It raises a number of interesting questions about what it means to be trans, as well as what it means to be queer, but it nonetheless seems to shut down the possibility for thinking of Max as sexually fluid or bisexual; he may have undergone an (outward) gender transition, but his sexuality can remain static.

Dylan never quite defines her sexual identity, but it is suggested in season 6 that her relationship with Helena has made her realize that she's a lesbian. When Helena sees her in her club, the following exchange occurs:

> *Helena*: "You were looking for a girl club? A lesbian girl club?"
> *Dylan*: "Yeah, you helped me with that."

Again, the show does not seem to have a problem with flirting with the homophobic stereotype that lesbians can "turn" women gay, but resolutely refuses to allow a character to identify consistently as bisexual, presumably because that would undermine the show's representation of lesbian sexuality. In the end, only one very minor and nonrecurring character maintains a consistent bisexual identity: Uta, who (surely not coincidentally) also happens to believe that she's a vampire.

Ultimately, *The L Word* attempts to alleviate the anxieties associated with bisexual identification, through both its initial tendency toward the stabilizing of identities and its willingness to embrace sexual difference and to depict sexuality as open and fluid. This attempt is compromised both by the very nature of bisexuality, its polysemy and its fluidity, and by the series' apparent desire not to alienate its core lesbian audience through the depiction of "too much straight sex"—even when at least one of the people engaging in said sex does not identify as straight. A sexual identity with so many different meanings and such varied manifestations cannot be done justice through one, or even two or three, representations. In the context of an utter dearth of such representations, each one bears the burden of embodying The (monolithic) Representation. And, as such, each inevitably falls short.

I maintain that serial television programming, among other audiovisual media, has the unique capacity to allow for more variegated, complex representations of bisexuality, and of sexuality in general. *The L Word*'s examination of sexuality comprises the most complex treatment of female bisexuality to date, but there is still much to be accomplished in the ongoing struggle for representations of sexual diversity. Among the calls for butch characters and other less mainstream-palatable images of queer women on television, I would have liked to see more in-depth examination of the many forms that sexuality can take.

Notes

1. Technically, Phyllis Kroll (Cybill Shepherd) also exhibits bisexual behavior, in that she was married to a man and then begins to date women; but hers is depicted straightforwardly as a coming-out story, in which she realizes that she has been a lesbian all along.
2. I am indebted to www.AfterEllen.com for its timeline of lesbian and bisexual female characters on television.
3. I discuss this at length in a previous article, "'Kinda Gay': Queer Cult Fandom and Willow's (Bi)Sexuality in *Buffy the Vampire Slayer*," in Jes Batis, ed., *Supernatural Teens: Essays on Magic, Mutation, and Adventure* (New York: Lexington Press, 2011).
4. She does date one other man while with Lisa, and she continues to have sexual relations with him after she has broken up with Lisa. She mentions her interactions with this man to her friends, but after their first date we never actually see them together.
5. This reference is to "The Puppy Episode" of *Ellen*, in which Susan (Laura Dern) facetiously suggests to Ellen Morgan (Ellen DeGeneres) that lesbians who reach their quota of having "turned" other women gay win a toaster oven.

CHAPTER 9

Somewhere between Love and Hate: Disidentification and *The L Word*

Marnie Pratt

The L Word was by no means the first television program to have lesbian characters. Queer female characters had already been appearing on cable and on regular network shows for over 20 years when *The L Word* debuted in 2004. Often these characters were secondary or peripheral; however, *The L Word* was not even the first series to address contemporary issues through a lesbian main character. This distinction, of course, goes to *Ellen,* when its main character, Ellen Morgan (played by Ellen DeGeneres), made television history by coming out during prime-time television. However, *The L Word* was unique in that it contained a large cast of main characters who were almost entirely queer women, and these characters' lives, relationships, and political or social issues were the focus of the series. Additionally, by airing on a premium cable network, the show was subject to fewer regulations than a network drama and thus was allowed to depict certain scenarios in a more open manner.

Despite these innovations, the show's immense popularity, and the largely positive media recognition *The L Word* received, it failed to be universally hailed by the communities it aimed to represent. Queer presses, community spaces, and new-media networking sites were rich with arguments over whether or not the show signified a positive change for queer individuals within the larger culture or whether it was just as damaging as no representation at all, or even more damaging. These frequently were animated conversations with high levels of emotional investment.

In support of *The L Word*, viewers most often cite the excitement they feel over finally being able to witness images and stories similar to their own lives within mainstream culture. For example, a viewer posting on a discussion board about *The L Word* states:

> As a gay viewer, the desire to see yourself or your life represented on screen can't be underestimated.... It's why as dykes we'll watch any old crap just for an infrequent glimpse of a gay minor character because up until [*The L Word*] there have been so few opportunities to see *any* lesbians on TV let alone cool, sexy ones that are shown in a positive light. (honeytheif)

Similarly, another audience member proclaims her investment in the series by stating:

> As someone who grew up in the 60's, I've just got to say, watching this show each week is becoming almost a spiritual experience for me. Needless to say, I didn't see any lesbian role models on TV when I was growing up.... [I]t almost brings a tear to this middle-aged dyke's eye. (Tenderwolf)

These two reactions are neither extreme nor unique. Audiences often discuss how important *The L Word* is to them or how it has profoundly changed their lives.

The emotional investment of other audience members has taken the form of disappointment as they critique *The L Word*. This position is evidenced by a viewer post on the website *Gaydarnation*:

> Hate It—This bears no resemblance to my life at all! I'm so disappointed in *The L Word*. After all the hype, I really thought that it would be better than it is.... I honestly think that lesbians would be better off without this kind of thing on our screens. It just gives straight people new stereotypes to hurl at us. (Louise 2004)

A member of the online lesbian social networking site *Pink Sofa* provides another negative opinion when she states

> [I] can't understand why everyone is so obsessed with something that features such unrealistic looking women.... The whole thing seems to

me to be promoting an unrealistic image of femme lesbians that is aimed at pleasing straight men, and the vast majority of the cast are straight in real life. (maria14)

The last two quotes demonstrate the common opinion among dissenting viewers that the show's representations are inaccurate, damaging, or stereotypical.

However, regardless of the stance audience members have taken regarding the show, a powerful emotional investment often remains in their comments. They not only speak of watching the series despite disliking it, but also continue to seek out interactions with others in order to discuss their reactions. Such dedicated yet frequently conflicted responses led me to interrogate how a show like *The L Word* functioned for its viewers.

Over the course of the series' active years, I conducted an ethnographic study of its audiences.[1] This consisted of observing and interacting with virtual and physical-world audience communities through a variety of formats, including, but not limited to, message and discussion boards, viewing parties, premieres and fundraising events, blogs, online videos, and wikis. Additionally, I administered an anonymous survey to 110 participants from both online and real-world audience communities, which asked predominantly open-ended questions about *The L Word* and about popular culture in general. This chapter briefly summarizes some of the findings of this study.[2] I argue that Eve Kosofsky Sedgwick's theory of "the closet," when combined with a historical framework regarding queer invisibility, provides an initial means of contextualizing the reasons commonly cited by audiences for their reactions to *The L Word* (*Epistemology of the Closet*). However, ethnographic research also clearly illustrates that viewer responses do not fall neatly into a positive/negative binary. Therefore, I offer José Esteban Muñoz's theory of disidentificatory reception as a tool for further understanding viewers' reactions and for considering the possible sociopolitical value offered to viewers by engaging with cultural texts like *The L Word* (*Disidentifications*).

Investment in Visual Culture and Disidentificatory Reception

My contribution to the first edition of *Televising Queer Women* marked one of the first times I considered *The L Word* and, in fact, the chapter concluded with the questions I eventually sought to answer within the larger research project represented here. I suggested that perhaps investment on the part of queer audiences might be better understood by considering queer culture's long struggle with "the closet" and with visibility. In *Epistemology of the Closet*, Sedgwick discusses the unique nature of oppression for queer individuals. She describes the closet as ever-present and explains:

> Vibrantly resonant as the image of the closet is for many modern oppressions, it is indicative for homophobia in a way it cannot be for other oppressions. Racism, for instance, is based on a stigma that is visible in all but exceptional cases...; so are the oppressions based on gender, age, size, [and] physical handicap. (75)

Certain markers related to aspects of skin tone, physical ability, gender, or age may result in oppression for some marginalized groups; however at the same time, such traits also render these individuals visible. In other words, these traits they constitute them as existing in an identity. For queer individuals, who live within a dominant culture that assumes heterosexuality and compels the concealment of divergent selves, invisibility becomes central to their oppression. As a result, the investment in representations of self may be high for anyone occupying a marginalized identity, but for queer individuals, it is closely linked with the ability to exist at all.

I now find it is further useful to contextualize this oppression through invisibility within a larger historical framework. Several historians of queer culture have argued that homosexuality was not enabled as an identity category within the United States until around the turn of the twentieth century. During this time period, sexologists first began to alter their discourse on sexuality from addressing homosexual behavior to addressing homosexual identity.

Curiously, this historical time frame is also marked by another cultural shift that is crucial to understanding the importance of visual representations of self to queer individuals. The same moment marked by the emergence of a gay identity is also characterized by the development of numerous technologies related to visual culture, such as motion pictures and photography's use in advertising. "Whereas nineteenth-century advertisements had been informational, almost exclusively composed of words, the rise of photography and then cinematographic technologies enabled a shift to images in the early twentieth century," explains Alexandra Chasin (103). This trend toward the visual was not limited to cinema and advertising either. Book publishers were able to create more visual book jacket artwork and marketing campaigns because of cheaper printing costs, and although television did not become widespread within consumer homes until mid-century, the technology was developed in the 1920s, and had already begun to manifest itself within the public consciousness (Powers 7).

When taken together, Western culture's new emphasis on visuality emerged at essentially the same cultural moment as an identity group whose existence was strongly masked emerged. In other words, as the larger culture became enamored with new technologies of the *visible*, queer individuals began to form their own identities of *invisibility*. I argue that this clash of invisible identities with a heavily visual culture offers an initial framework for understanding the uniquely strong emotional reactions that queer audiences have to queer visual representations like *The L Word*.

Although the audiences with whom I interacted clearly exhibited a strong investment, it would be much more difficult, if not impossible, to come to any definitive conclusion as to whether or not they more often enjoyed or were disappointed by *The L Word*. For every conversation I observed or participated in that praised the series, there was another condemning it. The results of my survey were undeniably divided, as the percentage of respondents citing either positive or negative feelings for the series both came in at approximately 40%. However, this friction also makes *The L Word* a particularly interesting case study, in that individuals often expressed both types of reactions simultaneously. Viewers who proclaimed support for the show were also some of its harshest critics, and those who condemned it also found positive aspects to its existence. They found it difficult to either reject or enjoy the series wholesale, which truly highlights the complicated relationship these audiences have with *The L Word*.

Muñoz's theory of disidentificatory reception provides a tool for understanding such reactions. His concepts are valuable in part because, like *The L Word*'s viewers, he attempts to move beyond the "good dog/bad dog criticism" of cultural representations in order to offer a more nuanced analysis (9). He warns against the propensity for viewing identity as either essentialist or social constructivist, and instead argues that it is a production at the point where these two perspectives meet. "This collision," he explains, "is precisely the moment of negotiation when hybrid, racially predicated, and deviantly gendered identities arrive at representation" (6). In other words, identity formation occurs when the essential understandings of self clash with the socially constructed representations of that self.

Muñoz's focus on how minority identities are negotiated with cultural representations, and his speculations on the sociopolitical value of such practices are also immensely valuable for examining the audiences of this study, who not only make comments frequently related to a marginalized identity, but also tend to view the show and its communities through sociopolitical frameworks such as visibility, community-building, and escape from oppression. By explaining that we must always assume cultural representations to be homophobic, sexist, racist, and so forth, because they must exist within the dominant culture, the "majoritarian public sphere"), Muñoz illustrates that the minority self is constructed both in relation to and against these representations (4). Lesbians must simultaneously identify and disidentify with cultural images. Finally, through this performance of disidentificatory reception, minoritarian subjects rework or reconfigure aspects of otherwise problematic representations in order to maintain use value (6).

I argue that the viewers of this study participate in disidentificatory reception. Even though *The L Word* is a queer text, it still exists within a dominant culture that is always already homophobic, racist, sexist, classist, and so forth. Identity and identification are produced when these audiences' hybrid selves clash with the show's socially constructed representations of those selves. Audiences are simultaneously drawn to the show by the validation of one aspect of their identity and disillusioned when it comes into conflict with their other experiences or positionalities. This is supported not only by the many viewers who discuss identity, representation, and visibility, but also by the fact that reactions to *The L Word* frequently are talked about in terms of being a negotiation. Furthermore, since the majority of critiques related to representation and visibility touch upon intersecting identity categories, such as sexuality and race, sexuality and gender identity, and sexuality and class, it is clear *The L Word*'s viewers find it necessary to both identify and disidentify with cultural representations in order to maintain use value or, as Muñoz suggests (1), "seize social agency."[3]

Negotiating a Love/Hate Relationship with *The L Word*

Some of the ways in which *The L Word*'s audiences discussed their appreciation of the series were much like those of the consumers of any form of visual culture, in that they valued it for certain cinematic qualities or as a source of entertainment. For example, one respondent described it as "a glossy, fun show to watch," while other respondents described the series as having strong writing, directing, acting, or being "well shot."

It is interesting that those unhappy with the show also occasionally mentioned cinematic elements. "Sometimes I find the writing and/or editing of the show [to be] lacking," stated one respondent, "and I can't always understand the motive behind the different characters' behavior." When it came to such criticism, writing and acting tended to receive the most comments; there was a particular emphasis on displeasure over specific story lines. Several viewers made it very clear that formal elements were in fact quite important to them, and their harsh statements reflected this. For instance, one described the show as "an enormous waste of potential," and went on to complain, "the writing is often terrible, the performances uneven, the story lines ridiculous, the characters poorly defined, despite the fact that the show draws a lot of interest and participation by talented women."

Television can create a whole new world for audiences, and escaping into that world was another commonly mentioned reason for liking *The L Word*. The show was important to several respondents because it was seen as providing a temporary space in which queerness was acceptable, if not normative. For those who deal with discrimination on a daily basis, even brief moments of relief from that reality can be critical. One survey respondent confirmed this when she stated, "watching TV is about escapism, not about documentaries." Viewers outside of the survey had similar reactions, such as one message board poster who explained, "Whenever I feel sad of my situation I keep watching *The L Word* and somehow it makes my heart feel light...I may never be outed but this show makes me feel welcome [in] the world" (Stillinside 2007).

Another message board user also alluded to escapist emotions when she responded to a thread entitled, "You know you're an L addict when..." by replying, "When you suddenly realize, 'Hey I can't live in the same TV world as the L, but I sure as HELL love too!'" (Willintoadmit 2004).

Although the show did not provide a physical space, it could provide a temporary emotional refuge in which viewers could see expressions of sexuality similar to their own. For some viewers, this might have been the only place for them to experience such things; however, for others, this became a starting point for other connections.

The L Word's audiences also often made comments related to community and the building of community. Perhaps it is best summarized by one survey respondent, who stated, "*The L Word* and these [web]sites have expanded the community and its ability to network." This quote alludes to both communities related to the series and to the wider queer or lesbian community. Those communities surrounding the show varied in format; some existed solely online, but others manifested in the physical world. However, both types were valued as safe venues in which members could voice opinions, express desires, make friends, find support, and even acknowledge their sexuality. In fact, the latter two of these were fairly common occurrences, as the following posts illustrate:

> The show has also confirmed that I am without a doubt a lesbian and could never be with another man. (lezmom3)

> Without this show, I probably wouldn't have realized that I like women. (ilovebette)

The L Word has definitely helped me feel much better about myself and my sexuality. (lilWannaB3 ROcK$t@R)

Has the show affected me??—yes. I came out to three of my friends the other week, telling them I think I'm bisexual. I've known for a while that I might be. The show has helped me see [that] it's just as normal as being straight. (H)

For these viewers and others like them, the show and its communities eased the often difficult processes of self-acceptance and coming out; for others, it even fostered a consciousness of their own sexual identity. Their identities were in fact formed or came into being as a result of *The L Word*.

Community was generally cited as a reason for having a positive reaction to the series; however, this does not mean that those who disliked *The L Word* did not discuss it. For example, one respondent mentioned, "I watch it regularly with friends—and we all enjoy chatting about it, discussing what we like and hate about the show." This comment indicates that it was by no means necessary to hold an entirely positive feeling towards the series in order to participate within the communities. Another respondent made this even more evident by stating, "I can't deny that it makes me feel more a part of the lesbian community to be hating on [*The L Word*] with everyone else when the new episodes are airing." In other words, some individuals who expressed an unfavorable opinion of the show still wished to maintain a connection with the community. It even appeared as if some watched the series out of a sense of obligation, or interacted with it largely because it was just such a prominent feature of queer women's popular culture.

The above types of responses exemplify viewer investment in visual culture like *The L Word,* despite its inability to completely satisfy. These individuals desired a connection with others who watch the series or wanted the ability to temporarily escape into a less oppressive world, yet they failed to appreciate some or all aspects of the show. In such cases, reactions were closely intertwined with a viewer's marginalized identity. In order to receive the validation of their identity experienced through community and escape, these individuals must negotiate with *The L Word*'s unfavorable aspects. This investment and negotiation is perhaps even better illustrated, however, by those audience members who discussed visibility and representation.

Although cinematic aspects, escapism, and community were important to some of *The L Word*'s audience members, the justifications offered most often by viewers were related to visibility and representation. Viewers who felt positively towards the show tended to connect their reactions to the social and political power they believed were present in visibility politics. In fact, when asked about the political possibilities of popular culture like

The L Word, over half the survey respondents commented on visibility politics, and many argued that visibility in popular culture greatly benefits queer culture.

"It's a very important show," stated one respondent, "both politically and in terms of visibility but also I think personally—to see aspects of our lives reflected on television and a group of women who are living open, happy, successful lives…" Several other respondents replied similarly, as the following examples illustrate.

> *Survey 25*: More visibility [will] reduce the fear that people have which will lead to the end of discrimination.
> *Survey 71*: Visibility is the most important aspect to changing popular opinion, and I think that the more visibility a show offers is wonderful [sic].
> *Survey 70*: I think [visibility] is very important because it places a marginalized group into the mainstream popular culture. Anytime we (lesbians specifically, gays in general) can get exposure on a broader scale like this, I believe it helps "normalize" us in a world that fears what they do not understand or have not experienced.

These viewers, as well as many others I encountered, not only believe *The L Word* has expanded the visibility of queer individuals, but also think this visibility will bring social and political change for queer individuals.

Audiences commonly argued that such change would occur because the series educates the wider culture about queer issues. "The show helps raise awareness to gay issues and shows the gay point of view to people who aren't usually aware," stated one respondent. Another individual described *The L Word* as "a good show that hits on a lot of issues concerning lesbians." A third explained, "It's great for lesbians because it encourages acceptance from straight people who watch it, and it's important to see gay relationship issues dealt with."

A number of viewers also placed this visibility within a historical context. They argued that the series was important, given the chronology of existing queer female images, which one individual described as "totally fucked up murderers, sociopaths, or suicidal depressives." Another person conveyed a similar sentiment when she explained that she was "happy that there is a show in which lesbian characters are the focus and being lesbian is not seen as deviant or strange." These audience members argued that the show's images depicted queer women in more positive ways than previous popular culture had, and thus a proliferation of such images could "normalize" (a term employed by a few individuals) queerness.

Whether or not the show has or will actually create this kind of cultural change is the topic of another project entirely; however, it is important to note that for many of its supportive viewers, pleasure is clearly accompanied by a belief in the show's potential for social or political change. Conversely however, others find *The L Word*'s power to be detrimental.

Just as viewers who enjoyed the series praised its connection to visibility politics, its critics took issue with visibility by arguing that its representations are problematic. Some of the earliest concerns to gain attention related to the cast's appearance, as evidenced by the following statement made by series writer and actor Guinevere Turner during the first season (in "Lipstick Los Angeles"):

> One of the biggest complaints I hear from lesbians about the television show...is that the women on the show are all so girly and un-gay-looking. "Where's the big old truck-driving tattooed dyke?" one woman stood up and asked at a panel discussion with the creative team of the show. "I don't know any women who look like those women!"

The audiences with whom I interacted also discussed their concerns over the cast's appearance. More than one identified the series as too "glamorous." Another equated the women on *The L Word* with "runway models" and declared this as "not representative of the lesbian community."

Audiences' concerns over a glamorized image tended to be connected to two further critiques. In some cases, such depictions were seen as only representing one type of lesbian identity, the femme. For example, a message board thread entitled "Where are the butch women, where is the diversity?" began with the following post: "I am disappointed that it would focus in so squarely on feminine lesbians. I love femmes but I would love to see butches...being represented as well" (carameladye). Much of this post was met with affirming responses, such as one that states, "*The L Word* needs to bring a true butch onto the show. Out of all the lesbians I know, even the femmest of femme are more butch than the girls on the show. I love the girls, but I'd like to see something true to life" (YouAreSoAnalog). Other times, viewers raised concerns over glamorous depictions by relating them to class issues. Some simply labeled the show as "classist." Others elaborated with humor by critiquing the characters "way-too-skinny-bodies and super-privileged lives" or stating, "BLAH. Boring, rich, rich, white ladies. I don't know dykes like that." One comment addressed both class and the diversity of lesbian identities: "I dislike the fact that they really only show femme women, no butch women, and class isn't dealt with hardly at all."

Critiques of representation were by no means limited to these areas, though. In fact, virtually every identity category became an avenue for critique at some point. Viewers considered such depictions as either lacking or problematic. For example, the show was heavily criticized for the way it handled transgender identity and issues through the characters of Ivan (played by Kelly Lynch) and Max (played by Danielle Sea). Several survey responses labeled the series and its treatment of these characters as "transphobic" or claimed that it did "not handle trans . . . issues well." One also clarified these broader statements by adding, "I think having a transsexual person on *The L Word* is progressive; however, I think the creators could have explored the complexities of being trans more fully." This person provided examples of plotlines she found to be particularly lacking, such when Max takes street hormones early in his transition when he has no health insurance, and the depictions of his transition process as a whole. They argue that neither of these scenarios is given enough screen presence or explanation.

Such comments were also corroborated by discussions within message boards. When Ivan was abruptly removed from the series, there was a lot of confusion as to why. Many posters did not understand his behavior towards Kit (played by Pam Grier), which often resulted in a general dislike of the character. Similarly, when Max began taking hormones as part of his transition, he became quite angry and even violent towards other characters. This story line also became a topic of discussion, and it caused significant dislike for Max. Transgender and/or transpositive posters were sometimes offended by the negative reactions and comments regarding these characters, and they spent considerable time and energy attempting to defend them to other posters. Some even began entirely new discussion threads for addressing their concerns, such as "Ivan's 'Gender Issues' from an FTM Perspective," "Why does everyone hate Max?," and "A few things you can do to be more tolerant to transpeople." Meanwhile, other viewers simply expressed disappointment with the show, "Max is a sorry portrayal of an FTM. Very similar to my problems with Ivan Aycock, they still can't seem to get it right. While I like that they are trying to bring this very real subject to life through a show that touches so many viewers, I really think they defeated the purpose with Max" (YouAreSoAnalog).

Dissenting viewers who addressed representation also often discussed *The L Word*'s depictions of racial and ethnic diversity. Initially, the show received criticism for having only one nonwhite queer character (Bette, played by Jennifer Beals, was biracial). "We [black women] are as much a part of the lesbian culture as other ethnic/racial groups," begins one poster, "and if the show truly wants to encompass the entire lesbian culture [then] a black woman or women should be included. And I know it would help the show reach a much wider audience if black lesbians had a character on the show that they could identify with" (MyWhatAGirl). Another individual makes a similar critique: "I love Bette and the fact that her presence has forced some discussions about biraciality. But I crave more than that and wish there were more opportunities for diversity outside of some faces in a crowd every once in a while..." (Arkaycee). Some discussion board posters had even harsher words for the series, such as some who labeled the entire show as "racist" or others who elaborated: "[The fact] that there are seemingly no PEOPLE of color, particularly lesbians, that are attractive to each other is patently offensive... Showtime should consult with any critical thinking lesbian about diversity, race politics, relationships... this show REEKS!" (Bigsmooches).

Eventually the series' creators did introduce other characters of color, such as Carmen (played by Sarah Shahi), Papi (played by Janina Gavankar), and Tasha (played by Rose Rollins). Criticism then turned to how these characters were represented, as many thought they only replicated stereotypes. One viewer's message board post addresses this idea:

> Most of the characters on the show are white. When you have one representative of a certain group (Hispanic, Black, Asian, etc.), and that character is the ONLY character representing a certain group, I personally believe that you need to be careful not to make that particular character portray the negative stereotypes that society has made for that group whether it be race/religion/sexual orientation, etc. For example, is there a reason why there are no educated minority characters [that] weren't formerly drug addicts/alcoholics/from the ghetto, etc.? (Contra)

Another viewer discussed her similar unhappiness over stereotypical depictions in the character of Kit, "Kit is a recovering alcoholic who abandoned her son and is a mess... Again, not a good representative" (Storm).

Problems also arose because of the creator's decisions to cast actors in racial or ethnic roles that did not match their actual identities. Both Carmen and Papi were Latina characters, but Shahi is of Iranian and Spanish descent and Gavankar's heritage is Indian and Dutch. A viewer responds to the Shahi casting decision, "[An] Iranian girl playing Latina? Okay, okay, I love *The L Word*, but why is a girl from Iran playing a Latina?... I would have preferred it would be a real Latina playing Carmen" (Wordswork). Although some viewers argued that actors should be able to play any part, others found this highly offensive and even described it as a type of modern-day minstrel show. As with the other examples of concerns overrepresentation, these critiques regarding race and ethnicity became fuel for spirited discussions within the audience communities with which I interacted.

I assert that queer individuals have a specific relationship with the visual produced, because of their history of invisibility in a heavily visual culture. This is initially supported by the fact that when audiences discussed their reasons for liking or disliking the series, visibility and/or representation was mentioned more than any other reason. Regardless of whether they were pleased or disappointed with the series, viewers invested time and energy in engaging with others about it. Muñoz's disidentificatory reception is also particularly useful for understanding the comments made pertaining to visibility and representation. Although some viewers felt the series was important for raising awareness of queer issues, creating community, or permitting escape, the same individuals may have also been disappointed in the representations of certain identity categories or the handling of certain topics. Several of the above comments regarding representation mention one aspect of the show as "important," "progressive," or something they "love," yet the positive aspect is followed by a critique of another element. In fact, if there were ever a type of reaction that came close to being universal during my interactions with audience communities, it was this love/hate relationship dance. Nearly everyone I talked to at some point included variations of the phrases "I like *The L Word*, but..." or "I don't like *The L Word*, but..."

It is clear that the viewers of this study are simultaneously identifying with and disidentifying with *The L Word*. They create their identities, whether they are years old or newly formed, both in relation to and against *The L Word*'s representations. This negotiation is made even more visible by the many critiques of representation, which relate to intersections of sexual identity with other categories (race, class, and gender identity). If these individuals are to receive the validation to their sexual identity that comes from no longer being invisible and are to have the ability to observe visual images of themselves (something the rest of Western dominant culture has been able to do since the early 1900s), they must also navigate through the aspects they find objectionable.

Disidentification and the Seizure of Social Agency

Muñoz's work is useful to this study because he considers the sociopolitical value of disidentificatory reception. He argues that through disidentification "the minoritarian subject [is offered] a space to situate itself in history and thus seize social agency" (1). I posit that the seizure of social agency happens when viewers are able to maintain the sociopolitical frameworks of escape, community, and visibility that they so clearly value. There is a long history of queer individuals who, when empowered by a realization or recognition of their identity, began to engage differently with the world around them. For instance, early queer publications, social spaces, organizations, and other aspects of popular culture were often formed around the idea of making connections with people and fostering change for a marginalized group. The change may be as simple as experiencing a momentary release from discrimination or finding support and friendship in others, or it might be based in more traditional politics, such as lobbying for legislative changes or organizing events to raise awareness around particular issues.

The L Word has fostered similar types of activities within its audience communities. Whether they are discussing what they enjoy about a particular story line, offering support for a fellow viewer who is in the process of coming out to family and friends, or considering the complicated issues of racism within the wider queer community, people are engaging in a dialogue important to queer culture and queer lives. Muñoz sees immense value in "the formation of [such] counterpublics that contest the hegemonic supremacy of the majoritarian public sphere" (1).

Virtual communities present an additional way of thinking about the social and political agency brought about by disidentificatory reception. Fandom studies scholar Henry Jenkins refers to such groups as "knowledge communities," which, he argues, create a type of "collective intelligence" through their interactions (*Fans, Bloggers and Gamers* 27). "Knowledge communities," he explains, "form around mutual intellectual interests; their members work together to forge new knowledge, often in the realm where no traditional expertise exists; the pursuit of and assessment of knowledge [collective intelligence] is at once communal and adversarial" (20). I would extend Jenkins's idea beyond fandom to argue that *The L Word*'s viewers do not merely create a collective intelligence for the series itself; these audience communities also create a collective intelligence for queer culture more broadly. Discussions that began as praise or condemnation of the show often extended to address larger issues related to queer existence, such as coming out, homophobia, viable political action, and diversity concerns within the larger queer community, and reactions to *The L Word* have become linked to the understanding of wider minoritarian concerns. Considering queer culture's long history of invisibility, the value of such autobiographical documentation is unmistakable.

Notes

1. I intentionally use the terms *audience* and *viewers*, as opposed to *fans*, largely because I feel many of the individuals I encountered would not use the term

fan to describe themselves. This study illustrates the complicated relationship between these individuals and the series; therefore, I prefer more neutral terminology.

2. Regarding citations for ethnographic fieldwork: if individuals used screen names as a form of identification, that name has been used when citing their quotations in the research. However, if no citation is provided, the quote was taken from either the anonymous survey data collected or from personal interactions. I have presented quotations that are as close to their original format as possible, without corrections to grammar and/or punctuation. The only changes made were done for comprehension and readability.

3. To clarify, Muñoz theorizes disidentification in terms of both reception and production. In fact, many of the case studies he examines in his book exemplify the production aspect of disidentification. Although it is possible to argue that some of *The L Word*'s viewers also participate in this aspect, such as those who create fan fiction or *The L Word* parodies through *You Tube*, I have concentrated here on the aspect of reception. My study largely focused upon the consumption of and reaction to the show and stopped short of such forms of audience production as parodies or fiction.

CHAPTER 10

(Un)recognizable Lesbians: Young People Reading "Hot Lesbians" through a Reality Lens

Sue Jackson

In January 2011, an article bearing the headline "Gay and Lesbian Characters Are Popping Up on Shows for Young People" appeared in the *LA Times;* it was about the growing number of coming-out story lines in teen-targeted television shows (Jan 3, 2011). Compared to the early 1990s, today's young television audience is certainly somewhat more likely to encounter queer representations on their TV screens; some of the shows include lesbian characters. Since Ellen DeGeneres's highly publicized coming-out episode on *Ellen*, lesbian characters have appeared on our screens in shows such as *Friends, Sex and the City, Bad Girls, At Home with the Braithwaites,* and *Buffy the Vampire Slayer,* to name a few. As Rebecca Beirne notes in the introduction to the 2008 edition of this book, however, the portrayals of lesbians on television scarcely invite a progressive trajectory; rather the pattern is one of "advances and retreats" (Introduction 3). Thus, for example, although more ongoing inclusion of lesbian characters is in evidence (a stand-out example is the *The L Word*), fleeting appearances are markedly persistent (for example, on *Desperate Housewives* and *Grey's Anatomy).* As Diamond, Ciasullo, and Driver have observed, increased visibility hasn't necessarily brought increased diversity. The visibility of butch, black, poor, and teen lesbian women continues to be largely obscured. Where women of color have been included, there has been a trend toward "double othering," wherein lesbianism can be understood by an audience as a racialized phenomenon that reinforces a marginalized status and doesn't threaten white heterosexuality (see Hidalgo, chapter 5 of this volume). In recent years, the homogeneity of lesbian representation on television has been even more deeply carved out in the figure of the commercialized "hot lesbian." Depicted by Lizzie Thynne (202) as a commodifed figure used to sell anything "from Kronenbourg beer to Peugeot cars and sunglasses," the hot lesbian can be described as a "sexy," attractive heterosexualized product designed for consumption by the male gaze, in much the same way that heterosexual women may be cast as "eye-candy" for a male audience (see also Ciasullo, Garrity, and Tricia Jenkins).

In this chapter. the importance of lesbian representation on television is viewed from the perspective of a teenage audience—particularly, but not exclusively, that of teenage girls. The pressing need to gather audience readings of contemporary popular culture texts has been emphasized by a number of feminist media scholars, who point to the dominance of textual analyses in media/cultural studies research (for example, Kearney); this tendency is even more striking in the interrogation of queer media representation (Driver). Since media are significant cultural resources for young people in making sense of themselves and of their experiences, exploring their understandings of texts through audience research is important. In a culture where heterosexuality is normative and alternative expressions of sexuality are marginalized and regulated, media may, for some, provide the primary or only informational sources about queer possibilities for oneself. So too may media contribute to ways in which the queer sexuality of those in young people's social networks is understood and responded to.

The concept of media as a cultural resource informed the research project from which the material in this chapter is drawn. The broader project investigated high school students' perceptions of gay and lesbian representations on television; in this chapter we focus on a strand of that material, in which students discussed representations of lesbianism. Perhaps reflecting her media dominance (Tricia Jenkins), the presence of the "hot lesbian" was striking in participant responses. Our intention in this chapter is to contribute new perspectives on how the hot lesbian may function in relation to understandings of lesbian sexuality. At the same time, we hope that our work, by contributing material from a New Zealand study, deflects from the Americo-centrism of the literature observed by Beirne ("Introduction"), albeit in a small way. Given our focus on a young audience, we begin with a brief review of lesbian representation on television shows that are generally popular with teen viewers, before describing our research method and discussing our research material.

Lesbian Possibilities for Teen Viewers

The television viewed by young people in New Zealand is predominantly American-produced, but there is a scattering of British, Australian, and New Zealand productions. Relative to the portrayals of gay sexuality, the limited presence of lesbian characters is striking; this is particularly so in shows that have more specifically targeted a teen audience (for example, *Dawson's Creek, Home and Away, Neighbours, Beverly Hills 90210, My So-Called Life,* and *Glee*). This skewing of representation toward gay males has historical persistence and, as noted by Susan Driver (*Queer Girls and Popular Culture*), girl-girl sex has perpetually been shadowed in popular culture. Notable exceptions among shows for teen audiences include, in more recent times, *Buffy the Vampire Slayer, Degrassi: The Next Generation,* and *Once and Again.* The latter two did not screen in New Zealand. It's important to note that these shows featured lesbian relationships that offered more than a fleeting appearance; in the case of *Buffy*, the relationship included a sex scene.

Depictions of sex between lesbians are relatively rare on television; Beirne ("Introduction"), Torres, and Dow all have noted the desexualizing and minimizing of expressive sexuality and sexual desire in the lesbian characters, compared to heterosexual characters. In tandem with going beyond sex as titillation, *Buffy*'s producers also avoided recuperation of a developmental narrative in which same-sex desire is constructed as an adolescent crush, a phase that the teens will grow out of en route to mature heterosexuality (Driver).

Although representations of lesbianism in *Buffy* may be less than ideal, there does seem to be more substance in terms of relationship, compared with the proliferation of hot lesbian representations in other shows. Among shows attracting a younger audience, *The OC* provides a good example: Melissa and Alex are both "white, rich, beautiful, and slender," and Melissa ultimately decides she is heterosexual after all, resurrecting the heterosexual maturation narrative (Driver; see also Burgess, chapter 6 of this collection). As Driver notes, however, there is a dearth of shows that feature teenage lesbians; in this adultcentric television arena, the richest source of representations are to be found in shows branded as suitable for adult audiences; in New Zealand these are shows screened outside of prime time, during hours known as "the watershed," when adult content may be aired. Sitcoms such as *Sex and the City,* comedy/dramas in the manner of *Desperate Housewives,* and soap dramas such as *EastEnders, Coronation Street,* and the New Zealand soap drama *Shortland Street* have all at some point featured lesbian characters; these shows may potentially hold some attraction for a teen female audience (Buckingham and Bragg). The first lesbian character on

Coronation Street was teenager Sophie Webster, although she did not appear until 2009. Representations in the British soaps have arguably conformed to the "seamier side of relationships" (Buckingham and Bragg) that marks their genre. These contrast starkly with the heterosexualized lesbians of both the American and New Zealand shows. Ciasullo, drawing on the earlier (now dated) television examples of the "thin, perfectly coiffed" brides in the *Friends* lesbian wedding, and the lesbian couple on *Mad about You,* suggests that such heterosexualization of lesbians reifies the femme and obliterates the political, feminist butch. Alternatively it could be argued, as does Eves, that the media representation of a femme lesbian brings overdue recognition to femme lesbians on the viewing side of the screen, for whom visibility may only be achieved through a butch partner.

The American shows cited above also exemplify the treatment of same-sex desire as temporary or experimental. In *Sex and the City,* for example, Samantha's heterosexual identity was reaffirmed once her passionate affair with Maria ended. Similarly, in *Desperate Housewives,* Katharine's liaison with lesbian character Robin is but a briefly-lit candle, although the episode deals well with the emotional aspects of a first same-sex desire. The depictions of lesbianism as transient in both these shows suggests "heteroflexibility," a term popularized by Diamond, and accords with a fashionable, chic, styled lesbianism (Jackson and Scott) wherein woman-woman sex is seen as "exciting," "safe," "fun," and, it is important to note, completely unthreatening to one's being heterosexual (Wilkinson).

Although *Shortland Street*, the only New Zealand–made program of relevance here, has heavily appropriated the hot lesbian since 2004 (Maia, Jay and, more recently, Nicole), the lesbian characters were firmly anchored in the show until Maia's departure in 2011. Thus, unlike some shows, in which the characters are defined only in terms of their sexual otherness, *Shortland Street*'s characters are portrayed dealing with everyday issues, from homophobia to child care. On the other hand, recuperation of heterosexuality has also featured in story lines through, for example, both Jay's and Maia's affairs with male characters. Nicole, first introduced as Maia's new partner in 2009, declared herself later in the show to be bisexual and, with Maia's departure from the show, she has since been in a heterosexual relationship.

The question of interest to this chapter is what meanings young audiences may make of the kinds of lesbian representations, "hot" or otherwise, that are made available to them on the small screen. That the heterosexual audience is generally more aware of "lesbian" sex displays as acts of performance than they are of heterosexual portrayals is perhaps, at least in part, influenced by the knowledge that the actors portraying them are (often) "really" heterosexuals. For example, a sceptical audience attributed the MTV Britney Spear–Madonna kiss, and subsequent comments about it, as a media ploy to attract a male audience (Diamond). Diamond suggests that this interpretation precludes a subversive reading of the kisses as a challenge to the heterosexual/homosexual dichotomy. Moreover, when girl-girl sexualized acts are framed as staged performance, they lend themselves to being read through a lens of the pornographic male fantasy of observing women having sex with women (Jenefsky and Miller). The matter of how straight and lesbian women or girls make sense of viewing girl-girl sex has been given relatively little attention in feminist scholarship. Straight and lesbian women make different readings of such portrayals as to, for example, whether the girl-girl sex is understood as "lesbian." As Wilton points out, such sense-making is "a contested process determined as much by lesbian/non-lesbian reading as by lesbian/non-lesbian text" (5). Similarly, Moritz observes that the complexity of television texts leaves them particularly open to a variety of often-contradictory readings. Lesbian viewers may variously enjoy, subvert, resist, or appropriate mainstream representation of "lesbians" (Clark; Simms).

Acknowledging the central importance of complexity in readings that may be made of television texts, we now turn to our focus in the remainder of the chapter: How young people "read" contemporary representations of media lesbians, and to what extent such representations inflect their own constructions of lesbian sexualities? However a purportedly lesbian text may be read, for us the importance lies in its possibilities, especially for queer girls, for making meanings, finding connections, and accessing a language with which to talk about experiences and feelings.

At the same time, we recognize the possibilities in media to harness and reproduce damaging and limiting stereotypes and to create new "impossibilities." Gross, for example, notes that if young people consume only heterosexual versions of sexuality and have no access to alternative sources of information (for example, in their social environment), they may "have little choice but to accept the media stereotypes they imagine must be typical of all lesbians and gay men" (16). Robert Cover similarly argues that a relatively inexperienced young audience is more likely to naively accept heteronormative representations if they are not provided with alternatives to stereotypical information. However, the viewpoints of both of these authors appear to position youth as an uncritical audience that simply absorbs everything that is watched, read, and listened to. Conversely, a growing body of research illustrates that young people are critical consumers, as seen in Buckingham and Bragg's 2004 investigation of young people's responses to sexual content in the television programs they watch. Distinctions between notions of audiences as passive and active are not as clear-cut as they may seem (Blackman), but in this chapter we view young people as actively making sense of the lesbian representations they encounter in the media.

Details of the Study

As indicated previously, the material we discuss in this chapter has been drawn from a broader study about television representations of homosexuality. A full description of the study is available in an earlier publication (Jackson and Gilbertson), and only a brief account will be given here. Our research took place in an inner city New Zealand high school that serves a broad ethnic and socioeconomic population. The study involved single-sex focus groups with 16– to 18-year-old high school students, predominantly Pakeha[1] (non-Maori New Zealanders). There were 12 male students and 13 female students in the groups. The school was selected for both its diverse student population and for its active support of lesbian, bisexual, and gay (LBG) students. However, we did not actively recruit LBG students, since these identity categories might have deterred students who engaged in same-sex relationships but did not use a sexual identity label. We considered it important to include heterosexual perspectives, since representations may be a primary source of heterosexual students' information about LBG relationships.

We recruited students through information sessions at a senior high school assembly and met with those choosing to take part, in groups of 6 or 7 students. Tamsyn Gilbertson conducted the interviews. These sessions were audiorecorded and were transcribed for subsequent analyses.

To stimulate discussion in the groups, we incorporated a selection of clips from TV shows featuring characters identified as gay or lesbian; these were used at various stages of the focus-group session. The clip of relevance to our exploration of talking about representations of lesbianism was from New Zealand's only local soap drama, the long-running *Shortland Street,* which at the time featured two long-standing lesbian characters. Screened in prime time, the show targets the 15- to 25-year-old demographic and regularly features teenage story lines and characters, although not teen lesbians.

The scene presented to focus groups portrayed two adult lesbian characters, Jay Copeland (Jaime Passier-Armstrong) and Maia Jeffries (Anna Julienne), who had been in the show for several years. Although they were not the first lesbian characters to be featured on *Shortland Street*, Jay and Maia were the first long-term lesbian couple in the show, and they were also a first for a New Zealand television drama, because they featured the legalization of their relationship though a Civil Union[2] ceremony. The scene

selected for discussion occurred during a separation between the two characters. Jay had recently returned to New Zealand after living in Australia
for a short period of time. Maia was living with another woman. The scene
shown to participants began with Jay and Maia getting into bed together,
ostensibly to "talk all night" as recently reunited friends. However, it soon
became apparent that Maia had something else in mind, and, after initial
reluctance on the part of Jay, the two women kiss passionately. The scene
ends with this kiss.

Discussions generated rich material, offering both uniform and distinct
perspectives about representations of homosexuality on television. Our analyses of transcribed material were informed by poststructuralist approaches
to discourse analysis (for example, Gavey; Willig) that view "talk" as both
productive of and produced by the cultural fabric of people's everyday lives.
Thus, in the context of our study, we understand young people's talk to
be illustrative of the myriad discourses in circulation about lesbian, gay,
and bisexual sexualities, as well as a site for rupture to those discourses.
At the same time, we do not hold young people's accounts to be the way
they "really" perceive lesbian sexuality, but consider them as a particularized
story produced within a discussion with other students and an interviewer
who was some two to four years older than they were.

The particular story that we focus on in this chapter is the way participants made sense of "authenticity" of representations through comparative
readings of the "hot lesbian" against "not hot dykes" and the known lesbians in everyday life. In the extracts presented in the following pages, participants' names have been changed to protect their identities, and it should
also be noted that the text is written as spoken, so it, for example, includes
repeated words.

"Pretending to Be Gay"

Although the topic of authenticity peppered participant discussions of both
gay and lesbian representations on television, the matter of realism assumed
a markedly greater presence in discussions about lesbianism. Audience
research with young people suggests that although they clearly differenti-
ate the "fantasy" elements of a television show, the line between fiction and
"realism" is nonetheless blurred, since its possibilities can be visualized in an
imagined future (for example, see Granello's study on *Beverly Hills 90210*).
Accuracy seems to be a central criterion in evaluations of "realism," assessed
in terms of how well a portrayal approximates what young people are familiar with in their daily lives (Buckingham and Bragg). In Buckingham and
Bragg's study of how young people viewed sexual content on television, for

example, the viewers said that *Friends* lacked reality because "real people in their twenties don't act like that" (170) and *Coronation Street* was likewise deemed unrealistic because of its depiction of numerous concurrent affairs.

Somewhat similarly to these previous studies, we found a critical stance toward portrayals that participants considered to be a poor imitation of what lesbians might do in "real life." In some moments, this critique related to the absence of explicit sex; in others, it was the depiction of lesbianism as "experimental" and constructed within norms of heterosexualized attractiveness. In making such critiques, participants demonstrated an acute awareness of television shows as a product for audience consumption. For example, sanitized portrayals were seen to offer a palatable version of lesbianism that would not alienate a heterosexual audience. The matter of a show's ratings intersected with such considerations; students constructed the "hot lesbian" in particular as designed to attract an audience while simultaneously meeting requirements of palatability.

Another aspect of authenticity that was discussed by participants related more to the production of a show in terms of the scripted activity and the actors' abilities to perform a lesbian role in a convincing way. Rosa, for example, talked about how straight actors playing lesbians couldn't relate to it, resulting in their looking uncomfortable with kissing or touching. She also explained how the actors' discomfort "just makes you feel very uncomfortable." In some cases, it was the transparency of performance that drew critique, as with the girls' comments about the actors portraying Maia and Jay in the clip from *Shortland Street*:

Tamsyn: So you said they're not gen...[3] they don't really fit the lesbian type. What, what is the lesbian type, do you reckon?
Genna: No, they just seem like...they'd like guys, in real life, which they pretty obviously do.
Kat: They look like street girls pretending to be gay.
?[4]: Mmmm.
Kat: They're just like experimenting. They don't look like it's a lifestyle choice. They look like, they're, like, hey look we're in the bed together. Oh, I threw away the pillow, let's make out.
[*Laughter.*]
Tamsyn: So are you thinking, not really, doesn't look like a serious full time...How do you think they would have done it to make it look like a serious full time...?
Kat: Umm, I'm not really...Well, act like a normal couple. Just, they weren't acting like a couple. They were acting like a bunch of teenage girls and...

Sasha: That kind of set the scene as like a slumber party.
Kat: Yeah, like, "How are we supposed to stay up and talk all night.
  Woo, pillow fight." But yeah…

Earlier in the discussion, the girls had described the *Shortland Street* lesbians as not fitting the "lesbian type." The clarification sought by Tamsyn comes not by way of addressing what a lesbian type *is*, but what she is not, and in so doing, the girls construct notions of the authentic through the inauthentic lesbian. In part, the lack of authenticity perceived by the girls draws in the on-screen, off-screen distinction of straight women playing lesbian roles and, perhaps implicitly associated with this, a failure to convincingly portray "real" lesbian women. Part of Kat's critique also orients to a construction of lesbianism as "temporary," a passing phase or an experiment. Feminist critiques similarly note the way that heterosexualization maintains the possibility of recuperation into normative heterosexuality (for example, Ciasullo; Diamond). So too are notions of experimental lesbianism particularly found in constructions of teenage girls' lesbian desire (Sue Jackson; Tricia Jenkins) and in a developmental trajectory of moving toward maturity and proper heterosexuality (Burgess; Driver). Kat makes explicit teenage referencing in her account of the pillow fight, which she takes as further evidence of an inauthentic, trivializing portrayal. By way of contrast, an implicit signaling of an authentic lesbian can be found in Kat's comparative constructions of "a normal couple" who have made "a lifestyle choice," pointing to a construction of lesbianism as a serious, more stable, and consciously decided way of life: as a choice.

"A Girlfriend Who Is Real"

We found a fluid movement between media and lived experience in students' talk, as in those occasions where they compared a media representation with lesbians they knew in everyday life. At a later point in their discussion, Kat and Gemma's group talk at length about people at school who are homophobic, and Kat relates a story about her sister, who identifies as a lesbian. A discussion about "lesbian stereotypes" follows and is ultimately drawn back into media portrayals:

Sasha: Yeah, but um, but yeah you you definitely, I think camp gay guys
  have got, are are really cool at the moment, but um but lesbians are
  still underdeveloped in terms of everything.
Kat: Oh well guys think it's hot but they don't necessarily wanna like
  see it.

Kristen: But not but not dykey lesbians, they're not hot.

Kat: Yeah yeah.

Kristen: It's only...

Kat: And then they're not accepting because it's not hot. Like, guys don't accept things that aren't hot, they don't...

[*omitted text*]

Gemma: My friends would, but yeah, they're friends. [*Laughs.*] They ah, like um like with like, I do think, like an actual person they might like. I don't know just just for chicks I've just realized like there's there's so many stereotypical lesbians. There's you know there's the lesbians who aren't probably real lesbians or whatever and then there's the you know man hating lesbian, you know and feminist and stuff, there's no real faces that you can identify [as] lesbians that you might know with, like there's just not that many...

Kat: And in the media too there's like there's...

Gemma: People, like there's not examples of being best friends and, with her and a girlfriend who is real, you know.

In the "real-life" world being referenced early in the discussion, the "cool" status of being gay, compared with the "underdeveloped" status of being lesbian, contrasts with the rapid rise of a "cool" lesbian visibility in the media, notably in the shape, quite literally, of the hot lesbian. A feminist scholarship's articulation of the heterosexually stamped hot lesbian as designed for a male gaze (for example, Ciasullo, Tricia Jenkins) finds compatibility with the girls' discussion here in a construction of boys as accepting "hot" lesbians but not accepting "dykey" lesbians, who are "not hot." Gemma differentiates her male friends from the generalized "other" in having the potential to "like" a lesbian who didn't meet the "hot" criteria; this seems to trigger a pondering about the absence of lesbianism's "real faces," obliterated in the stereotypical representations of lesbians as "probably" not real or as "manhating" feminists. Although she doesn't elaborate about the "probably" not real lesbian, one possibility is that she refers to the chic, commodified, and heteroflexible "hot lesbian." For Gemma, these flawed stereotypes belie a "real" lesbian relationship, which would involve friendship; thus the TV portrayals lack resonance with "real" lesbians whom the viewers may know in the lived world.

"I Haven't Really Seen Any Butch Lesbians on TV"

The "dykey" lesbian referenced in Gemma's group had a counterpart in talk about the "butch" lesbian as the other to the "hot lesbian." Across the discussion groups, "butch" stood as a stereotypical category, no more "real" than the "hot lesbian," but, unlike the hot lesbian, she drew little, if any, affective response. The structure of the butch stereotype is elaborated in the boys' talk below. The group had been talking at some length about the "acceptance" of lesbians relative to gays—in particular, about the idea that the acceptance was related to (a) invisibility, for example, "lesbians don't have as distinct sort of characteristics;" "nothing gave off a lesbian vibe" and (b) the "hot lesbian's" appeal to "horny boys." We take up the continuing discussion from this point:

> *Tamsyn*: So you said horny boys? Like could you elaborate?
> *Bart*: No, it's just like, I dunno. You could almost see it as like being a . . . I mean it it depends what where and you know what where you're coming from what attitude you have but one of the views is that if if you are quite . . . I dunno if you see it as quite a sort of male-orientated world, you know, the whole guys getting off to lesbians thing. I mean that, that could have something to do with it. I mean, yeah.
> *Matt*: Like at the same time you said there aren't any women gay stereo-types. I mean they weren't really stereotypical lesbians but quite often there's the girl who's really into her soccer and . . . (*Bryn*: Yeah) and dressed as like a guy and . . .
> *Josh*: Short hair . . .
> *Matt*: . . . doesn't shave and stuff and . . . But at the same time there's also . . . (*Bart*: Yeah) . . . the real girly girl. I dunno.
> *?*: I mean it's . . .
> *Matt*: But most of the gay girls I know are nothing like that so . . .
> *Tamsyn*: Nothing like?
> *Matt*: Nothing, nothing like nothing like um nothing like the stereo-typical lesbian.

Bart sets out the construction of a voyeuristic male "getting off" on looking at "hot lesbians" in careful terms, not owning the view personally but work-ing within a frame of generalized possibility (indicated in the punctuation of his talk with "I dunno," "if," and "you"). While the "butch" stereotype is not named, the joint construction of a lesbian within terms characterized as "masculine" connotes such a reading—she plays a "masculine" sport, adopts a masculine dress code, shuns body hair removal, and sports short-styled hair. A polarizing binary is established through Matt's reference to the butch counter of the "real girly-girl," a description that evokes the figure of the "hot lesbian." However, when held up to a mirror of the lived world, neither the butch or "girly-girl" stereotype is deemed to reflect what Matt knows of lesbians, leaving open the possibility that stereotypes may be fantastical rather than "real."

The absence of a "butch" lesbian stereotype, in contrast to a saturating presence of a hot lesbian on the small screen, garnered particular attention in discussion groups.

> *Rosa*: I haven't really seen any butch lesbians yet on TV.
> *Anya*: No. That will be the next step.
> *Rosa*: Yeah. We'll get there.
> ....
> *Tamsyn*: So would you think that that would be a positive step or...?
> *Rosa*: Yeah, I think so. I mean, it's showing just another aspect of it.
> *Siobhan*: It's just real. It's not.
> *Rosa*: I mean it's showing another...
> *Siobhan*: It's not just for sleazy men. I mean it's for...
> *Rosa*: Yeah.

The inclusion of "butch lesbians" in television shows is constructed by the girls in this group within a progressive narrative as a "next," "positive step" in lesbian representation that shows another face of lesbianism. The "realness" of butch lesbianism is underscored both by the insertion of "Reality TV" as a source for staging butch lesbianism and, more specifically, by Siobhan's comments that butch lesbianism is "real" and, unlike the "hot lesbian" identified earlier in their talk, is not designed to appeal to "sleazy men." Disparagement of "hot lesbian" and "not real" representations typified much of our participants' talk about television portrayals of lesbians, as shown in another excerpt from the same group's discussion:

> *Rosa*: I think also with the gay guys they make them more stereotyped and when they put lesbian couples they make them more normal, like they do have very out there stereotypical gay guys.
> *Riley*: So it's easier to [*indistinct*]
> *Anya*: Yeah, they do.
> *Siobhan*: It's not like, "ah ha."
> *Rosa*: Its not like the stereotypical like butch lesbian couple on TV. It's always young, pretty...
> ?: Yeah it is, yeah.
> *Anya*: Yeah, they've used, like I watched the *OC* the other day and...
> [*Indistinct conversation, multiple voices*]
> *Riley*: It was just, it's always weird. It's not like unrealistic; it's just not real.

Rosa: It's always two pretty girls…
?: Yeah, exactly.
Rosa: …it's never like
Siobhan: So it's catering more for men than for women.
Rosa: Yeah.
?: Yeah.
Rosa: I mean like, you, you think, well they look normal and then you know they act normal, however you perceive normal to be and, but then, I don't know, it just doesn't work as you would see a lesbian couple in real life.

The girls' discussion explores the notion of normality in relation to depictions of lesbians on television. As the talk progresses, the meanings of "normal" can be seen to orient around the notion of appearance. Whereas the stereotypical gay guy is, in Rosa's view, more likely to stand out, (perhaps through a camp appearance, although this is not stated), the lesbian portrayals conform to standard representations of women on television— "always young, pretty." As observed by Ciasullo, one of the ways this normalizing, heterosexualized appearance functions is to, paradoxically, heighten invisibility; "hot lesbian bodies" convey "above all, sameness to mainstream images of heterosexual bodies" (595). This sameness is caught in Siobhan's comment about the absence of an "ah ha" realization moment. So too does the homogenizing of lesbian representation as white and middle class obscure the plurality of lesbianism—not only the absence of a "butch stereotype," as Rosa notes, but also the diverse positions in between and outside of butch-femme categorization. Young women in Driver's study *Queer Girls and Popular Culture,* for example, found identification in ambiguity such as androgyny or boy/girl fusion ("birls").

The American television show *The OC* was a frequently cited example of "hot lesbian" representations across discussion groups, and here the girls also use it to characterize the kind of representation they have been discussing—a lesbian constructed to cater to men. Riley makes the intriguing comment that the portrayal "is not unrealistic" but "just unreal," and while it is difficult to untangle what seems to be a contradiction in terms, one possibility is that the show displays realism but the portrayal of lesbianism does not. She later clarifies her position by making a comparison with "real life," in which a lesbian couple neither behaves nor looks like the hot lesbians depicted on television. Taken together, the girls' views expressed here offer an aware and incisive critique of the hot lesbian that recognizes her narrow construction in normalizing and heterosexualizing discourses, as well as her derailing of other forms of lesbian expression. As in other examples of students' discussions presented here, their critique is particularly informed by what they consider to be "real," from their knowledge and experience of lesbianism in their everyday lives.

Concluding Commentary

At the beginning of the chapter, we stated our intention to explore how participants' understandings of lesbian sexuality connected with their readings of the "hot lesbian." In the main, our exploration points to a place of rejection and alienation, with the hot lesbian archetype being seen as an unhelpful figure in imagining possibilities for being or for becoming lesbian. From the perspectives of our participants, the hot lesbian is not representative of lesbians in a lived world (see Marnie Pratt's discussion of representation, "This Is the Way We Live...and Love!"), but rather is a normalized, heterosexualized figure produced to titillate and lure male viewers. Our participants' talk recognized the hot lesbian as a narrow, exclusionary, exclusive figure whose visibility on television speaks to white, pretty, slim, middle-class girls, rendering alternative expressions of lesbianism—in particular, butch women—invisible. Participants identified how, in looking like all of the other pretty straight women on television, the "lesbian" becomes unrecognizable, and even explicitly sexual acts may be understood as experimental displays between women who are "really" heterosexual.

Although I do not argue that televisual lesbians ought to somehow obviously convey lesbianism through appearance, the issue of erasure accomplished through the hot lesbian is, as others have noted (most particularly Ciasullo; Diamond; and Jenkins), a significant one in terms of underrepresentation. Lesbian erasure accomplished through the hot lesbian is heavily reinforced by the accompanying absence of other forms of lesbian sexuality, leaving a landscape that Ciasullo describes as "at once incredibly full and altogether empty" (605).

The resonances of our participants' critiques of the hot lesbian with those of feminist scholars such as Ciasullo, Tricia Jenkins, and Diamond are strong. What we learn from our viewers' perspectives is the strong part that the knowledge of lesbians in their everyday "real" world plays in informing those critiques, which is important. We would be cautious about interpreting such comparative readings as "what young people do," given that we were talking with students in a school where homosexual visibility is made safe. In other words, these students have, at the very least, a school-specific cultural resource in the "real world" to draw on in making sense of lesbian sexuality. On the other hand, this referencing of the cultural resources of social and peer networks in readings of the "unreal" in popular culture has been more broadly found in critiques of American shows by Israeli girls

(Reznik and Lemish) and by British young people (Buckingham and Bragg). In a different medium than television, Dawn Currie has articulated a practice of comparison reading used by girls in her study of girls' magazines; comparison reading refers to the way in which experiential and discursive (sociocultural) knowledge intersect in a process of assessing "the truth status of the text" (277).

However, for girls exploring their sexuality who do not have experiential referents in their everyday lives, the exclusions produced by the hot lesbian may present a challenge, for how can "sexy fat femmes, poor dykes, queers of color, androgynous girl-boys and butch and trans-youth" (Driver 9) recognize themselves in her apparition? The normalizing and essentializing brush of the hot lesbian may present nonheterosexual sexuality more as impossibility than possibility for girls' own negotiation of sexuality. However, dismissing the hot lesbian as "unreal," as do our participants, may function to erase femme lesbian identity and may position butch as the "genuine" version of being lesbian. Such a possibility permeated the notion of butch lesbians as subjects in reality TV, although the mention of "butch" also largely references a stereotype, rather than a reality. Although we cannot conceive of our participants as a typical young audience, their critical perspectives on the circumscribed representation of lesbian sexuality through the "hot lesbian" highlights the need for much greater complexity in constructions of queer characters. Acknowledging television's "problem" of how to make lesbianism both different and not-different (Torres) and moving beyond the dominance of the unidimensional hot lesbian requires pushing past universalizing sameness into sexual plurality.

Acknowledgments

We wish to thank the students who so were so willing to discuss and share their views with us and also the school for allowing us to work with the students and providing us with the facilities to do so. Additional thanks go to Tamsyn Gilbertson for her help in compiling the data.

Notes

1. Maori are the indigenous people of New Zealand. *Pakeha* is the Maori term for nonindigenous New Zealanders.
2. According similar rights as marriage, the Civil Union Act came into New Zealand law in 2005 for same-sex and other-sex couples.
3. Series of dots denote a brief pause that sometimes involves another speaker interjecting.
4. ? denotes that we were unable to identify the speaker on the recording.

CHAPTER 11

Queering Teen Television: *Sugar Rush,* Seriality, and Desire

Whitney Monaghan

Susan Driver's *Queer Girls and Popular Culture: Reading, Resisting, and Creating Media* was the first major study of queer girls appearing in and engaging with popular film, television, and music. It tells a very predictable story about the representation of queer adolescents in television. Writing in 2007, about series from the early 2000s, Driver noted that while "narratives of gay adolescent boys coming out" have become more visible within the teen genre, "lesbian, bisexual, transgender and questioning girls remain very hard to find on the television dial" (58). When queer teens are represented, Driver writes, they are often restricted to the "special" coming-out narrative. This is a format that emphasizes a "brief moment of visible difference" but disavows the possibility of the television narrative to "expand and contextualise [the] experiences" of being young and queer "beyond dramatic scenes of revelation" (58).

Writing in the 1990s, in an essay on *Melrose Place,* Dennis W. Allen identified the singular narrative function of queer characters within television narratives: that of the revelation of their sexual identity. And in 2001, Anna McCarthy (*"Ellen:* Making Queer Television History") asserted a fundamental incongruity between queerness and television, writing that "the problem that queerness poses for television's representation politics" is "the difficulty of making same-sex desire uneventful, serial, everyday"

(609). Although much has changed in the years since these accounts, with series such as *Queer as Folk, The L Word, The Real L Word,* and *Lip Service* all including "ongoing narrativisation" (Davis and Needham 7) of queer/ lesbian life, the revelatory-based representation remains pervasive, particularly within the genre of teen television. As Glyn Davis and Gary Needham discuss in *Queer TV: Theories, Histories, Politics,* "the revelation of a character's homosexuality [often] quickly leads to narrative redundancy after said disclosure. Most of the gay and lesbian characters…have little to do after they come out, and more often than not they eventually get written out" (7). Davis and Needham further note that when queer characters do continue to appear in television narratives after coming out, "the fate of such characters is often to have the queer aspects of their lives (sex, love, queer friends and spaces, homophobia) elided" (7).

Further, when queer girls appear in popular film and television, queerness is often characterized as a transient phase, entered into during a liminal period of adolescence. In this phase, queer desire, sex and/or romance is framed as acceptable practice for heterosexual desire, sex and/or romance (see *Lost and Delirious,* dir. Lea Pool, 2001; *Cruel Intentions,* dir. Roger Kumble, 1999); as a form of teenage rebellion (see Alison Burgess's discussion of *The O.C* in this volume); or alternatively, as a lesson or "issue" to be dealt with (see Rebecca Beirne's discussion of *Neighbours* in "Screening the Dykes of Oz"). Engaging with these ideas, Driver writes that, "A brief shy kiss, a tomboy transgression, an 'innocent' crush, and playful flirtations are often valued only as temporary departures from a normative course toward feminine heterosexual adulthood" (7). That is, within many television series, queer desire is represented only on the condition that it dissipates upon maturation into "feminine heterosexual adulthood" (Driver 7) or at the very least, into a more "mature" stage of (heterosexual) adolescence.

One program that does move beyond such limited characterization is the UK series *Sugar Rush* (2005–2006). A teen comedy about a "15-year-old virgin" named Kim (Olivia Hallinan) who is "sexually obsessed" with her straight best friend, Sugar (Lenora Crichlow), *Sugar Rush* follows Kim's attempts to deal with her newfound desires as she adjusts to living in a new city with her eccentric family. This chapter argues that *Sugar Rush* serializes a traditionally closed narrative, drawing out and extending the coming-out narrative and ultimately moving beyond it, thus opening the possibility for more nuanced representations of the queer teenager, in which the "queer aspects" of life—"sex, love queer friends and spaces, homophobia" (Davis and Needham 7)—are featured prominently. However, in order to emphasize the significance of *Sugar Rush*, it is necessary to contextualize the series, both historically and generically.

Broadly speaking, teen television is a genre associated with adolescent concerns and/or the teenage audience, with genre-specific story lines that "touch on coming of age issues, but also on questions of the self, identity, gender, race and community" (Ross and Stein 1). Ross and Stein note that a wide range of texts can be considered teen television, "from programs nominally about teens but directed at older audiences to programs not defined as teen but featuring teen characters, themes and concerns. Teen TV can include half-hour-long sitcoms and hour-long melodramas, network television, subscription TV, MTV and reality TV" (5–6).

Along with having a focus on the concerns of adolescents, a teenage audience, and a unique format that combines the traditional episodic series with the "punctuated seriality of soap operas" (Ross and Stein 8), this genre is, as David Oswell suggests, "ironic, critical and sassy" (44). I would add that the teen genre is also characterized by a foregrounding of the high school setting, which often serves as a microcosm of society. The teen genre functions on a specific ideological level, as Caralyn Bolte has argued, often operating as a "means to interrogate contemporary cultural ideologies" (94) and fill the gaps left by adult-oriented programming. Indeed, Glyn Davis writes that the teen series holds "great promise" for screening "lives, desires and issues that are often ignored, stymied or cursorily treated by television (and other media)," including those of the queer teen (131).

In her introduction to the first edition of *Televising Queer Women*, Rebecca Beirne noted that gay and lesbian characters finally appeared to be moving into this teen genre. The Canadian teen series *Degrassi Junior High* (1987–1991) was one of the first series to do this, dealing with issues of teen homosexuality in an episode titled "Rumor Has It" (episode 1.6), in which a teenage female character developed a crush on a female teacher after hearing a rumor that the teacher was a lesbian. However, it took more than a decade for lesbian sexuality to really begin to permeate teen-oriented programming and for the queer girl to become a recognizable figure within these teen spaces. (See Beirne, "Television's Queer Girls," for further discussion.) From 2000–2002, the supernaturally themed series *Buffy the Vampire Slayer* (1997–2003) featured an ongoing relationship between young witches Willow (Alyson Hannigan) and Tara (Amber Benson) that has been discussed as one of the more positive teenage lesbian story lines (see Driver, Battis). However, despite these praises, the representation of the Willow/Tara relationship has garnered much criticism (see Bartlem; Beirne, "Queering the Slayer-Text;" Davis "Saying It Out Loud;" Mendlesohn) particularly for its conflation of lesbian sexuality and magic (Bartlem, Davis). Both Mendlesohn and Beirne focus their critiques on the desexualization of Willow; Beirne notes that the Willow/Tara relationship positions Willow as "a 'safe' normalised gay character," while removing "her potential to be confident, dangerous, powerful and seductively queer" ("Queering the Slayer-Text" par. 19). Further, although *Buffy the Vampire Slayer* sits quite firmly within the teen genre—as evidenced by its initial focus on the high school setting, its attention to "adolescent concerns" and its marketing to teen audiences—Willow's relationships with women began in college, rather than high school. As such, Willow is figured both as teen and nonteen— that is, adult—over the course of the series, troubling definitions of her queer identity or her relationships with women as "teenage." Nevertheless, *Buffy the Vampire Slayer* is significant as it did serialize the queer television narrative beyond the "special" episode format through its depiction of Willow. Upon Tara's death in 2002, a further relationship between Willow and "potential slayer" Kennedy (Iyari Limon) was developed, which was significant, because it worked against the logic of the dominant queer teen narrative, a logic in which the queer story line is situated as "phase" or mere "exploration" (Sweeney, 34). "Never before," writes Driver, "has a queer girl been given so much space to grow, hesitate, struggle, and assert her powers across a broad range of teen and young adult experiences" (62).

The early 2000s, however, marked a slight return to the pervasive representation of the queer girl as an ephemeral figure in many television series. For example, although teenage characters Jessie (Evan Rachel Wood) and Katie (Mischa Barton) had an extended relationship on US drama series *Once and Again* (1999–2002), in 2002, the conservative Australian soap *Neighbours* (1985–present) featured a brief story line in which lesbian character Lana (Bridget Neval) kissed her heterosexual best friend Sky (Stephanie McIntosh) in 2004. The two characters remained friends, but the story line ended rather predictably with Sky confirming her feelings for her boyfriend and Lana leaving the series shortly after. (For further discussion of this see Beirne, "Screening the Dykes of Oz"). Later in 2004, a relationship began between Marissa (Mischa Barton) and Alex (Olivia Wilde) in US series *The O.C* (2003–2007); a story line that Alison Burgess notes "began as something new and exciting, representing a nuanced and fluid understanding of women's sexuality," but that eventually "reified the dominance of homophobic and heteronormative discourses in popular culture" (211–212). The year 2004 saw a similarly problematic queer story line in the US series *One Tree Hill* (2003–present), which has been discussed by Michaela Meyer in terms of its depiction of "transitional bisexuality" that is, bisexuality as a transitional identity between heterosexuality and homosexuality (374). Within this story line, the queer girl character Anna (Daniella Alonso) deliberated over her sexual identity, outing herself as bisexual (episode 2.15), but two episodes later declared that she was, in fact, gay (episode 2.17). Not surprisingly, Anna then disappeared from the series, in line with the dominant depiction of the queer girl character "as existing only to engage with as 'an issue,' and having little narrative value beyond that" (Beirne, "Dykes of Oz" 7).

A significant shift occurred in 2005 with the emergence of a number of teen series featuring prominent lesbian story lines, taking us beyond these kinds of problematic characterizations. The first of these was *Sugar Rush*, which premiered in June of 2005 on Channel 4 in the UK. In November of 2005, just a few months after *Sugar Rush* hit television screens through the UK, *South of Nowhere* (2005–2008), an ensemble drama that dealt with issues of racism, violence, bullying, drug abuse and most notably, teen homosexuality, premiered on the now-defunct tween-oriented network The N, which endeavored to provide "an authentic voice for teens to help them figure out their lives" (The N Mission Statement, cited in Ross 61). Finally, also in November of 2005, *Degrassi: The Next Generation* (2001–present) featured a prominent queer girl story line, as queen-bee Paige (Lauren Collins) engaged in an on again/off again relationship with bad-girl Alex (Deanna Casaluce) until October of 2007.

Thus, by the end of 2005, three very different representations of queer girlhood were simultaneously circulating on mainstream television. *Sugar Rush, South of Nowhere,* and *Degrassi: The Next Generation* were incredibly significant series because they pushed the boundaries of traditional teen programming, placed queer female teenagers at the center of their media landscapes, and opened up new possibilities for queer teen representation. From this point onwards, television viewers began to see less of the transient queer teen character type—those appearing out of nowhere, creating a complication in the narrative, and then disappearing—and more of the queer teen character who was either the protagonist of a series or a major character in an ensemble. However, while *South of Nowhere* and *Degrassi: The Next Generation* focused on an ensemble of teenage characters and were thus able to explore a wide variety of teen "issues," including those of teen homosexuality, *Sugar Rush* was perhaps the most significant of these, because Kim was the central character. Foregrounding Kim's desires and experiences in this manner, *Sugar Rush* not only achieved complex characterization of a queer girl, but also a depiction of a queer teen lifestyle that had never before appeared on television.

As earlier noted, Glyn Davis ("Saying It Out Loud") suggests that the teen series "offers great potential for the representation of teen lives and desires, including those [of] queer teens" (131). Within the serial format, according to Davis,

One of the key elements here is longevity: the sheer length of a long running series allows for the development of characterisation, and substantive narrative depth and complexity; further, particular issues and storylines can breathe and develop in some detail and at a slow (and thus potentially more realistic) pace. (131)

While *Sugar Rush* was by no means a long-running series, because it only aired for two seasons, I argue that it can be understood in Davis's terms, when compared with prior representations of the queer girl—that is, as a series allowing for greater depth of both characterization and narrative, a more prominent exploration of the "queer aspects" of life, and an elongation of a traditionally limited queer story line, which lets the entire series act as an interrogation of queer desire.

The first episode of *Sugar Rush* opens with an image of two girls—Kim and Sugar—alone at the carnival. The lyrics of the song "No Sleep Tonight" by girl band The Faders—"Can't stop this feeling, you can't run away/Baby I'm what's on your mind/you can't stop this feeling, there's no escape/No sleep tonight, you won't get no sleep tonight"—reverberate around the carnival as Kim and Sugar spin around and around on a carnival ride. As the two girls lean in to kiss, the camera cuts to a shot of Kim in bed alone, her eyes firmly closed. The sound of the reverberating music is replaced by the sound of vibration and the first of her internal voice-overs begins, "Ok. This is the twenty-first century. A fifteen-year-old using a toothbrush to masturbate about her best friend really shouldn't be that big a deal." (episode 1.1)

"After all," Kim says, "This *is* Brighton: Sin City;" then she goes on to introduce her family and the reason for their recent move. Arriving at the introduction of herself, Kim immediately expresses her desire for Sugar. Here the camera cuts to Kim's perspective as she looks in the direction of Sugar, leaning over a pool table, with her pool cue and long necklace directing the viewer's gaze to her breasts, which are right at the center of the frame. The camera lingers over Sugar's body as Kim's voice-over continues, "The girl I'm sexually obsessed with. She'll do anything, say anything, have anything. Well, anything with a dick and that's the problem. She's not gay and I don't want to be." Throughout the remainder of this episode, Kim attempts to overcome her crush on Sugar by losing her virginity. However, the episode concludes in the same place where it began. Kim lies in bed alone, masturbating with an electric toothbrush. The closed circular format of the narrative within this first episode sets up an audience expectation for the progression of the series: an expectation that the narrative of each episode will focus on the same lustful pursuit and follow a similar trajectory. It is not surprising that this narrative format is paralleled in many of the further episodes, in which Kim either attempts to overcome her "sexual obsession" with Sugar or attempts to have sex with Sugar, but ultimately ends up in the same place of unfulfilled desire.

As the series progresses, Kim goes to further and further lengths in her hilarious attempts to overcome this "Sugar addiction" (episode 1.9). She moves from secretly lusting after Sugar to stealing her underwear, considering date rape as a viable seduction method (episode 1.3), and intervening in her relationships with men (episode 1.5), before deciding that she can no longer maintain the secrecy of her desires. When Sugar continues to reject her romantic advances, Kim turns to an ex-gay religious youth group, looking for a "cure" (episode 1.8). This first season, according to Natalie Edwards was concerned, primarily, with "unfulfilled queer desire" as "emphasis was placed on Kim's *solo* sexual activities, rather than her sexual interactions with other girls, underscoring a more general commentary on the frustrations resulting from thwarted teenage sexuality" (Edwards par. 9). Maintaining the emphasis on queer desire, Kim prays,

> Dear God. Please stop me perving over Sugar and help me find a fit guy to perve over instead. Or if it turns out that you're ok with the whole same-sex thing, stop Sugar messing me about and help her find her way into my bed. (episode 1.8)

Far from the brief flirtations with lesbianism as exemplified by *Degrassi Junior High, Neighbours,* or *The O.C,* the elongation of Kim's "sexual obsession" through the seriality of the narrative allows the entire series to act as an interrogation of queer desire. Stylistically, throughout this first season, the camera often takes on Kim's perspective, lingering distractedly over Sugar's body and offering a visual manifestation of Kim's desire. Indeed, Kim's desires remain emphasized in this manner, despite the fact that the second season of *Sugar Rush* features a mostly absent Sugar. As Edwards argues, "If series one was principally about the containment of *unexpressed* queer desire, series two was rather more about its release" (par. 9).

The second season begins in very much the same way as the first. We return to the carnival ride, although this time Kim appears to ride alone. Her voice-over informs viewers that "It's 18 months since I hotwired a car, stole my mum's credit card and had hot lesbian sex with my best friend, Sugar. And things are going great." With this, Kim leans to her right, revealing a woman on the carnival ride with her. They kiss and she continues, "Really great," as another woman appears to her left. They too kiss, but Kim's voice-over quickly interrupts, "yeah right." The image of the carnival is replaced by an image of Kim alone in bed. "Life is back to normal, nothing's changed... Well, my toothbrush has seen better days" (episode 2.1).

As noted by Glyn Davis and Gary Needham, when queer characters continue to appear in television narratives after coming out—their primary narrative function—"the fate of such characters is often to have the queer aspects of their lives (sex, love, queer friends and spaces, homophobia) elided" (7). *Sugar Rush* does not do this. Rather, it revels in exploring the "queer aspects" of its protagonist's life. This focus spans the entirety of the second season, but initially emerges from the prison setting, where the incarcerated Sugar tells Kim that it is time for her to "get a life" (episode 2.1). Where the first season focused intently on the negotiation of identity and the angst associated with unfulfilled queer desires, the second season shifted this attention to the negotiation of space and community and, equally, to the expression of queer desire.

In this first episode, Kim is introduced to queer sex, love, friends, and spaces after accidentally bumping into a girl named Saint (Sarah Jane Potts), who is carrying a bag of sex toys. In this scene, dildos and vibrators spill to the ground and Kim helps to collect them. Following the girl to the sex shop—The Munch Box—Kim muses that she could, "just walk in there and ask her out" but does not have the courage to do so. Instead, she purchases an assortment of sex toys as the lyrics of the song "Would you . . . ?" by British band Touch and Go reverberate around the room—"I've noticed you around/I find you very attractive/would you go to bed with me?" The shop girl eventually asks her out to the local lesbian club—the Clit Club—where Kim meets an attractive and manipulative older woman.

At the conclusion of this episode, in a return to the beginning and a parallel to the narrative circularity of the first episode of season one, Kim again bumps into the shop girl; this time she walks away with her number. Edwards notes that *Sugar Rush* offers a "cosmopolitan perspective" (par. 14) as it presents its audience "with a selection of queer characters who interact with and are, to a greater or lesser extent, integrated into the (predominantly heterosexual) wider community" (par. 15). This cosmopolitanism, writes Edwards, is strongly linked to the "backdrop of queer arenas" that constitute its location (par. 17). The Clit Club and Munch Box are among these primary "queer arenas" that Kim finds herself (both literally and figuratively) within. The "queer aspects" of life, including the negotiation of space and community, are foregrounded within the serial format of *Sugar Rush* against this backdrop. Notably, this connection between identity, community, and space is established when Kim faces difficulties in reconciling her old life with her new one (episode 2.4). In this episode, Sugar notes, "I get it all right, you're a proper grown up lezzer with your lezzer friends and your dodgy bar" (episode 2.4). It is also significant that later episodes see Kim initiating other characters into these queer spaces, as she gains confidence within them.

As the second season focuses primarily on the expression and fulfilment of queer desire, *Sugar Rush*'s serial format maintains the emphasis on both desire and sex that propelled the narrative of the first season. Through this, as Edwards suggests, "The frustrations which beset her [Kim] throughout the first series [are] supplanted by the dilemmas which result from her often unsophisticated navigation of her queer sexual identity" (par 9.). The second season sees Kim engaging in sexual activities including bondage and role-play while also feeling anxious about her sexual inexperience. When thinking about sleeping with Saint, Kim expresses these anxieties through voice-over:

> Thinking about all of the things I wanted to do with her was fine. But in reality, satisfying the girl who worked in the sex shop was a frightening prospect. What if she had accessories I'd never seen? What if I couldn't strap them on right? What if I put the wrong end in the wrong place? (episode 2.3)

Moving beyond the limited nature of the coming-out narrative, *Sugar Rush*'s seriality allows for the depiction of more complex queer characters, lives, and desires as well as questions such as these to be asked, for the first time, on teen television.

In previous work, I have argued that *Sugar Rush* represents a significant departure from the prevalent trope of "coming out as coming of age" (Monaghan 58), in which coming out is represented as a means of transgressing the boundary between adolescence and adulthood. I argued this to be problematic, because the conflation of the coming-out moment with the coming of age moment has often resulted in the "adultification" of the queer teen character, offering little room for complex representations of queer adolescents. Moreover, within such story lines, the coming-out moment is typically portrayed as a narrative climax, and thus the act of coming out becomes "not only an end in itself, but *the* end" to this singular narrative (Bronski 20).

Sugar Rush's deviation from this "closed" narrative format is achieved through the fact that Kim comes out a number of times over the course of the series. Each episode begins with a voice-over that acts as an assertion of her status as a "fifteen-year-old queer virgin" or some variation thereof, constantly reminding the audience of the queer desires driving the narrative. When Kim does finally come out to Sugar, in what should traditionally be the climax (and thus mark the conclusion) of her story line, she finds herself inarticulate and it is Sugar who must speak for her.

Sugar: Well maybe you like me then. Ha-ha…what?
Kim: [*silence*]
Sugar: Oh my god. My god. You fancy me.
Kim: I've got to go. (episode 1.6)

Kim does articulate her sexuality in a later episode, in which she tells the annoying son of her neighbors that she cannot date him because she is "gay" (episode 1.9). This is followed by an immediate internal monologue/voice-over in which Kim optimistically informs the audience that "For the first time I was out and proud" (episode 1.9). Kim is, however, not "adultified" through these encounters, as the series ultimately disentangles the complex processes of coming out and coming of age. After coming out over the course of the first season, Kim remains firmly positioned within the liminal state of adolescence. The second season, however, is devoted to her "intensely introspective questions about the self, love, sex, and ultimately coming of age" (Monaghan 65).

Within the series, Kim's queer desires are contrasted with those of Sugar, as Sugar's brief flirtation with lesbianism within season 1 (most explicitly within episode 1.7 and episode 1.10) engages with the dominant depiction of lesbianism as a phase. After learning of Kim's sexual attraction, Sugar flirts with the idea of desiring women, telling Kim that she has had enough of opposite sex: "More trouble than what their worth. I reckon it's time I found other ways to enjoy myself" (episode 1.7). After an extended montage of the day's events in which Kim and Sugar act like a couple, they go out to the local nightclub. Shadows roll over their faces as they dance closely and intimately. A man approaches them, asking whether they are lesbians, to which Sugar quickly replies, "Yes."

In previous episodes, the camera takes on Kim's physical point of view, often leering at Sugar's body; however, here the movement and framing of the camera, lighting and soundtrack come to represent Kim's emotional point of view. The camera orbits Kim and Sugar as they kiss; close-ups of lips, eyes, and colored lights fill the frame. This is replaced by a moment of shadowy darkness and when the lights return, they kiss again. The music here abruptly transitions from a light dance track to a softer song, performed by a single piano. The camera continues its orbit as Kim's voice-over optimistically asserts, "Tonight I was living the dream." However, this dream is soon shattered as Kim discovers that the kiss was, for Sugar, just an experiment and another way of "turn[ing] on loser guys" (episode 1.10). Sugar later argues that this kind of experimentation is acceptable so long as it is not permanent (episode 2.3), thus reiterating the figuration of queer desire as an aberration or interruption. However, Kim's story line challenges this dominant depiction; her queer desires are represented with a degree of permanence that is unmarred throughout the entire series and are extended beyond a brief experimentation.

Writing in 2001, Anna McCarthy argued that "same-sex desire plays a deeply antagonistic role" within television's "temporal structures" ("*Ellen: Making Queer Television History*" 597); that queerness itself poses a problem for the televisual medium, stemming from the great difficulty of "making same-sex desire uneventful, serial, everyday" (609). Through the emphasis on Kim's desire as a driving narrative force across the series as a whole, *Sugar Rush* challenges these arguments. Rejecting the narrative format of the "very special episode" in which queerness has often appeared on television, its format successfully renders same-sex desire as "serial" and "everyday" but importantly, never boring. *Sugar Rush* is significant because it is one of few programs to serialize this classically "closed" and limited queer narrative, a narrative typically focusing solely on the revelation of homosexuality.

However, as a teen series it is even more unique. Although *The L Word* achieved this narrativization of queerness prior to *Sugar Rush*, opening up the possibility for complex queer characters, lives, and story lines, and there has been further queer/lesbian-oriented programming, such as *The Real L Word* and *Lip Service*, these series still focus on adult characterization, narratives, desires, and lives. Even *Buffy the Vampire Slayer*, a teen-oriented series, framed its prominent queer character, Willow, as an adult; her queer story line began in the college setting. Privileging the queer adult over the queer teen in this manner serves to render queer teen experience invisible within popular discourse and reinforces the problematic configuration of the queer girl as an ephemeral character type, thus positioning queerness itself as a transient phase. However, *Sugar Rush* places this experience at the very center of its narrative, interrogating the surfaces of queer desire and opening up the possibility for more complex characterizations of the figure of the queer girl. To return to an earlier quote by Driver (7), *Sugar Rush* frames Kim's sexual subjectivity not as a "temporary departure from a normative course toward feminine heterosexual adulthood," as is the case with many teen series, but rather as a viable alternative and a driving narrative force.

CHAPTER 12

Out for Life: Makeover Television and the Transformation of Fitness on Bravo's *Work Out*

Dana Heller

I'm Jackie Warner and this is my world. It's a world of hard bodies and beautiful faces. (episode 1.1)

With this seductive voice-over, Bravo introduced *Work Out*, a new reality series based on the life of Los Angeles entrepreneur and fitness trainer Jackie Warner, about her launching of Sky Sport and Spa, a private, state-of-the-art gym that caters to the Beverly Hills elite. The show's first season, which aired in the summer of 2006, focused on Jackie's determined efforts to get her new business off the ground and to establish productive working relations with her team of professional trainers, a diverse crew whose engaging personalities make them not only readable as character types, but perfect foils for Jackie's dogmatic management style. Additional tensions arose from Jackie's struggles to balance her demanding professional life with her private life, as viewers bore intimate witness to the collapse of her four-year romantic relationship with Mimi, her jealousy-prone Brazilian girlfriend with a penchant for biting.

Although mocked by one critic as "*The Apprentice* in sweatpants" (Laura Fries), *Work Out* emerged as Bravo's most successful new show of 2006 ("Work Out," bravotv.com). The second season, which aired in the spring of 2007, trained its lens more voyeuristically on Jackie's private life, and in particular her reentry into the Los Angeles dating scene, which prompted some to remark that the show might have been aptly retitled *Make Out* (*Work Out Reunion*). However, audiences also gained insight into Jackie's strained relationship with her mother, a former Baptist turned Mormon, who morally disapproves of her daughter's lesbianism. They watched Jackie launch her clothing line of gym-to-street workout attire and they became more intimately acquainted with Sky Sport and Spa's clients, mainly through Jackie's launching of Sky Lab, an intensive two-week fitness program. And fans were saddened, as was the series' cast, to learn of the sudden loss of one of the Sky team, Doug Bladsdell, whose death from kidney failure at age 44 provided the season's emotionally climactic conclusion.

Prior to the third season of *Work Out*, intense speculation circulated on message boards and fan blogs as to what surprises it might hold in store: "Will Jackie finally meet her match...? Will the other trainers continue to live in fear and mockery of Jackie's bravado? Will someone finally get too much exercise instead of too little? And how much more crying and protein shakes can we really take?" ("Work Out" bravotv.com) In many ways, season 3 of *Work Out* continued to develop three interrelated themes, which it is the purpose of this essay to consider: First, rehearsing long-standing American historical tendencies for the social promotion and commercial marketing of physical fitness, in the very instance of demonstrating the individual body's capacity to resist and redefine the terms of its conditioning. Second, reinforcing the concept that Ella Taylor has called the "television work-family" (Ella Taylor 14), the tendency "of American television to recruit its most potent images and forms, to reproduce its foundational myths, and to resolve its most debilitating social contradictions through narrative studies of the unstable boundaries of industry and intimacy, the reproduction of wealth and the reproduction of life, the public performance of labor and the private performance of intimacy, domesticity, and sexuality," as I have described elsewhere (Heller "States of Emergency"). And third, it will celebrate the "powers of transformation," a myth system that organizes countless reality makeover formats in markets around the world by manufacturing belief in our individual and shared capacities for radical self-reinvention (Bratich 6–22).

Power Transformations

In *Work Out*, this latter notion is unequivocally defended by Jackie's ethos that her clients should achieve not just a better body, but "a lifestyle change" (1.1). This belief is further championed by Jackie herself, a working-class girl from Ohio who got herself to Hollywood and metamorphosed into a glamorous, successful fitness mogul. (Her father, a Vietnam veteran, committed suicide when she was 18.) However, while *Work Out* demonstrates the core strength of the makeover mythos, it also highlights its flexibility and its adaptability to changing social and televisual contexts. We see this most vividly in the series' handling of Jackie's lesbianism, which throughout *Work Out*'s two years has remained the one aspect of her life absolutely not subject to alteration. Indeed, viewers quickly learn that Jackie is openly gay and uncompromising in her sexual self-definition.

In the series premiere, a male client tests her to see if she might be persuaded to date a man, reasoning coyly that "some people have interests in many things."

"I'm not one of those people," Jackie responds, with pointed finality (1.1). In a subsequent episode, Jackie lays it out: "I gotta tell you for the record," she says, looking decisively into the camera. "People do not choose to be gay" (1.4). From here, *Work Out* continually reinforces Jackie's conviction that while bodies, behaviors, and lifestyles can be positively broken down and transformed, homosexuality remains at least partially genetic, inherent, and wholly compatible with aspirations to individual fitness, social well-being, and national health.

Implicitly then, the series' focus on Jackie's self-assured sexual identity, her savvy approach to business management and fitness training, her messy breakup with Mimi, and her drama-fraught relations with her real-life television "work family" raise a number of questions relevant to recent transformations in health and fitness television programming. For example, how does *Work Out*'s unscripted premise contribute to the repositioning of lesbianism—with its long history of medical pathologization and cultural and religious demonization—as consistent with health and fitness administration? How do audiences and fans negotiate their own viewing pleasures and personal investments in diet and exercise in relation to the day-to-day lives, challenges, and conflicts faced by Jackie, her trainers, and their clients? What does the Bravo series ultimately reveal about the proper management and disciplining of bodies, sexualities, and desires? And how might these revelations reflect broader shifts in the programming and organization of social and national bodies?

To begin with, as social and cultural historian Harvey Green, in his 1986 book, *Fit For America*, has shown, the proper definition of "good health" has remained throughout American history a question of unrelenting controversy. Early America's evangelical faith in its own moral perfectibility—and by extension, in the perfectibility of its citizens—were threatened in the nineteenth century by waves of immigrants from Europe who seemed physically poised to economically outperform the overindulged and debilitated young men of America's major cities. The natural abundance and industrial prosperity that had been the boast of political orators became, in the vision of social reformers across the nation, a foreshadowing of the republic's undoing, as the sedentary habits, heavy diets, political and religious passions, and nervous stress of middle-class Anglo-Saxon Americans appeared to render them weaker and less able to compete than the new foreigners who were arriving. Fears of "race suicide" and labor unrest gave way to calls for the nation's men and women to improve their "edge" through physical strength training and improved dietary habits.

The calls emanated from secular medical professionals, faddists, and quacks, as well as from nonsecular advocates for "muscular Christianity," such as Luther Gulick, who turned the Young Men's Christian Association into a fitness organization (Green). The result of these many calls, and the new programs, agencies, and activities they spawned, lead to a national obsession with fitness and to a growing marketplace for the advertising and consumption of new commercial products, foodstuffs, and equipment for improving the body—and, by extension, the soul.

In all of this, the health of the individual was understood as tantamount to the health of the nation, and women were not excluded from this moral responsibility. In the pre–Civil War era, middle-class women were encouraged to eschew the fashionable sedentary feminine activities of the time—reading, piano, drawing, and needlework—and perform vigorous housework as a means of strengthening their reproductive capacities. They were criticized for adhering to the custom of tight-lacing by educators and social critics such as Catherine Beecher, who was among the first to argue for an essential connection between the development of physical fitness and the attainment of natural beauty (Green). The nineteenth-century appearance of this equation, as Green notes, registered a fundamental shift in America's perception of the ideal female form from ample portliness to a leaner feminine muscularity.

Despite women's participation in calisthenics and other supervised forms of light exercise, serious muscle building and participation in competitive sports such as football and boxing would remain positive attributes of American masculinity, particularly given their associations with power, violence, and male superiority over those perceived as other to the nation. Still the twentieth-century development of mass consumer culture often relied upon the image of energetic, sensually vivacious womanhood to promote physical culture products and the promise of bodily transformation to men and women alike. Following on the success of innovators such as Eugene Sandow and Bernard McFadden in linking health to sexual attractiveness and potency, Charles Atlas (an Italian immigrant born Angelino Siciliano) capitalized upon fears of male sexual inadequacy, distributed through the medium of popular comics, to sell his "dynamic tension" fitness system, which promised to turn scrawny Macs into the heroes of the beach.

With the establishment of commercial radio in the 1920s, boxing matches, college football, and baseball games penetrated into American living rooms with unprecedented immediacy. Television's invention in the 1920s and its development as an electronic commercial broadcast medium in the 1930s and 1940s promised a new technological format for the delivery of popular spectator sports and advertising. However, it would not be not until after World War II, with television's mainstreaming into the mundane fabric of middle-class American domestic life, that "the godfather of fitness," Jack LaLanne, the son of French immigrants, would see the medium's potential for delivering health and fitness programming to American audiences. Following on the success of the Oakland, California, health and fitness spa that he opened in 1936, *The Jack LaLanne Show* began broadcasting in 1951, thus becoming the first lifestyle health and fitness program in American television history. It remained on the air until 1984.

Since *The Jack LaLanne Show* first invited television viewers to work out with Jack in the privacy of their own homes, many fitness programs, gurus, and fashionable methods of weight loss and physical conditioning have come and gone on American television, both network and cable. Adding to this, exercise videos, launched by Jane Fonda in the early 1980s, seized upon the entrepreneurial potential of VHS technology as a new inducement for women and men to regard exercise as something uniquely suited to the television screen and to the intimate space of home.

These recent developments are part of the long historical view of America's fitness obsession, as we can discern from certain recurring motifs. Physical fitness remains variously linked to moral ideologies and their management via developing technologies and consumer practices; debates over proper exercise and diet have continue to reflect debates over proper gendering and sexuality; questions of individual fitness similarly continue to mirror questions of social and national fitness; and finally, and perhaps most obviously in its recent forms, our preoccupation with working out—more than simply a register of cultural narcissism or fear of death—remains "an expression of the desire for community and emotional bonding in a culture of men and women alone" (Green 323).

Flexing the Family

Work Out amplifies these characteristics in clearly marked ways as it stages, wittingly or not, debates over the ethics of care, morality in the workplace,

proper mothering, proper gendering, familial loyalties, and national lega-
cies. Much of this is communicated in the screen time devoted to Jackie's
trainers. Only 8 out of the 22 trainers she actually employs appear on the
series. These 8 were selected in part due to their distinctive personal styles,
which produce not only a dramatic sense of "good TV" but also a social
microcosm of human expressiveness and human need. They are Brian (the
southern "ladies' man" and alpha male); Rebecca (the sassy, exhibitionistic
flirt); Andre (an African American former military officer, whose traditional
values are exercised with quiet tolerance); Jesse (the catty, effeminate gay
man, and one of Jackie's closest confidantes); Erica (a reserved and aloof
beauty and a recovered bulimic); Zen (the "funny" girl who sidelines as
a stand-up comic); Doug (the avuncular elder of the group, and "everyone's best friend"); and Gregg (an African American musician and aspiring
recording artists who appears only in season 2).

In their first-season interviews, they frequently refer to their competitive
yet affectionate dealings with one another in terms of natural familial inti-
macies and rivalries. Brian introduces himself and his coworkers by explaining, "We are like a family here." Later he dismisses his initial distrust of the
new hire, Jesse, by contending that, "If you wanna be in this family, I will
have you in this family" (1.1). Even Sky Lab clients reiterate the familial
ethos that binds them to their otherwise grueling boot camp sessions and
pitiless trainers, as Tess does in admitting, "I really formed a family with
these people" (*Work Out*, "Reunion," episode 2.9, 2007).

In these instances, the concept of family becomes unmoored from its
legal or biological meanings to suggest that professional labors performed in
the name of administering or attaining better health are extensions of the
caring bonds and nurturing loyalties that organize the private family. At the
same time, the rhetoric of familialism works to naturalize the disciplinary
constraints of capitalism and its management of time, bodies, and produc-
tivity by suggesting that when we surrender ourselves to the governance
and surveillance of the workplace, we experience the most meaningful and
emotionally gratifying relationships that life has to offer.

In *Work Out*, this idea is reinforced by the near-total absence of trainer
backstories or individual histories. Viewers know comparatively little about
where the trainers come from, who their loved ones are, or how they spend
time when not at work, unlike what they know about the personal history of
Jackie, which is a critical part of the series' narrative arc. The upshot is that
trainers appear to have no serious relationships, sexual or otherwise, beyond
the incestuous web of professional affiliation, competition, loyalty, and
betrayal that the demanding, high-stress fitness industry compels. When
Zen introduces her new boyfriend to the trainers, she quips, "Welcome to

our dysfunctional family" (2.7). The remark serves to intensify the perceived emotional stakes of the trainers' on-camera interactions with one another and with Jackie. This is made more complicated by the fact that Jackie's efforts to nurture intimacy and trust with the crew do not always blend well with her imperious managerial style. "My place, my rules, and that's how it has to be," she asserts in the series premiere. Her need to be in control and her tendency to criticize trainers for performing beneath expectations result in frequent clashes and eruptions of pique, many of which direct the narrative arc of episodes, as trainers gossip among themselves and offer their individual analyses of the latest scandal or spat.

In the premiere, for example, Jackie corrects Brian's training technique in front of a client, which sends him into a rage. He complains about her to the other trainers. Jackie likewise complains about him to the trainers in whom she chooses to confide. Rebecca "privately" offers her assessment of the situation for the camera: "I think Jackie and [Brian] are both type A alpha males" (1.1).

Collisions and catty confrontations, many involving complicated tensions around the appropriate performance of gender and sexuality, are central to *Work Out*'s depiction of fitness administration. In this sense, Jackie's gym represents a liminal space, a site of constant negotiation and debate over the proper social posturing and correspondence of bodies, genders, and desires. Jackie admits this to be a general dilemma not only in the gym, but in modern life in Los Angeles, when she says, "It's hard to decipher who's gay and who's not in this town anymore" (1.1). In her self-presentation, Jackie likewise resists prescribed sexual and gender scripts and the social codes that organize them. "A gym is a very different environment," she claims. "There's flexibility in our environment" (*Work Out*, "Reunion," episode 2.9). Jackie's "flexibility" is evident in the way she combines "alpha male" butchness in work-related matters with a chic lipstick lesbian style sense. Politically she identifies as a "strong woman and feminist" who has "a hard time with someone…just playing the sex card" (1.2). However, she performs her own sexuality openly and playfully, signifying as queer while showing a marked preference for straight-looking femmes and heterosexual women, around whom she admits to being a sexual predator. At age 37, she is happily and even somewhat recklessly nonmonogamous. "Being a slut, I've decided, works for me," she says on *Work Out*'s "Reunion" episode, yet she is so invested in her reproductive future that she consults a doctor about the possibility of having her eggs frozen for later fertilization. In short, *Work Out* traffics lavishly in the seeming contradictory niches and gaps of social gendering, along with sexual, oedipal, and political identities. But, true to Annette Hill's claim that reality television is essentially about "border territories," or spaces in which relations of information and entertainment, and fact and fiction, are tested and reimagined (2), *Work Out* revels in subversive border regions that render unrealistic all normative notions of femininity and masculinity, heterosexuality and homosexuality, and butch and femme roles within the stereotypical formation of lesbian subjectivities. Good health, from this standpoint, may require that we reshuffle the codes of gender and sexuality according to our own flexible relational circumstances.

After the obligatory extended recap of the first season's notable interpersonal crises, the second season of *Work Out* opens with Jackie's summary of what she has thus far accomplished: "My trainers and I bonded like a family," she proclaims (2.1). From here, season 2 unfolds through documentation of a total boundary breakdown, as Jackie, following her final split from Mimi, begins casually dating her employee, Rebecca, who has heretofore identified as heterosexual. Subsequent episodes follow the bemused and disturbed reactions of the Sky Sport "work family" through these incestuous travails. It's "the most unethical thing that anyone can do" (2.4) says Jesse of Jackie's behavior, although he later accuses Rebecca of opportunistically dating the "boss" only to get more screen time for herself (*Work Out,* "Reunion" episode). It is "unprofessional," claims Brian, clearly chafed (2.4). And Andre comments that no man wants to stand by passively and see "his boss with women that he secretly desires" (2.4).

Through it all, Jackie defends her actions as something she "deserves," a healthy and joyful stage in her adjustment to single life. Moreover, she understands it to be ethically consistent with the "flexibility" of the fitness industry. "Trainers sleep with trainers, trainers sleep with clients," she rationalizes (2.4). However, fans responded very negatively to Jackie and Rebecca's relationship, and in such numbers that Jackie was caught off guard. "I had no idea the attention that we would get," she admits in the "Reunion" episode, before announcing her decision to continue dating Rebecca privately and only off camera.

In contrast to the routine insubordination and drama at Sky Sport and Spa, Jackie's biological family history is presented as one of misfortune and loss. Indeed, a recurrent theme of the *Work Out* is Jackie's strained relationship with her mother, whose strong religious convictions cannot be reconciled with her daughter's sexuality and her aspirations to one day marry a woman and have a child. At the conclusion of season 2, Jackie returns to her hometown in Ohio in order to resolve their difficulties and make amends with the painful memory of her father, who returned from Vietnam suffering from mental illness. The episode stages the return of the prodigal daughter as putting to rest both personal and national trauma, as Jackie visits her father's grave for the first time with her mother, and as she acknowledges the imprint that national history has left upon her. Although her father took his life long after the war in Vietnam had ended, Jackie comes to see that "he was a casualty of that war" (2.7).

Meanwhile, back at Sky Sport, Jesse is faced with a revelation concerning current history and the latest American war in Iraq. He is training a male model and actor who works in the gay porn industry. As it turns out, the actor is also a former marine who served in Iraq on the administrative board for homosexual conduct. The contradiction confounds Jesse, as his client confides—between crunches – that his experience in Iraq was nothing except "pointless" and sad (2.7).

Cut back to Ohio, where Jackie's visit appears to be bringing about a positive shift in family relations, as we watch her mother proudly standing witness as Jackie delivers an inspirational address to a large crowd of admiring students at her former high school. Gratified that the visit has been a success, Jackie returns to L.A., where she describes her time in Ohio as a "rebirth with my mother" (2.7). The theme of rebirth, however, is soon paired with the theme of death, as she returns home only to learn of the passing of her trainer, Doug, from kidney failure. By turn, the trainers address the camera in tight focus, each contributing to the spectacle of tears and emotional outpouring that Doug's death inspires. Brian sums up their feelings in saying that he will remember Doug, "like a member of my family" (2.5).

At such moments, we begin to get a sense of the multiple meanings inherent in the program's title. Treadmills, protein shakes, and entrepreneurial growth are mere trace elements within the larger transformational labor process that *Work Out* champions as part of our individual, social, and national health consciousness. *Work Out*, Jackie insists, is really about "working life out" ("Jackie's Blog," May 10, 2007). In other words, life is an extreme sport, the goal of which is emotional catharsis, the key to strengthening ourselves individually and collectively. Indeed, the fitness ethos that the program advocates is one that requires full disclosure and reconditioning of inner processes. In Jackie's gym, and in her boot camps, physical change matters less than the restored sense of self-worth that disclosure brings about. The "beautiful faces and hard bodies" that constitute Jackie's world are thus markers of an open and flexible interiority that informs our modern middle-class vision of health and our notions of comprehensive fitness. *Work Out* is a docudrama that contributes to the history of fitness culture, as well as to the evolution of "factual entertainment" television, by presenting physical health and well-being as a set of intimately relational signifying practices, which when flexed properly will reveal and transform our "reality"—beginning with our authentic inner selves.

Outing the Real

Another way of putting this is that "reality" on *Work Out* is something that needs to be continuously "outed" in the interests of wellness. Indeed, Jackie's uncompromising openness about her sexuality and her confidence as a gay woman going up against the corporate rat race is entirely consistent with this ethos, as it signals her authenticity and her awareness of the moral obligations that come with it. Fans of the show, both gay and straight-identified, affirm this on message boards and posts to Jackie's personal blog. For example, Cindy writes, "I watch the show every week and I love your honesty. You just put it out there and it's real." And this from "Semaj Taylor:"

> Well tonight was the first time i seen your show and yes...i am just totally in love with it. Why? Well for one it REAL its not some made up stuff that people already [plan] whats going to happen. it's REAL people REAL problems, and REAL life. What more could you ask out of a show?

Fans repeatedly claim to be inspired by Jackie's authenticity and the truthfulness of the challenges she faces, and this—they further claim—makes it possible for them to see themselves in a new light and with new hope for retrieving the value of authenticity in their own lives. The external manifestation of this process is physical exercise, as Priscilla suggests in writing, "Well, I just wanted to let Jackie know that she's really inspired me. I can't wait until the doctor okays me working out again, but when he does, I'm workin' out!" ("Jackie's Blog")

Also important to consider from an industry perspective is the extent to which the Bravo cable television network (which is owned by NBC Universal) has capitalized on the cultural chic of a simple three-letter word: "out." "Out" has become the veritable signature of Bravo's original reality programming, with niche series such as *Blow Out*, which focused on celebrity hair stylist Jonathan Antin's launching of a salon in L.A., and *Flipping Out*, which centers on obsessive-compulsive real estate speculator Jeff Lewis, who buys houses and resells them for profit. This series of shows, along with other popular queer-friendly programs such as *Boy Meets Boy* (2003), *Queer Eye for the Straight Guy* (2003–), *Queer Eye for the Straight Girl* (2005), the Emmy-nominated *Kathy Griffin: My Life on the D List* (2005–), and *Welcome to the Parker* (2007), cater directly to gay and lesbian audiences and tastes and, in the eyes of *New York Times* television critic Alessandra Stanley, has successfully elevated Bravo to the status of "premiere gay network, even though it is not labeled as such."

Moreover, Bravo's slogan, "Watch What Happens," reflects its investment in branding itself as reality, precisely by claiming that its programming is unformulated and spontaneous. Implicit in its slogan is Bravo's recognition that dramatic self-disclosure and submission to surveillance remain the twin guarantors of authenticity and spontaneity, "the promise of the real in reality TV" (Andrejevic 108). Like Sky trainers, Sky clients too become integral players in *Work Out*'s drama of authentic self-retrieval. "I'm ready to get back to the person I know I am," says Tess in an interview that marks her preparedness to begin a journey towards weight loss, but more importantly towards an ethical unity of inner self and outward performance, a moral obligation that obesity and ill health have seemingly compromised (1.3). Resistance is part of journey, and Sky clients do on occasion rebel, backslide, and/or fail. However they can be redeemed through theatrical emotional candor, by admitting failure and self-revulsion, and by otherwise turning themselves inside out for the camera and for Jackie, who appears to derive tremendous satisfaction from their abjection. "I get a joy from doing my job well," she admits. "And I get a joy from just breaking someone down" (1.1). In one episode, Jackie works Tess out so strenuously she vomits. But even this, which Jackie treats lightly, is seen as a positive step toward weight reduction, and even more important, as a purge of inner toxins that must be outed—in this case, literally. As part of this process, Sky Lab clients give up control of their bodies to be tested, measured, weighed, analyzed, and monitored, their food input and physical exertion output scrupulously recorded and continuously assessed. Even the trainers are required to surrender their bodies for weigh-ins, fat density checks, and rigorous boot camps, which, as one trainer observes, Jackie orchestrates but never participates in herself.

The information that Jackie exacts from the bodies of clients and trainers at the gym is revealing of how well they care for themselves, and by extension a measure of how well they might care for others. The cultivation and maintenance of fitness is thus coextensive with an "ethics of care," which Annette Hill locates at the core of much contemporary reality television programming. *Work Out* is a reality program that is fundamentally about caring for one's own self as the most effective means of caring for others. However, Jackie's proficiency in caring for others does not translate into her private conduct. The challenges she faces in realizing her personal goals—a stable marriage and family—remind viewers that Jackie is neither flawless nor consistently in charge of her own impulses and desires. In other words, she appears conspicuously lacking in certain aspects of self-knowledge—an embodiment of the directive (albeit paraphrased), "Trainer, train thyself."

However, it is precisely this inconsistency—the supremely fit and powerful health guru reduced to a chew toy for her petulant girlfriend, and to angry self-condemnation in therapy—that produces viewer interest and involvement with Jackie, both as a "real" individual and as a living symptom of shifting technologies for the screening of sexualities elsewhere defined as "non-normative" and immoral. In this way, *Work Out* invites viewers to engage with ethical debates about the normalization of homosexuality and lesbianism in American society. Jackie is in this sense a flashpoint, an embodied site of ethical conflict and transformation. And, indeed, Jackie's celebrity status is largely rooted in the disjuncture between her public function as fitness instructor *par excellence* and her self-exposure as a less than responsible cultivator of self-knowledge. This encourages fans of the program to analyze Jackie's ethics; some of them encourage her to care for her "self" just as attentively as she does her business and her body. We see this tendency, for example, in the following message from "a fan:"

> In all honesty, I absolutely love this show and I just want to point out that you may be great at everything else in you [sic] life, but it has been recorded/filmed that when it comes to relationships, you may need some help... ("A Fan," Jackie's Blog)

Here, the implicit understanding is that health-based reality television lends itself to ethical analysis of what it means to be fit—a condition measured not only by our capacity to care for others, but by "the self's relation to itself" (Gauntlett 124–128), which requires that we commit to our own emotional and psychological improvement through the application of ethical techniques that Michel Foucault called "technologies of the self" (*The Use of Pleasure*).

This quest leads Jackie and her girlfriend Mimi to seek couple's counseling from Dr. Shirley Impellizerri, an L.A. therapist. In their first session, while discussing the difficulties they have communicating with one another, Mimi's anger is triggered and she abruptly stands up and leaves the office. Jackie is left alone with "Dr. Shirley," who, feigning curiosity, asks her, "Why are you in this?" (2.1)

"Because I'm fucked up," Jackie blurts out in frustration. She falls silent while the camera lingers over her, maximizing the power and urgency of her confession. But viewers who have been watching the series up to this point will likely be gratuitously affirmed in what they've understood all along: "This relationship is my addiction," Jackie recognizes. With this admission, she continues seeking individual therapy, claiming that she hopes to discover "why I attract the people I attract" (2.1).

Jackie enters therapy in order to transition out of her situation with Mimi and to positively transform the quality of her future relationships.

Her meetings with Dr. Shirley comprise a contemplative leitmotif throughout season 2, although Jackie's scenes with Dr. Shirley provide very little by way of dramatic revelation. Rather, Jackie's decision to pursue therapy is a logical extension of the overarching narrative that frames Jackie as a fitness folk hero, and a distinctively American folk hero at that. Jackie's individual history is evocative of a national makeover mythos, as it rehearses the familiar tale of westward flight toward freedom and new open spaces for the exercise of one's instincts and innermost desires. In this mythos, the American West—and California in particular—represents the preeminent locus of self-recreation, opportunity, and youthful experimentation.

In national literature, popular culture, and mass media, California has long served as a receptacle for all who gravitate toward the farthest western boundaries of the nation and the national imaginary—from Huckleberry Finn to Sal Paradise. Not insignificantly, the mythology also has a central place in twentieth-century US histories of queer migration, as young gays and lesbians from the nation's more culturally conservative heartland sought refuge in politically and socially progressive locations such as San Francisco in the 1950s and 1960s, and West Hollywood 1970s and 1980s. As a conveyor of fantasies that speak to national idealism as well as to minority community aspirations, California is where one goes to discover and authenticate new self-meanings—new ways of being. Like physical culture, therapy culture has become an integral part of the service industries that cater to middle-class self-management and to the meanings we've come to associate with the labors of authenticity, including the productive work of being "out."

Indeed, Jackie has often attributed the success of her show and the breadth of her fan base to the fact that she is originally from America's heartland, and proud of it. At the same time, she recalls what it meant to grow up isolated, lonely, and closeted in a stifling small town: "Growing up a gay teenager . . . I constantly felt that I was going to be exposed" (2.7). That her quest for self-actualization should lead her to Hollywood, to the celebrity fitness industry, and to Dr. Shirley's Beverly Hills office is probably no great surprise, but it is ironic that Jackie's teenage fears of lesbian exposure should have led her to become an object of exhibitionistic self-disclosure on national television. In this respect, no body on *Work Out* is more willingly appropriated, scrutinized, and picked over than Jackie's own. Alongside the glamorous PR photos featuring her famous abs and frequent camera shots of her buff body in sports bra and spandex, we see Jackie exhausted and cranky, fidgeting uncomfortably on Dr. Shirley's sofa, drinking to excess (the tabloids claim she was arrested for DUI in the fall of 2006), making out with women in public bathrooms, puffy-eyed from lack of sleep, and moping about her house in baggy pajamas. When asked about the magnitude of her exposure on the show, Jackie admits that it often goes too far, but she accepts it all as part of her service to others. She explains, "I was raised with a mentally ill parent and I made a conscious effort to expose that and to expose therapy because I think it's tremendous for people. I think my relationship issues and why I choose these mates is very relatable to people. I think a lot of people make [dumb] choices, even though they're high achievers in other areas of their lives. I hear it over and over" (Belge).

On one hand, Jackie's vision of *Work Out* as a public health service is consistent with her primary passion, "which is changing people's lives" (2.1). And fans of the show do repeatedly testify to the life-altering influence of Jackie's struggles, as this message from "Lucy" eloquently explains:

> I have suffered from disabling Fears my whole life, phobias, panic attacks, so on. Jackie Warner has given me permission to accept myself warts and all and see the world as a challenge not a threat. My favorite quote I keep in my purse at all times now is when she spoke at her high school and used the word "Reinvention." It gave me hope. Thank you Jackie Warner. ("Lucy Beard" on Jackie's Blog)

But in conclusion, let's be real: while *Work Out* may improve the health practices of some adoring fans, the success of the program has contributed as much—if not more—to Bravo's fiscal health, not to mention Jackie's own financial fitness (the "Reunion special" reveals that a private work-out session with her now costs $400 per hour). However, the net effect of so much selfless self-disclosure and compassionate self-exposure is an expression of longing for shared meanings and experiences in a media-saturated culture that continues to link lesbianism to deviance, mental illness to shame, and health to private consumers and agencies. This is not the case on Bravo's *Work Out*, where being "out" functions as a flexible metaphor for ongoing debates over what it means to be healthy and fit at this moment in history, a moment defined by cultural shifts in the perception of normative sexuality; economic shifts that require self-maintenance, mobility, and adaptability within capitalist labor forces; and representational shifts within the television industry itself. Given these conditions, could it be possible that the long-predicted revolution in American health care will be televised? "Thank you, Jackie Warner."

CHAPTER 13

Switching Affects: Anxious Narratives of Lesbian Representation in Spanish Television[1]

Maite Escudero-Alías and
Mónica Calvo-Pascual

In the last few years, Spanish television has undergone an unprecedented shift in the representation of nonheteronormative sexualities. Although until very recently, there was simply no cultural room for gays, lesbians, transsexuals, and other sexual and gender minorities, with the arrival of the twenty-first century, and especially with the 2004 political change in Spain that allowed same-sex marriage and adoption, there is a sense in which the lives and desires of gays and lesbians have merged into a romanticized paradise of visibility and existence. Prior to this change, at the threshold of this century, and under the rule of a right-wing party, the introduction of gay characters into television series had already taken place. Current representations of lesbian identity and desire in Spanish television attest to a subtle mechanism of lesbian visibility, which, paradoxically, lies at the core of the recent political, legal, and social changes.[2]

This association between politics and lesbian visibility as is shown in Spanish television series is a key to fully diagnosing the ways in which lesbianism, despite its proliferation and increasingly positive representation, "has not constituted a steady narrative of progress, but rather has been marked by advances and retreats, breakthroughs and hiccups, sometimes even all within the same program" (Beirne, Introduction to 2008 edition, *Televising*

Queer Women 3). Moreover, the representation of lesbianism in specific genres such as soap operas or period dramas has become essential for the articulation of different narratives and their potential to produce alternative affective responses in the lesbian spectatorship. Unlike sitcoms, which usually display a more limited topography of emotions, such as laughter and joy, soap operas and period drama have the capacity to generate myriad affects, thus opening up new configurations of both positive and negative affective qualities. In what follows, then, our contribution will analyze the presence of lesbian characters in Spanish soap operas and period dramas as ambivalent sites of affect production: on the one hand, their overt visibility posits the very possibility and potentiality of articulating lesbian desire and identification, thereby displaying pleasurable and joyful affects for lesbian audiences, but on the other, precisely because most enactments of affects convey negativity and violent unnaturalness, the rhetoric of lesbian visibility becomes an aporia in itself—that is, an irresolvable paradox, to echo the words of literary critic Cathy Caruth when she defined the concept of trauma (*Trauma*).

On Lesbians and Affects

By bringing trauma studies to the fore, we do not intend to analyze the category of lesbian as traumatic, but rather to invoke the very premises of unrepresentability and unthinkability that characterize trauma theory when looking at lesbians. In the same way that the traumatic event exceeds and defies language, creating an epistemological and ontological crisis, so does the lesbian in contemporary Spanish television series. According to Judith Butler, the lesbian still "fails to conform to those norms of cultural intelligibility, since they [lesbians] appear only as developmental failures or logical impossibilities from within that domain" (*Gender Trouble* 17). This is not to say that lesbians cannot be represented, but that their representations fail to articulate a queer discourse, other than being assimilated into the dominant culture. The trauma of representing the unrepresentable, then, conceives of the lesbian as someone who is simultaneously known and unknown, since only representations that do not pose any threat for the patriarchal order in terms of politics, aesthetics, and ethics are positively depicted. For a start, all the lesbians portrayed in these series have been conveniently and safely packaged inside the progressive politics of same-sex marriage recognition; also, they all embody the beauty standards of "lesbian chic;" and finally, their presence denotes the absence of butch characters. The reduction of a great part of lesbians to nonexistence and invisibility may reinforce the idea that the butch lesbian has become the emblem of a threatening phantom caused by the shameful condition of her sexuality (Castle 2). Not surprisingly, in order to keep the domains of the political and social order intact, the butch lesbian must be erased or else, shown, punished, and then violently killed.

This said, our chapter tackles lesbian representation in Spanish television not as an (im)possible narrative of trauma, which may show the devastating psychic lives of lesbian characters as well as their painful self-scrutiny together with feelings of worthlessness and powerlessness, but as a narrative of affects, capable of addressing those lesbian affects and desires that are not yet expressed. In their study of affects, Gregg and Seigworth insist on the idea of "affect as potential: a body's *capacity* to affect and be affected" (2). Drawing upon the oft-cited quotation by Spinoza, "no one has yet determined what the body can do" (3), Gregg and Seigworth's work on affects addresses this "not-yet" as a contingent site for change and transformation of ethical, aesthetic, and political dimensions, all at once. This means that, due to their ephemeral and malleable condition, negative affects can be transformed into positive or yet-to-come affects.

The potential of affects to be attached and connected to other affects was first pointed out by psychologist Silvan Tomkins in his seminal work *Affect Imagery Consciousness*,[3] in which he argued that the affect system has both self-rewarding and self-punishing characteristics, which can be temporarily transformed into negative and positive responses respectively. Tomkins' theories have been thoroughly analyzed by literary and cultural critics such as Eve K. Sedgwick (*Shame and Its Sisters* and *Touching and Feeling*) and Sara Ahmed (*The Cultural Politics of Emotion* and *The Promise of Happiness*), who have focused on the malleability of the affect of shame as a key trait to explore a promising structural and semantic freedom for minority identities, especially for queers and nonwhite people. To gain such a freedom would require affects such as shame, disgust, and guilt—often attached to nonnormative bodies—to be revitalized by positive affects like interest, joy, or excitement.[4]

Admittedly, with the exceptions of *Hospital Central* and *La República*, most lesbian representations in Spanish television series are narratives of self-doubt, rage, or shame, thus underpinning potential audience feelings of alienation and self-devaluation. Rebecca Beirne rightly points out the importance of affect investments in lesbian images since "television can also produce intense affective relationships" (Introduction to first edition, *Televising Queer Women* 2) that may influence the spectator. For the lesbian spectator, then, it is essential both to develop sites for positive identification and to launch a series of resetting affects, capable of neutralizing the pernicious ones that most lesbian narratives enact.

In *The Promise of Happiness* (2010), Sara Ahmed argues that the fantasy of happiness is linked to a set of social indicators that function as predictors of happiness, such as heterosexual marriage and stable families and communities. However, Ahmed is not so much interested in launching a critique upon such a traditional account of happiness as in developing "unhappy archives that emerge from the feminist killjoy, the unhappy queer and the melancholic migrant" (17). The creation of these unhappy archives does not literally mean praising negative affects over positive ones but rather seeking productive accounts of affects aimed at casting new ontological pathways— in our case, for lesbian existence in (Spanish) television series.

Similarly, inspired by the work of Ann Cvetkovich, who attempts to find creative ways to challenge the traumas resulting from inhabiting lesbian identities, David Eng and David Kazanjian call for "productive rather than pathological, abundant rather than lacking, social rather than solipsistic, militant rather than reactionary" ways of approaching deleterious images of loss and absence (ix). Following this line of argument, we would like to rework those heterosexist discourses that have dehumanized and, by extension, prompted a set of negative affects around the figure of the lesbian.[5] Thus, if any cultural meaning must be a negotiated process in relation to identity categories, geographical positions, and differences, we must certainly look for the pleasures of narratives which, despite their heteronormative *modus operandi*, offer subversive room for feeling differently. Yet, we must not forget that, within mainstream television, the redefinition of lesbian affects in affirmative terms becomes a further intricate task, for in the (re)production of the dominant ideology, hegemonic aesthetics, ethics, and politics must remain intact.

Again, we feel that any attempt to represent the lesbian outside the negative-oriented affects in which she is often positioned becomes an aporia in itself, at least in commercial television series aimed at increasing ratings in order to make a profit for the network. In order to depathologize those negative affects attached to the figure of the lesbian, albeit temporarily, it is important for us to stick to evanescent structures of feeling that help us reconstruct our identities. According to Ahmed, affects are sticky and depend on the objects and/or persons they are attached to, thus being dependent on a structural contingency in which the role of reception becomes essential. As Ahmed puts it:

> To be affected by another does not mean that an affect simply passes or leaps from one body to another. The affect becomes an object only given the contingency of how we are affected. We might be affected differently by what gets passed around. (*The Promise of Happiness* 39)

Indeed, the lesbian spectator can be affected differently by discarding painful feelings and sticking to joyful emotions instead—after all, all the lesbians depicted in these soap operas experience intense feelings of love, friendship, or comradeship. Due to the structural malleability of affects, then, it is possible to swiftly feel different. In pointing out the intensity and temporality of affects, there is always a reminder of the potentiality of the narrative to be interpreted and *felt* in heterogeneous ways, ranging from alienation to proximity; from collective anxiety to cheerful sympathy; and from anger or rage to pleasure and joy. It is precisely the contingency of these shifting structures that must be grasped in order to produce counternarratives of lesbian feeling.

(Con)textual Analysis of Lesbians in Spain

Soap operas that include lesbian characters in Spanish television can be divided into two groups, depending on two distinct yet interrelated features: their sociohistorical settings and approaches to lesbianism as an issue, and the channel on which they are broadcast. On the one hand, commercial channels like Antena 3, Cuatro and Telecinco generally produce series based on present-day affairs and contexts, adopting a contemporary perspective on non-normative sexuality that sways between political correctness and outrageousness, according to the channel's political positioning (Antena 3 is highly conservative while Cuatro and Telecinco are more liberal, even though the latter are owned by former Italian Prime Minister Silvio Berlusconi). On the other hand, state-run public channel TVE1 tends to locate its programming in the past, where nostalgia frequently merges with political criticism and the stand on lesbianism sometimes verges on the anachronistic.

Bearing in mind the strong antigay politics of the Partido Popular (PP) government (1996–2004), which barred every left-wing attempt to assimilate homosexual couples, it is no surprise that the earliest lesbian appearances on TV took place on commercial rather than state-run television. Our analysis focuses on the presence of lesbians as regular characters, leaving aside one-off appearances in soap operas and period dramas.[6] The first regular character to be defined as lesbian—albeit only temporarily—in a Spanish television series was Clara del Río (Laura Manzanedo) who appeared in the teen soap *After Class* (*Al salir de clase*, Telecinco, 1997–2002), broadcast daily with an ensemble cast that numbered more than a hundred primary characters over five years. The series centered on the lives of a large group of high school students in Madrid, who fluctuated between being friends and enemies, fell in and out of love with one another, and had the anxieties and problems of upper middle-class urban preadults. Within this context,

Clara (1998–2001) was presented as a surly adolescent who came out as a lesbian to her friends, a disclosure that was met with suspicion and disdain. Unfortunately, her sexual identity was stereotypically portrayed as a "phase" provoked by her traumatic history of childhood sexual abuse and failed relationships with boys.

What is interesting in this representation is the shift in spectatorial identification promoted by the changes that the character went through. While Clara was portrayed as a lesbian, she was depicted as a mentally unbalanced, aggressive girl who was rude to her classmates and even set fire to the home of a straight friend who rejected her. This disturbing, disagreeable character no one could possibly identify with suddenly changed when she got professional psychological attention, after which she became not only heterosexual, but also sweet, sexy, and the center of attention for male characters. The move from marginality and abjection to centrality and affection in this conversion narrative stands not only as an index of the mainstream perception of lesbians at that time, but also acts as an off-putting extra load on lesbian teens' problems of identification. It functioned to awake only negative affects: contempt and disgust in the straight audience, and shame and humiliation or anger and rage in the lesbian spectator. For, although the lack of queer characters is harmful, especially for young people in the process of identity formation, having only one character who is rejected by everyone is even worse, indicating that the target audience was strictly heterosexual and the token lesbian was just a problem to be "cured."

This approach changed to a certain extent in the very early 2000s, when television companies in Spain became aware of the potential of lesbian audiences. Since girl-on-girl titillation has proven so popular with audiences, some other series on commercial channels have introduced token lesbian characters in the last two decades. One of them deserves some mention for the novelty it introduces, even though it does not escape stereotyping. *Hay alguien ahí* (*Is there someone around?* Cuatro, 2009–2010) was a short-lived horror series, focusing on the paranormal murders that take place after a group of friends in their early twenties invoke spirits in the protagonist's new house. In this context, the third victim is secondary character Amanda Ríos (Esmeralda Moya), a sweet, blonde twenty-year-old seduced by Nieves Bruc (Bárbara de Lema), her best friend's mother. Amanda is the sensitive daughter of a successful opera singer who is always abroad—and it is the figure of the absent mother that is implied to prompt Amanda into Nieves' bed. Nieves, on her part, is depicted as a perverse married woman, mother of the equally perverse Silvia (Marina Salas). She seduces Amanda as part of her plan to win back her husband's attention, setting a trap for Amanda in which she becomes the unwilling part of a threesome. After a suggested scene of sexual abuse on the husband's part, Amanda is kidnapped by a masked man and is finally found dead.

Needless to say, this is but another stereotypical representation of lesbianism as deviance caused by the need for a mother figure, and the young woman is soon eradicated by death. For her part, Nieves' behavior adds to the traditional association of bisexuality and viciousness. Yet, an interesting combination of affects was brought to life, since the terror and distress provoked by the series' plot merged with excitement and joy in lesbian spectators as woman-on-woman sex was more explicitly shown than ever before on Spanish television, giving it the same treatment as straight sex in the series—even if only for the sake of audience ratings.

One cannot say the same about *Hospital Central* (Telecinco, 2000–present), the most representative series including lesbian protagonists, who were ironically referred to as "the girls with no tongues" in lesbian blogs (El Aviaducto) for the underrepresentation of their physical relationship. Nevertheless, the prime-time soap awakened positive identification by means of resetting affects when the sociopolitical circumstances demanded it. As we have discussed elsewhere (Calvo and Escudero "We Are Family?"), *Hospital Central* marked an turning point in the way Spanish television made lesbianism visible. The relationship between ugly-duckling head nurse Esther García (Fátima Baeza) and sexy doctor Maca Fernández-Wilson (Patricia Vico) went hand in hand with the development of political change in Spain: Maca, a lesbian pediatrician, made her appearance in *Hospital Central* in season 8 (2004), falling in love with the previously heterosexual nurse, who had a history of failed relationships with men. They married as soon as the law on same-sex marriage was actually passed in Spain, when it became the third country in the world to legalize homosexual marriage. Despite such political associations, their relationship has never posed a threat to the heteronormative system: both characters are straight-looking femmes with no interest in feminist and queer politics, living in an entirely straight community where they are the oddity. Sex between the two was never explicitly shown or suggested—in contrast to their straight counterparts within the series—and they were soon redirected towards the realm of domesticity, as the mothers of three children.

Maca and Esther's relationship (2004–2010) revitalized *Hospital Central*'s audience rates, capturing the attention of the whole Spanish lesbian community. Blogs and forums mushroomed on the Internet to discuss every detail of the episodes, and several LGBT associations gave awards to the actresses for their positive interpretation of the characters and their consciousness-raising role in Spanish society (see Arranz, López, and Santos). Even though it is not free of stereotypes and flaws, the portrayal of their love story became an emblematic cornerstone of lesbian representation in Spain. Some of the flaws include the lack of realism in the all-too-perfect acceptance of lesbianism on the part of every single colleague in the hospital,and the weakness of their family, suggested by the fact that Esther has a one-night stand with a man and gets pregnant while Maca is on maternity leave, reinforcing the idea of lesbian availability for straight sex. As Charlotte Ashton put it when dealing with the concept of the "post-lesbian," a suitable label for Esther,

> The reason for post-lesbianism's current popularity with the mainstream media lies in the fact that it doesn't *look* or *act* any differently from other forms of accepted femininity. For as long as men can look at post-lesbians and see sexy women they want to fuck, and who indeed might even fuck them back, they will not consider that they have been forced to concede any ground. (172)

In 2009, *Hospital Central* takes a different turn when, on the verge of divorce caused by Esther's infidelity, Maca has an affair with newly arrived psychiatrist Vero (Carolina Cerezuela), an exuberant, blonde femme fatale This new relationship is conversely portrayed in highly sexualized terms, with recurrent scenes of passionate kisses and casual sex in closets and changing rooms, since the combination of these two women fits more adequately into the male fantasy of pseudolesbian sex. This evidence of straight-male-oriented voyeurism mirrors the words of Showtime's executive vice president of original programming when Showtime first aired *The L Word*: "lesbian sex, girl-on-girl is [a] whole cottage industry for heterosexual men ... [T]he straight men are going to sexualize beautiful lesbians anyway. Let's educate them along the way" (quoted in McCroy 42). Indeed, this parenthesis of erupting, adulterous sexuality seems to be part of the lesson that lesbian couples are just like any others, since Maca and Vero's affair ends amicably and Maca returns to her family life with Esther and the three children—conceding to the much-demanded wishes of the lesbian audience.

The spectator's identification with the couple is reinforced and settled for good when both characters leave the series in season 19 (2010), through a narrative device that is ennobling but not without fault. Esther is offered the chance to start a new career as a writer of fairy tales in Argentina, and the couple decide to move there. Maca is at the time the head of the E.R. (emergency room) and offers to stay until a new head is appointed. When doubts assail her and she is tempted to stay at the hospital in a position she has long desired, her shift of feeling is mirrored by a parallel story of teenage lesbian love.[7] Eighteen-year old Alma (Marina Salas) has a seventeen-year-old girlfriend, Sol, who is in a coma due to kidney failure. Sol has been going through dialysis all her life and is tired of this dependence to the point of feeling suicidal. Despite Sol's parents' rejection and insulting attitudes, Alma is so in love with Sol that she offers one of her kidneys for a transplant and delivers an exalting speech pleading for her love. This moves Maca, prompting her to take the first flight to Buenos Aires, where she is warmly received by her whole family (19:10). The fact that Maca and Esther leave the series together after Alma's epic speech reinforces the audience's empathy and identification with the couple, as well as transmitting affects like joy for the happy ending and excitement at the prospect of the characters' new beginning together.

As can be expected from the portrayal of previously underrepresented groups, close scrutiny of *Hospital Central* reveals certain shortcomings. For instance, the series never interrogates governmental assimilationist policies as it shows only gender-conforming lesbians. As Candace Moore and Kristen Schilt observe in their discussion of *The L Word*, representing only pretty feminine women who are indistinguishable from straight women may initially challenge "straight viewers' misconceptions that all lesbians are visually identifiable," but "it neglects to show that butch and masculine-identified lesbians are an equally important part of the culture.... It also allows the show to maintain a crossover audience by avoiding confrontational identities" (168). Not only Maca and Esther, but also every minor character in *Hospital Central* who is defined as lesbian, like Maca's former lover and the mentally unbalanced woman Esther flirts with, are feminine married mothers. As Samuel A. Chambers argues (85), "television, like any other cultural artifact, participates in the constitution of our reality.... Television, to put it starkly, proves political because of the way it participates in the reproduction of norms (and therefore culture, and therefore reality)." In this sense, *Hospital Central* denies the existence of and respect to the non-femme sector of lesbians, who are denied a degree of the possible affects inspired by the series because of its restrictive depiction of lesbianism. Yet, despite its many flaws, *Hospital Central*'s breakthrough is that it has gone beyond the "coming-out narratives, and de-sexualized storylines revolving around parenting" (Warn, Introduction to *Reading the L Word* 5) to which most lesbians on TV are confined. Lesbianism indeed stopped being an "issue" in the series, with the lesbian couple's relationship placed at the same level as straight ones in terms of plot, complications, and imperfection.

We move now to the analysis of series aired on public television. *Amar en tiempos revueltos* (*Love in Turbulent Times*, TVE1 2005–present) is a daily ensemble period drama dealing with life in a Madrid neighborhood during the Spanish Civil War and the early Franco years. A lesbian plot starts in its fourth season (2009), set in the mid-1950s. Primary character Ana Rivas

(Marina San José) is the rich heiress of a successful department store who secretly falls in love with Teresa García (Carlota Olcina), a humble village girl who migrates to Madrid and works as a shop assistant in the Rivas department store. After becoming friends with Ana, Teresa meets and marries "good cop" Héctor Perea (Javier Collado). Ana, meanwhile, marries Teresa's brother Alfonso (Alex García), a watchman turned boxer, in order to be closer to Teresa. Teresa is a very conventional woman in terms of moral values; Ana is portrayed as unusual for her time, since she was educated abroad. The plot is full of familiar elements: Ana sleeps with Hector before Hector and Teresa get engaged, thus diverting onto the man her desire for a woman. Also, there is a clear distinction between the upper-class sophisticated woman who initiates the relation and the rural traditional one who lets herself be loved and is afraid of loving a woman because it seems to be unnatural. Their relationship is emblematic of representations of lesbians as available for sex with men: both characters simultaneously sleep with each other and with their husbands, until Ana asks for divorce and Alfonso batters and rapes her. Only when Alfonso dies in an accident does Teresa decide to leave her husband and move to Santander with Ana, now pregnant with Alfonso's child. The double life motif reinforces the characters' sexual indecision, but it is only fair to acknowledge that this is fitting in the context of the period drama: the only options available for women over their twenties in Franco's times were to get married or embrace religious life. Being single, not to speak of lesbian, was simply not a socially acceptable option. In this vein, it is also worth mentioning that the reference to divorce is anachronistic, since divorce was not legally recognized in Spain until 1981. The fact that Teresa works in a store after getting married is also anachronistic. Working-class women had to quit their jobs immediately before getting married; the role of breadwinner was available exclusively to men in Franco's attempt to keep the heteropatriarchal system intact.

The anxious way the relationship is portrayed by the series is entirely dependent on the drama's audience: as a midafternoon program, most of its spectators are old-age pensioners. The producers no doubt felt that, as this audience was the most conservative sector of society, the lesbian relationship had to be tackled in a chaste and tentative way, though leaving space for a younger part of the population—lesbian students and part-time workers—to be attracted to the series. The increase in lesbian audience share with the introduction of these characters was again noticeable, as were the number of websites and forums devoted to commenting on the lesbian subplot and the LGBT associations' awards the actresses received for their performances. Apart from the commercial reasons to include this plot, it also provided an investment of certain emotions like empathy and sympathy on the part of an older audience that, having grown up during Franco's dictatorship, could find it difficult to understand the possibility of sexual dissidence.

To close our analysis, we discuss another period drama, appearing on TVE1, which recently has included a lesbian subplot: *14 de abril: la República* (2011–present), a spin-off of *La Señora* (TVE1 2008–2010), which focuses on the restless years prior to the Civil War. Encarna (Lucía Jiménez) is a single mother, a feminist, and anarchist activist who left her child behind in Asturias to embark on a political career in Madrid. There she meets Amparo Romero (Marta Belaustegui), an anarchist agent and alleged communist spy of German descent who runs an avant-garde cabaret. Significantly enough, the series' "golden minute" or audience peak was during a dream Encarna had that depicted her kissing Amparo multiple times.

This approach to lesbianism can be considered a positive one for several reasons. First, the two female characters involved are quite average in their looks, neither prototypically feminine nor masculine, and thus not prone to being identified with the scenario of male-fantasy pseudolesbian sex. Then, they are strong independent women with political and feminist engagements who place their professional pursuits over their family lives. Their attitudes are not anachronistic, as they are located in one of the most revolutionary and progressive periods of Spanish history—the Second Republic, when women were enfranchised and divorce was legal. Besides, the idiosyncrasy of these characters allows for the verisimilitude of the lesbian scenes, as they lived in an avant-garde intellectual environment where it was possible for women both to follow a professional career and to engage in "alternative" relationships. Undoubtedly, the display of positive emotions and affects such as commitment, interest, pleasure and self-confidence attest to the importance of showcasing lesbianism as a feminist option since, historically, feminist lesbians are rarely depicted, much less in a television series (Gimeno). Encarna and Amparo can be enthusiastically welcomed as representative of feminist lesbians who have been fighting for our rights and visibility and who, more often than not, are hidden from history.

Conclusion

Despite historical, political, and social differences, the representation of lesbians in Spanish television generally follows the same pattern as the Anglo-Saxon ones: standard feminine beauties engage in relationships that boost audiences and help mediate public opinion and social concern about the sociopolitical changes that have taken place in the last few years regarding the legal recognition of same-sex partners and marriage. Yet within these representations working-class, butch, and other queer lesbians do not find a symbolic space where they can become visible and can offer affective relationships with audiences. Such a discursive impossibility of representing *other* lesbians prevents complex and intense affective exchanges among a diversity of lesbian characters and audiences. That is, identification, respect and empathy are only allowed for certain portrayals of lesbians (who, paradoxically, do not correspond to the average lesbian in Spain). Nevertheless, as we have argued in our contribution, the representations of lesbians are ambivalent because, although they show many flaws, the creation of new positive affective sites must not be underestimated. These lesbian representations offer varying affects, and, through the absence of the butch lesbian, show the sharp anxieties of lesbiphobia and shame that most narratives enact for economic and political reasons. As powerful discourses of hate propagation, these feelings bring about what Ahmed has called "a politics of discomfort" (*The Cultural Politics of Emotion* 148), arguing that the psychic costs and alienation of lesbians living outside the limits of cultural and social intelligibility are in fact very high. Yet, Ahmed points out that the ambivalence of these discriminatory structures may indeed allude to a self-rewarding component because "the non-fitting or discomfort opens up possibilities, an opening up which can be difficult but exciting" (154). Given the malleability of affects that has been discussed throughout our study, lesbian bodies, even those that are not represented at all, can be reoriented towards unofficial, yet-to-be paths of love, endurance, and hope.

Notes

1. The research carried out for the writing of this essay has been financed by the Spanish Ministry of Science and Innovation (MICINN) and the European Regional Development Fund (ERDF) (code HUM2007–61035). The authors are also grateful for the support of the Government of Aragón and the European Social Fund (ESF) (code H05).
2. As late as 2011, despite the seven million nonwhite people that have arrived in our country for the last ten years, Spanish dominant culture in general and television series in particular simply do not show any concern for representing these identities. While we can certainly say that the first step has been the introduction of white gay and lesbian characters in mainstream culture, it is also true that the lack of reference to nonwhite queer identities and lesbians points to a national anxiety towards racial difference, which may be due to Spain's backwardness regarding the representation of identity categories other than white. As we argued elsewhere (2009), there is a great paradox in our culture: on the one hand, the legal advances have been enormous, but on the other, the social and cultural acceptance of difference is still far from being assimilated. Moreover, as we see it, this backwardness is also related to the lack of academic

departments and institutions devoted to studying nonwhite representations of identities, for unlike Anglo-Saxon culture, Spanish universities do not have a long tradition of race, cultural, or queer studies.

3. All quotations from this work have been taken from a revised version selected and edited by Sedgwick and Frank in 1995.

4. Silvan Tomkins distinguishes among positive affects interest-excitement, enjoyment-joy), negative affects (distress-anguish, fear-terror, shame-humiliation, contempt-disgust and anger-rage), and resetting affects (surprise-startle), which can neutralize the negative force of harmful affects (74).

5. Rather than favoring reworking strategies of lesbian desire and identification from feminist psychoanalytic viewpoints such as those posited by Laura Mulvey with her concepts of scopophilia and fetishism, Elisabeth Cowie's multiplicity of positions to all subjects or the ethnographic approach to the problematic of seeing/being seen carried out by Lola Young (1996), we would like to redefine the lesbian look by highlighting the affects it suggests, since only by evoking and recognizing multiple possibilities of affect production can we move beyond teleological meanings of lesbian representation in contemporary television series.

6. For further information on the representation of lesbians in Spanish sitcoms see Calvo and Escudero "We Are Family?"

7. This structure replicates the episode in which Maca and Esther's relationship starts (8.7). In her coming-out process, Esther's feelings are reassured when she meets a couple of lesbian girls in love in the emergency room, desexualizing the relation from the start (for more information see Calvo and Escudero "We Are Family?").

References

American Civil Liberties Union. "ACLU Fact Sheet: Chronology of Bottoms v. Bottoms, A Lesbian Mother's Fight for Her Son." American Civil Liberty Union Online, April 29, 2001. http://www.aclu.org/news/n050797c.html

"A Fan." Jackie's Blog. Bravotv.com. July 5, 2007 (accessed October 23, 2007). http://www.bravotv.com/blog/jackiewarner/2007/05/its_about_working_life_out.php#comments

Affinity. Directed by Tim Fywell. ITV1, 2008.

Ahmed, Sara. *The Cultural Politics of Emotion*. Durham, NC, and London: Duke University Press, 2004.

———. *The Promise of Happiness*. Durham, NC, and London: Duke University Press, 2010.

Akass, Kim, and Janet McCabe, eds. *Reading Sex and the City (Reading Contemporary Television)*. London and New York: I. B. Tauris, 2004.

Akass, Kim, and Janet McCabe, eds.. *Reading The L Word: Outing Contemporary Television*. London and New York: I. B. Tauris, 2006.

Allen, Dennis W. "Homosexuality and Narrative." *Modern Fiction Studies* 41, 3–4 (1995): 609–634.

All Kinds of Families. Directed by Liz Garbus and Rory Kennedy. Lifetime Television, 2001.

Ally McBeal. Created by David E. Kelley. Fox, 1997–2002.

America's Next Top Model. Created by Tyra Banks. UPN/CW, 2003.

Anderson-Minshall, Diane. "Sex and the Clittie." In *Reading the L Word*, ed., Kim Akass and Janet McCabe. London and New York: I. B. Tauris, 2006. 11–14.

Andrejevic, Marc. *Reality TV: The Work of Being Watched*, Lanham, MD & Oxford: Rowman and Littlefield, 2004.

Arkaycee. "More Black Lesbian Couples." *Showtime Message Boards*, 28 Jul. 2006 (accessed 28 Sept. 2011). http://discussion.l-word.com/viewtopic.php?t=12203&highlight=race

Arranz, Pilar. "Esther (Fátima Baeza) y Maca (Patricia Vico) celebran el Día del Orgullo Gay." Supertele. June 28, 2005 (accessed June 19, 2007). http://www.supertele.orange.es/supertele/carticulos/87236.html

Ashton, Charlotte. "Getting Hold of the Phallus: 'Post-Lesbian' Power Negotiations." In *Assaults on Convention: Essays on Lesbian Transgressors*, ed., Nicola Godwin, Belinda Hollows, and Sheridan Nye. London: Cassell, 1996: 157–174.

Associated Press. "Cynthia Nixon Switches Roles." CBSNews.com. September 24, 2004 (accessed March 17, 2005).http://www.cbsnews.com/stories/2004/09/24/entertainment/main645556.shtml

Atkin, Hillary. "From Hopeful to Household Name." *TelevisionWeek,* January 28, 2008: 24.

Ausiello, Michael. "*Buffy* Creator Titillates the Audience." *TV Guide,* August 5, 2000 (accessed July 2006. http://www.tvguide.com/News/Insider/default.htm?rmDate=05082000

Australia's Next Top Model. Created by Tyra Banks. FOX8, 2005–.

Bad Girls. Created by Maureen Chadwick, Eileen Gallagher, and Ann McManus. Perf. Mandana Jones, Simone Lahbib, and Alicia Eyo. ITV1. 1999–2006.

Barthes, Roland. *Image—Music—Text.* Trans. Stephen Heath. New York: Hill and Wang, 1977.

———. *Camera Lucida: Reflections on Photography.* 1980. Trans. Richard Howard. New York: Hill and Wang, 1981.

Bartlem, Edwina. "Coming Out on a Hell Mouth." *Refractory: a Journal of Entertainment Media,* vol. 2 (2003) (accessed November 11, 2011). http://www.refractory.unimelb.edu.au//journalissues/vol2/edwinabartlem.html

Battis, Jes. "'She's Not All Grown Yet:' Willow as Hybrid/Hero in *Buffy the Vampire Slayer.*" *Slayage: The Online International Journal of Buffy Studies* 8 (2003) (accessed November 11, 2011). http://www.slayage.tv/essays/slayage8/Battis.html

Beifuss, John. "Sex and the City 2: An Epic of Tackiness." GoMemphis.com, May 27, 2010. http://www.gomemphis.com/news/2010/may/27/movie-review-sex-and-city-2-epic-tackiness/

Beirne, Rebecca. "Queering the Slayer-Text: Reading Possibilities in Buffy the Vampire Slayer." *Refractory* 5 (2004) (accessed November 20, 2011). http://refractory.unimelb.edu.au/2004/02/03/queering-the-slayer-text-reading-possibilities-in-buffy-the-vampire-slayer-rebecca-beirne/

———. "Embattled Sex: Rise of the Right and Victory of the Queer in *Queer as Folk.*" In *The New Queer Aesthetic on Television: Essays on Recent Programming*, ed., James R. Keller and Leslie Stratyner. Jefferson, NC: McFarland, 2006, 43–58.

———. "Dirty Lesbian Pictures: Art and Pornography in *The L Word.*" *Critical Studies in Television* 2.1 (2007): 90–101.

———. "Introduction: A Critical Introduction to Queer Women on Television." In *Televising Queer Women,* ed., Rebecca Beirne. New York: Palgrave Macmillan, 2008, 1–15.

———. "Lesbian Pulp Television: Torment, Trauma and Transformation in The L Word." *Refractory* 11 (2007) (accessed Novemver 20, 2011). http://refractory.unimelb.edu.au/2007/09/04/lesbian-pulp-television-torment-trauma-and-transformations-in-the-l-word-rebecca-beirne/

———. "Television's Queer Grls." AfterEllen.com. 2008. (accessed March 15, 2009). http://www.afterellen.com/TV/2008/5/queerteengirls?page=0,0

———. "Screening the Dykes of Oz: Lesbian Representation on Australian Television." *Journal of Lesbian Studies*, 13.1 (2009): 25–34.

Rebecca Beirne, Ed. *Televising Queer Women: A Reader.* New York and Basingstoke: Palgrave Macmillan, 2008.

Belge, Kathy. "Lesbian Life Interviews Jackie Warner." October 9, 2007. http://lesbianlife.about.com/od/lesbianactors/a/JackieInterview.htm

bell hooks: Cultural Criticism and Transformation. Dir. Sut Jhally. The Media Education Foundation, 1997.

Benkov, Laura. *Reinventing the Family.* New York: Crown Publishers, Inc., 1994.

Bennett, Dan. "Producers Like Telling the Truth with Showtime's *The L Word.*" *Video Store Magazine,* December 21, 2004 (accessed November 20, 2011). http://www.homemediamagazine.com/news/producers-telling-truth-with-showtimes-l-word-6973

Berlant, Lauren, and Michael Warner. "Sex in Public." In *The Cultural Studies Reader,* 2nd ed. Simon During, ed. New York: Routledge, 1999, 354–367.

Bigsmooches. "So, We're Not Supposed to Say Anything about the Racism?" *Showtime Message Boards*, January 14, 2004 (accessed September 28, 2011). www.sho.com/site/message/thread.do?topicid=103056&boardid=268&groupid=12

Blackman, Lisa. "Self-Help, Media Cultures and the Production of Female Psychopathology." *European Journal of Cultural Studies* 7.2 (2004): 219–236.

Bociurkiw, Marusya. "It's Not About the Sex: Racialization and Queerness in *Ellen* and *The Ellen DeGeneres Show.*" *Canadian Woman Studies.* 24, no. 2–3 (Winter–Spring 2005): 176–182.

Boddy, William. *Fifties Television: The Industry and Its Critics.* Chicago: University of Illinois Press, 1993.

Bolte, Caralyn. "'Normal is the Watchword': Exiling cultural anxieties and redefining desire from the margins." In *Teen Television: Essays on Programming and Fandom,* ed., Sharon Marie Ross and Louisa Ellen Stein. Jefferson, NC: McFarland 2008, 93–113.

Bolter, Jay David. "Critical Theory and the Challenge of New Media." In *Eloquent Images: Word and Image in the Age of New Media*, ed., Mary E. Hocks and Michelle R. Kendrick. Cambridge: MIT Press, 2003, 19–36.

Bratich, Jack Z. "Programming Reality: Control Societies, New Subjects, and the Powers of Transformation." In *Makeover Television: Realities Remodelled*, ed., Dana Heller. London: I. B. Tauris, 2007, 6–22.

Bronski, M. "Positive Images & the Coming Out Film: The Art and Politics of Gay and Lesbian Cinema." *Cineaste* 26.1 (Winter 2000): 20.

"Brooke Shields." *Internet Movie Database.* May 11, 2001 (accessed November 20, 2011). http://us.imdb.com/BPublicity?Shields,+Brooke

Brown-Bowers, Amy. "Who Is '*The L Word*' for?" *The Toronto Star,* October 11, 2005: D02.

Bryant, Wayne M. *Bisexual Characters in Film: From Anaïs to Zin.* New York: Harrington Park Press, 1997.

Buckingham, David, and Bragg, Sara. *Young People, Sex and the Media: The Facts of Life?* Houndsmill: Palgrave, 2004.

Buffy the Vampire Slayer. Created by Joss Whedon. The WB/UPN, 1997–2003.

Burgess, Allison. "There's Something Queer Going On in Orange County: The Representation of Queer Women's Sexuality in *The OC*." In *Televising Queer Women,* ed., Rebecca Beirne. New York: Palgrave Macmillan, 2008, 211–227.

Burgess, Helen, Jeanne Hamming, and Robert Markley. "The Dialogics of New Media: Video, Visualization, and Narrative in *Red Planet: Scientific and Cultural Encounters with Mars*." In *Eloquent Images: Word and Image in the Age of New Media*, ed., Mary E. Hocks and Michelle R. Kendrick. Cambridge: MIT Press, 2003, 61–85.

Burston, Paul, and Colin Richardson. Introduction. In *A Queer Romance: Lesbians, Gay Men and Popular Culture*, eds. Paul Burston and Colin Richardson. London: Routledge, 1995, 1–9.

Butler, Heather. "What Do You Call a Lesbian with Long Fingers? The Development of Dyke Pornography." In *Porn Studies*, ed., Linda Williams. Durham, NC: Duke University Press, 2004, 167–197.

Butler, Judith. *Gender Trouble: Feminism and the Subversion of Identity*. London and New York: Routledge, 1990.

———. *Bodies That Matter: On the Discursive Limits of "Sex."* New York: Routledge, 1993.

Califia, Pat. "Gay Men, Lesbians, and Sex: Doing It Together." *Public Sex: The Culture of Radical Sex*, 2nd ed. San Francisco: Cleis Press, 2000, 191–198.

Calvo, Mónica, and Maite Escudero. "We Are Family? Spanish Law and Lesbian Normalization in *Hospital Central*." *Journal of Lesbian Studies* 13.1 (2009): 35–47.

Candy Bar Girls. Created by Sarah Burton and Helen Orton. Channel 5, 2011.

Capsuto, Steven. *Alternate Channels: The Uncensored Story of Gay and Lesbian Images on Radio and Television*. New York: Ballantine Books, 2000.

Carameladye. "Where Are the Butch Women, Where Is the Diversity?" Showtime Message Boards. November 15, 2004.(accessed September 28, 2011). www.sho .com/site/message/thread.do?topicid=103056&boardid=268&groupid=12

Caruth, Cathy, ed. *Trauma: Explorations in Memory*. Baltimore and London: The Johns Hopkins University Press, 1995.

Case, Sue Ellen. "Toward a Butch-Femme Aesthetic." In *Lesbian and Gay Studies Reader,* eds. Henry Abelove, Michele Aina Barale, and David M. Halperin. New York and London: Routledge, 1993, 294–306.

Castle, Terry. *The Apparitional Lesbian: Female Homosexuality and Modern Culture*. New York: Columbia University Press, 1993.

Chambers, Samuel A. "Heteronormativity and *The L Word*: From a Politics of Representation to a Politics of Norms." In *Reading the L Word*, ed., Kim Akass and Janet McCabe. London & New York: I. B. Tauris, 2006, 81–98.

Champagne, Christine. "Gaywatch: Ellen's New Talk Show," Quoted on *Gay.com* April 24, 2002 (accessed October 25, 2005). http://www.gay.com/entertainment /news/?coll=pno_Entertainment&sernum=544&page=1; also at http://ellen.4th dimension.info/forum/showthread.php?t=278

Chasin, Alexandra. *Selling Out: The Gay and Lesbian Movement Goes to Market*. New York: Palgrave Macmillan, 2000.

Ciasullo, Anna. "Making Her (In)visible: Cultural Representations of Lesbianism and the Lesbian Body in the 1990s." *Feminist Studies* 27 (2001): 577–508.

"Cindy" on Jackie's Blog. Bravotv.com. May 1, 2006 (accessed October 5, 2007). http://www.bravotv.com/blog/jackiewarner/2007/05/you_can_go_home_again.php

Clark, Dana. "Commodity Lesbianism." In *The Lesbian and Gay Studies Reader*, eds. Henry Abelove, Michele Barale, and David Halperin. London: Routledge, 1993, 186–201.

Contra. "Stereotypes in *The L Word*." *Showtime Message Boards*. February 20, 2007 (accessed September 28, 2011). http://discussion.l-word.com/viewtopic.php?t=14439&highlight=race

Cosmopolitan. February 1981 issue: Cover.

Cotter, Catherine Louise. Co-ordinator, Media Committee, Lesbian Feminist Liberation Inc. Letter to television networks. New York, 11 Feb. 1975. Located in Lesbian Herstory Archives, Brooklyn, NY, (accessed September 2004).

Couldry, Nick. *Media Rituals: A Critical Approach*. London: Routledge, 2003.

Cover, Robert. "First Contact: Queer Theory, Sexual Identity, and 'Mainstream' Film." *International Journal of Sexuality and Gender Studies* 5 (2000): 71–89.

Cowie, Elizabeth. "The Popular Film as a Progressive Text—a discussion of *Coma*—Part 2." In *Feminism and Film Theory*, ed. Constance Penley. London and New York: Routledge, 1988, 104–140.

Crawford, Lucas Cassidy. "Transgender without Organs? Mobilizing a Geo-Affective Theory of Gender Modification." *Women's Studies Quarterly* 36.3/4 (2008): 127–43.

Creekmur, Corey K., and Alexander Doty. Introduction. In *Out In Culture: Gay, Lesbian, and Queer Essays on Popular Culture*, eds., Corey K. Creekmur and Alexander Doty. Durham, NC and London: Duke University Press, 1995, 1–11.

Cruel Intentions. Dir. Roger Kumble. Columbia Pictures, 1999.

Currie, Dawn. *Girl Talk: Adolescent Magazines and Their Readers*. Toronto: University of Toronto Press, 1999.

Cvetkovich, Ann. *An Archive of Feelings: Trauma, Sexuality, and Lesbian Public Cultures*. Durham, NC and London: Duke University Press, 2003.

Davis, Glyn. "Saying It Out Loud: Revealing Television's Queer Teens. In *Teen TV*, eds. Glyn Davis and Kay Dickinson. London: British Film Institute, 2004, 127–140.

Davis, Glyn, and Gary Needham. "Introduction: The pleasures of the tube." In *Queer TV: Theories, Histories, Politics,* eds. Glyn Davis and Gary Needham. Routledge: London, 2009, 1–12.

Deeken, Aimee. "Syndies Score in February." *Mediaweek* 15.11 (March 14, 2005): 30.

DeGeneres, Ellen. *My Point…And I Do Have One*. New York: Bantam, 1996.

Degrassi Junior High. Created by Kit Hood and Linda Schuyler. CBC Television, Canada. 1987–1991.

Degrassi: The Next Generation. Created by Linda Schuyler and Yan Moore. CTV, MuchMusic, Canada. 2001–.

Diamond, Lisa. "'I'm Straight, But I Kissed a Girl': The Trouble with American Media Representations of Female-Female Sexuality." *Feminism and Psychology* 15 (2005): 104–110.

Doane, Mary Ann. "Film and the Masquerade: Theorizing the Female Spectator." In *Feminism and Film*, ed., Ann Kaplan. Oxford: Oxford University Press, 2000, 418–436.

Dolan, Jill. "Fans of Lesbians on TV." *FlowTV* April 25, 2005 (accessed September 15, 2011). http://flowtv.org/2005/04/fans-of-lesbians-on-tv-the-l-words-generations/

Dow, Bonnie. "*Ellen*, Television, and the Politics of Gay and Lesbian Visibility." *Critical Studies in Media Communication* 18 (2001): 123–140.

Driver, Susan. *Queer Girls and Popular Culture. Reading, Resisting, and Creating Media*. New York: Peter Lang. 2007.

Dyer, Richard. *Stars*. London: British Film Institute Publishing, 1979.

Edwards, Natalie. "From Minority to Mainstream: Channel 4's Queer Teens." *Journal of e-Media Studies* 2.1 (2009): http://journals.dartmouth.edu/cgi-bin/WebObjects/Journals.woa/2/xmlpage/4/article/325

El Aviaducto. "The D Word … ¡Ya era hora!" Blogspot. January 25, 2006. (Accessed July 26, 2007). http://elaveturuta.blogspot.com/2006/01/d-word-ya-era-hora.html

Ellen. Created by Carol Black, Neal Marlens, and David S. Rosenthal. ABC, 1994–1998.

Ellen DeGeneres: The Beginning. HBO. July 23rd, 2000.

Ellen: The Ellen DeGeneres Show. NBC, 2003–.

"Ellen Tearfully Talks of King." *Windy City Times*, March 5, 2008, 19.

Eng, David, and David Kazanjian. *Loss: The Politics of Mourning*. Berkeley: University of California Press, 2003.

Entertainment Weekly. 6 October 2000: Cover.

Epstein, Jeffrey. "Prime Time for Gay Youth." *The Advocate,* April 27, 1999: 60.

ER. Created by Michael Crichton. Perf. Laura Innes, Noah Wyle, and Anthony Edwards. NBC, 1994–.

Esterberg, Kristin G. *Lesbian and bisexual identities: Constructing Communities, Constructing Selves*. Philadelphia: Temple University Press, 1997.

Esterberg, Kristin G. "The Bisexual Menace or, Will the Real Bisexual Please Stand Up?" *Handbook of Lesbian and Gay Studies,* ed., Diane Richardson and Steven Seidman. London: Sage, 2002, 215–227.

Eves, Alison. "Queer Theory, Butch/Femme Identities and Lesbian Space." *Sexualities* 7 (2004): 480–496.

Exes and Ohs. Created by Michelle Paradise. Logo, 2007–.

Fonseca, Nicholas. "*The L Word* Series Finale: Who Killed Jenny Schecter? And Does it Even Matter?" *Pop Watch*. Entertainment Weekly. March 9, 2009 (accessed September 15, 2011). http://popwatch.ew.com/2009/03/09/the-l-word-seri/

Foucault, Michel. *The History of Sexuality*, Volume 1. New York: Vintage Books, 1990.

———. *The Use of Pleasure: The History of Sexuality,* Volume 2. trans. Robert Hurley. London: Penguin, 1992.

Friends. Created by David Crane and Marta Kauffman. NBC, 1994–2004.

Fries, Laura. "Work Out." *Variety,* July 17, 2006 (accessed October 1, 2007). http://www.variety.com/review/VE1117931098.html?categoryid=32&cs=1

Gamson, Joshua. "Sweating in the Spotlight: Lesbian, Gay and Queer Encounters with Media and Popular Culture." In *Handbook of Lesbian and Gay Studies,* eds. Diane Richardson and Steven Seidman. London: Sage Publications, 2002, 339–354.

Garrity, Jane. "Mediating the Taboo: The Straight Lesbian Gaze." In *Straight with a Twist,* ed., Calvin Thomas. Urbana: University of Illinois, 2001, 191–231.

Gauntlett, David. *Media, Gender and Identity: An Introduction.* London: Routledge, 2002.

Gavey, Nicola. *Just Sex? The Cultural Scaffolding of Rape.* London: Routledge, 2006.

Geen, Jessica. "Lesbians and Bisexuals 'Not Represented Enough' on the BBC." Pinknews.co.uk September 30, 2010 (accessed November 21, 2011). http://www.pinknews.co.uk/2010/09/30/lesbians-and-bisexuals-not-represented-on-the-bbc/

Gimeno, Beatriz. *Historia y Análisis Político del Lesbianismo: La Liberación de una Generación.* Barcelona: Gedisa Editorial, 2005.

Gitlin, Todd. *Inside Primetime.* New York: Pantheon Books, 1983.

Glamour. February 1981: Cover.

Gomery, Douglas. "*Brian's Song*: Television, Hollywood, and the Evolution of the Movie Made for TV." In *Why Docudrama? Fact-Fiction on Film and TV,* ed., Alan Rosenthal. Carbondale and Edwardsville: Southern Illinois University Press, 1999, 78–100.

———. "Television, Hollywood, and the Development of Movies Made-for-Television." In *Regarding Television*, ed., E. Ann Kaplan. Los Angeles: The American Film Institute, 1983, 120–129.

Graham, Paula. "The L Word under-whelms the UK?" In *Reading The L Word*, ed., Kim Akass and Janet McCabe. London and New York: I. B. Tauris, 2006, 15–26.

Granello, Darcy. "Using Beverly Hills 90210 to Explore Developmental Issues in Female Adolescents." *Youth & Society* 29.1 (1997): 24–53.

Green, Harvey. *Fit for America: Health, Fitness, Sport and American Society.* New York: Pantheon Books, 1986.

Gregg, Melissa, and Gregory J. Seigworth, eds. *The Affect Theory Reader.* Durham, NC, and London: Duke University Press, 2010.

Greven, David. "The Museum of Unnatural History: Male Freaks and *Sex and the City.*" In *Reading Sex and the City*, eds. Kim Akass and Janet McCabe. London: I. B. Tauris, 2004, 33–47.

Gross, Larry. *Up From Invisibility: Lesbians, Gay Men, and the Media in America.* New York: Columbia University Press, 2001.

Habermas, Jürgen. *The Structural Transformation of the Public Sphere: An Inquiry into a Category of Bourgeois Society.* 1989. Trans. Thomas Burger. Cambridge: MIT Press, 1991.

Halberstam, Judith. *Female Masculinity.* Durham, NC: Duke University Press, 1998.

Halberstam, Judith. "The I Word: 'I' for Invisible, as in Real-World Lesbians on TV." *Girlfriends.* February 2004: 18.

———. "I Love The L Word Not." *Girlfriends.* January 2004: 38–40.

Halperin, David M. *Saint Foucault: Towards a Gay Hagiography.* New York: Oxford University Press, 1995.

Hamming, Jeanne E. "Whatever Turns You On: Becoming-Lesbian and the Production of Desire in the Xenaverse." *Genders* 34 (2001) (accessed July 14, 2007). http://www.genders.org/g34/g34_hamming.html

Handy, Bruce. "He Called Me Ellen Degenerate?" *Time* (April 14, 1997), 86.

———. "Roll Over, Ward Cleaver." *Time* (April 14, 1997), 78–85.

Hankin, Kelly. *The Girls in the Back Room: Looking at the Lesbian Bar.* Minneapolis: University of Minnesota Press, 2002.

Hantzis, Darlene, and Valerie Lehr. "Whose Desire? Lesbian (Non)Sexuality and Television's Perpetuation of Hetero/Sexism." In *Queer Words, Queer Images: Communication and the Construction of Homosexuality*, ed., R. Jeffrey Ringer. New York: New York University Press, 1994, 107–121.

Harding, Jenny. "Making a Drama out of Difference: Portrait of a Marriage." In *The Good, the Bad and the Gorgeous: Popular Culture's Romance with Lesbianism*, ed., Diane Hamer and Belinda Budge. London: Pandora, 1994. 119–131.

Harrington, C. Lee. "Lesbian(s) on Daytime Television: The Bianca Narrative on *All My Children*." *Feminist Media Studies* 3.2 (2003): 207–228.

Hastie, Nicki. "It All Comes Out in the Wash: Lesbians in Soaps." *Trouble & Strife* 29/30 (1994/1995): 33–38.

Heartbeat. Created by Harry Winer. Perf. Kate Mulgrew, Laura Johnson, and Gail Strickland. ABC, 1988–1989.

Heffernan, Virginia. "The Perils of Pleasant, Or Spacey, on Talk Shows." *New York Times* (Sep 16, 2003): E5.

———. "It's February; Pucker Up, TV Actresses." *The New York Times* February 2005. February 1, 2006. http://www.nytimes.com/2005/02/10/arts/television/10heff.html?ex=1265778000&en=81966f6411ba81ad&ei=5090&partner=rssuserland

Helber, Steve, photographer. "1996 Out 100." *Out Magazine* December-January (1997): 95–104.

Henry, William A. "Gay Parents: Under Fire and on the Rise." *Time,* September 20, 1993, 66–71.

Helford, Elyce Rae. "Feminism, Queer Studies and the Sexual Politics of *Xena: Warrior Princess*." In *Fantasy Girls: Gender in the New Universe of Science Fiction and Fantasy Television*, ed., Elyce Rae Helford. Lanham, MD: Rowman & Littlefield, 2000, 135–162.

Heller, Dana. "States of Emergency: The Labors of Lesbian Desire in *ER*." In *Televising Queer Women,* ed., Rebecca Beirne. New York: Palgrave MacMillan, 2008. 83–98.

Heller, Dana, ed. *Loving the L Word,* London: IB Tauris, forthcoming.

Herman, Didi. "'Bad Girls Changed My Life': Homonormativity in a Women's Prison Drama." *Critical Studies in Media Communication* 20.2 (2003): 141–159.

Hidalgo, Melissa. "Going Native on Wonder Woman's Island: The Eroticisation of Lesbian Sexuality in *Sex and the City.*" In *Televising Queer Women,* ed., Rebecca Beirne. New York: Palgrave Macmillan, 2008, 121–133.

Hill, Annette. *Reality TV: Audiences and Popular Factual Television.* London and New York: Routledge, 2005.

Hinds, Hilary. "*Oranges Are Not the Only Fruit:* Reaching Audiences Other Lesbian Texts Cannot Reach." In *Immortal Invisible: Lesbians and the Moving Image,* ed., Tamsin Wilton. London: Routledge, 1995, 52–69.

Hocks, Mary E., and Michelle R. Kendrick, eds. *Eloquent Images: Word and Image in the Age of New Media*. Cambridge, MA: MIT Press, 2003.

Holmlund, Christine. "When Is a Lesbian Not a Lesbian? The Lesbian Continuum and the Mainstream Femme Film." *Camera Obscura* 24 (1990): 145–178.

hooks, bell. "Eating the Other: Desire and Resistance." In *Black Looks: Race and Representation*. Boston: South End Press, 1992, 21–39.

Hubert, Susan J. "What's Wrong with This Picture? The Politics of Ellen's Coming Out Party." *Journal of Popular Culture* 33.2 (1999): 31–36.

Hutchins, Loraine, and Lani Kaahumanu. "Overview." In *Bi Any Other Name: Bisexual People Speak Out*, ed. Loraine Hutchins and Lani Kaahumanu. Boston: Alyson Publications, 1991, 2–11.

The Incredibly True Adventures of Two Girls in Love. Dir. Maria Maggenti. Perf. Laurel Holloman, Nicole Parker, and Maggie Moore. Smash Pictures, 1995.

In Her Line of Fire. Dir. Brian Trenchard-Smith. Here, 2006.

Inness, Sherrie A. *The Lesbian Menace*. Amherst: University of Massachusetts Press, 1997.

"Jackie's Blog" Bravotv.com. May 10, 2007 (accessed October 12, 2007). http://www.bravotv.com/blog/jackiewarner/2007/05/its_about_working_life_out.php10 May 2007

Jackson, Stevi, and Sue Scott. "Sexual Anatomies in Late Modernity." *Sexualities* 7.2 (2004): 233–248.

Jackson, Sue. "'I'm 15 and desperate for sex': Doing and undoing desire in letters to a teenage magazine." *Feminism & Psychology* 15.3 (2005): 295–313.

Jackson, Sue, and Gilbertson, Tamsyn. "'Hot lesbians': Young people making sense of on and off-screen representations of lesbianism." *Sexualities,* 12.2 (2009): 198–224.

Jarvik, Lawrence. "It's Only a Movie: The Television Docu-drama and Social Issue Movie as The American Marketplace of Ideas." *Popular Culture Association in the South* (1988): 80–96.

Jenefsky, Cindy, and Miller, Diane. "Phallic Intrusion: Girl-Girl Sex in *Penthouse.*" *Women's Studies International* 21.4 (1998): 375–385.

Jenkins, Henry. "Searching for the Origami Unicorn: Media Convergence, Transmedia Storytelling, and the Matrix." Lecture given at Georgia State University, Atlanta. October 2003.

———. *Fans, Bloggers, and Gamers: Exploring Participatory Culture.* New York: NYU Press, 2006.

Jenkins, Henry. *Convergence Culture: Where Old and New Media Collide.* New York: NYU Press, 2006.

Jenkins, Tricia. "'Potential Lesbians at Two O' Clock': The Heterosexualisation of Lesbianism in the Recent Teen Film." *Journal of Popular Culture* 38 (2005): 491–504.

Johnson, Ted. "H'w'd, politics bring wedded blitz." *Variety,* May 26–June 1, 2008: 6.

Jonet, M. Catherine, and Laura Anh Williams. "'Everything Else Is the Same:' Configurations of *The L Word.*" In *Televising Queer Women: A Reader,* ed., Rebecca Beirne. New York: Palgrave Macmillan, 2008, 149–162.

Julien, Eileen M. *African Novels and the Question of Orality.* Bloomington, IN: University of Indiana Press, 1992.

Kaplan, Don. "Kiss Each Other, Girls, The Ratings Are Down." *New York Post,* January 28, 2000: 114.

Kearney, Mary Celeste. "Introduction: Girls Media Studies 2.0." In *Mediated Girlhoods,* ed., Mary Celeste Kearney. New York: Peter Lang, 2011, 1–14.

Kelleher, Terry. "Courting the Custody Issue." *Newsday,* September 22, 1996: 3.

Kelly-Saxenmeyer, Anne. "Articulating 'The L Word.'" *Back Stage West,* May 11, 2005: 6.

Kennedy, Roseanne. "The Gorgeous Lesbian in *LA Law*: The Present Absence?" In *The Good, the Bad and the Gorgeous: Popular Culture's Romance with Lesbianism,* eds. Diane Hamer and Belinda Budge. London: Pandora, 1994. 132–141.

Kessler, Kelly. "They Should Suffer Like the Rest of Us: Queer Equality in Narrative Mediocrity." *Cinema Journal* 50.2 (2011): 139–144.

Koehler, Robert. "*Zachary* Proves a Subject with no Verve." *Los Angeles Times,* September 21, 1996: F13.

Kort, Michelle. "Portia Heart & Soul." *The Advocate* (September 13, 2005): 40–46.

L.A. Law. Created by Steven Bochco and Terry Louise Fisher. NBC, 1986–1994.

Limon, John. *Stand-up Comedy in Theory, or, Abjection in America.* Durham, NC, and London: Duke University Press, 2000.

Lip Service. Created by Harriet Braun. BBC Three, UK. 2011–.

Lo, Malinda. "The Incredible Story of Ellen DeGeneres: The Rise and Fall and Rise Again of a Reluctant Lesbian Icon." *AfterEllen.com* February 2004 (accessed October 24, 2005). http://www.afterellen.com/People/ellen.html

———. "Review of *Tipping the Velvet.*" AfterEllen.com. September 2004. (accessed January 30, 2007).http://www.afterellen.com/archive/ellen/Movies/92004/tipping thevelvet.html

———. "Taking Stock of *The OC*'s Lesbian Storyline." AfterEllen.com. February 11, 2005. (accessed December 16, 2005). http://www.afterellen.com/TV/2005/2 /theoc/html

———. "Does *The L Word* Represent? Viewer Reactions Vary on the Premiere Episode." *AfterEllen.com* January 2004. (accessed May 3, 2006). http://www .afterellen.com/TV/thelword/reaction.html

Loomba, Ania. *Colonialism/Postcolonialism.* London and New York: Routledge, 1998.

López, Sara. "Premio Les Gai de Visibilidad." *Mundo Joven*. September–October 2005: 11–12.

Lost Girl. Created by M.A. Lovretta. Showcase, 2010–.

Lost and Delirious. Dir. Lea Pool. Lion's Gate Entertainment, 2001.

Louise. "Love It—Hate It: *The L Word*." *Gaydarnation.com*. September 2, 2004 (accessed September 28, 2011). http://gaydarradio.com/UserPortal/Article /Detail.aspx?ID=14625&sid=65

"Lucy Beard." Message posted 9 May, 2007 on "Jackie's Blog." (Accessed October 12, 2007). http://www.bravotv.com/blog/jackiewarner/2007/05/until_tomorrow.php

The L Word. Created by Ilene Chaiken, Michele Abbot and Kathy Greenberg. Showtime, USA. 2004–2009

Mad About You. Created by Paul Reiser and Danny Jacobson. NBC, 1992–1999.

Magoulick, Mary. "Frustrating Female Heroism: Mixed Messages in *Xena*, *Nikita*, and *Buffy*." *Journal of Popular Culture* 39.5 (2006): 729–755.

Majbritt [pseud.]. Photo of Alyson Hannigan and Amber Benson. July 26, 2006 http://www.alysonhannigan.dk/alypictures/alypub/idol/bp3.jpg

Mangels, Andy. "Lesbian Sex = Death?" Interview with Joss Whedon and Marti Noxon. *The Advocate* August 20, 2002: 70–71.

Maria14. "I Hate *The L Word*." *Pink Sofa*. 20 Jul. 2006. Web. (accessed 1 May 2008). http://www.pinksofa.com/guest/toast/toast.asp?sub=show&action=posts &fid=96&tid=1 90379

Marshment, Margaret, and Julia Hallam. "From String of Knots to Orange Box: Lesbianism on Prime Time." In *The Good, the Bad, and the Gorgeous: Popular Culture's Romance with Lesbianism,* eds., Diane Hamer and Belinda Budge. London: Pandora, 1994. 142–65.

Matheson, Whitney. "The annotated 'O.C.': Jan. 27 episode." *USA Today*. 3 February 2005 (accessed January 1, 2006). http://www.usatoday.com/life/tele vision/news/2005–02–02-annotated-oc_x.htm

McAlister, Melani. *Epic Encounters: Culture, Media, and U.S. Interests in the Middle East, 1945–2000*. Berkeley: University of California Press, 2001.

McCarthy, Anna. "Ellen: Making Queer Television History."*GLQ: A Journal of Lesbian and Gay Studies* 7.4 (2001): 593–620.

———. "'Must See' Queer TV: History and Serial Form in *Ellen*." In Mark Jancovich and James Lyons, ed., *Quality Popular Television: Cult TV, the Industry, and Fans*. London: BFI, 2003, 88–102.

McCroy, Winnie. "L for Invisible." *Washington Blade* 7 (2003): 42.

Mendlesohn, Farrah. "Surpassing the Love of Vampires; or, Why (and How) a Queer Reading of the Buffy/Willow Relationship Is Denied." In *Fighting the Forces: What's at Stake in Buffy the Vampire Slayer*, ed. Rhonda V. Wilcox and David Lavery. Lanham, MD: Rowman and Littlefield Publishers, 2002, 45–60.

Merck, Mandy. "Sexuality and the City." In Kim Akass and Janet McCabe, eds. *Reading Sex and the City*. London and New York: I. B. Tauris, 2004, 48–62.

Meyer, Michaela. "Representing Bisexuality on Television: The Case for Intersectional Hybrids." *Journal of Bisexuality*, 10.4 (2010): 366–387.

Millbank, Jenni. "It's about This: Lesbians, Prison, Desire." *Social & Legal Studies* 13.2 (2004): 155–190.

Millman, Joyce. "The Sitcom That Dare Not Speak Its Name." *San Francisco Examiner* (March 19, 1995): B1.

misterQ [pseud.]. "Amber Benson." Online posting. Ain't It Cool.com. December 1, 2004 (accessed July 22, 2004). http://www.aintitcool.com/tb_display.cgi?id =18005#787910

Mitchell, Peter. "De Rossi's nuptials in doubt after vote to ban same-sex marriage." November 6, 2008, *AAP General News Wire* .

Monaghan, Whitney. "'It's All in a Day's Work for a 15 Year Old Gay Virgin': Coming Out and Coming of Age in Teen Television." *Colloquy 19* (2010): 56–69.

Monteiro, Kate, and Sharon Bowers. "Too Queer for *Queer as Folk*: Identity, Patriarchy and the Lesbian Subject." Paper presented at the Southwest Popular Culture and American Culture Associations' Annual Conference. October 2002. Rpt. online. September 5, 2003. http://sharonbowers.com/GasNSip/QAFPaper.htm

Moore, Candace. "I Love *The L Word*." *Girlfriends,* Jan. 2004: 38–40.

———. "Resisting, Reiterating and Dancing Through: The Swinging Closet Doors of Ellen DeGeneres's Televised Personalities." In *Televising Queer Women*, ed., Rebecca Beirne. New York: Palgrave Macmillan, 2008, 17–31.

Moore, Candace, and Kristen Schilt, "Is She Man Enough? Female Masculinities in *The L Word*." In *Reading The L Word*, ed., Kim Akass and Janet McCabe. London & New York: I. B. Taurus, 2006, 159–171.

Moritz, Margeurite. "Old Strategies for New Texts: How American Television Is Creating and Treating Lesbian Characters." In *Queer Words, Queer Images: Communication and the Construction of Homosexuality*, ed., R. Jeffrey Ringer. New York: NYU Press, 1994, 122–56.

Mulvey, Laura. "Visual Pleasure and Narrative Cinema." *Screen* 16.3 (1975): 6–18.

Mulvey, Laura. *Visual and Other Pleasures.* Basingstoke: Macmillan, 1989.

Muñoz, José Esteban. *Disidentifications: Queers of Color and the Performance of Politics.* Minneapolis: University of Minnesota Press, 1999.

MyWhatAGirl. "Having African American Women on *The L Word* Could Bring a Different Type of Flavor to the Show." *Showtime Message Boards,* December 3, 2005 (accessed February 3, 2008). http://www.sho.com/site/message/thread.do? topicid=169850&boardid=107&groupid=12

Naughton, John. "*Buffy*: Here to Slay?" *Radio Times,* January 13, 2003: 28.

Neighbours. Created by Reg Watson. Network Ten, Australia. 1985–.

Newcomb, Horace. "Champagne of Television." *Channels 5* (1985): 23.

"Not Your Mother's Lesbians." Cover. *New York,* Jan. 2004.

Nyong'o, Tavia. "Queer TV, A Comment." *GLQ* 11.1 (2005): 103–105.

The O.C. Created by Josh Schwartz. Fox, 2003–2007.

"The O.C." *Fox Broadcasting Company.* December 16, 2005. www.fox.com/oc/

Olson, Michael. "Bewitching." *Stuff,* December 2001: 118+.

Once and Again. Created by Marshall Herskovitz and Ed Zwick. ABC, USA. 1999–2002.

One Tree Hill (2003– present)

Oranges Are Not the Only Fruit. Directed by Beeban Kidron, BBC, 1990.

Oswell, David. "A Question of Belonging: Television, Youth and the Domestic." In *Cool Places: Geographies of Youth Culture,* ed., Tracey Skelton, Gill Valentine, Routledge: London: New York, 1998, 35–49.

Page, Barbara. "Women Writers and the Restive Text: Feminism, Experimental Writing and Hypertext." *Postmodern Culture* 6.2 (1996). May 1, 2006. http://muse.jhu.edu/journals/postmodern_culture/v006/6.2page.html

People Magazine. March 17, 1980: Cover.

People Magazine. December 29, 1980: Cover.

Powers, Alan. *Front Cover: Great Book Jackets and Cover Design.* London: Mitchell Beazley, 2001.

Pramaggiore, Maria. "Straddling the Screen: Bisexual Spectatorship and Contemporary Narrative Film." In *Representing Bisexualities: Subjects and Cultures of Fluid Desire,* ed., Donald E. Hall and Maria Pramaggiore. New York: NYU Press, 1996, 272–297.

Pratt, Marnie. "This Is the Way We Live…and Love!: Feeding on and Still Hungering for Lesbian Representations in *The L Word.*" In *Televising Queer Women,* ed., Rebecca Beirne. New York: Palgrave Macmillan, 2008, 135–147.

Price, Deb. "Same-Sex Partners Both Need Parental Rights to Protect Best Interest of All." *The Detroit News* 17 November 1995. 29 April 2001 http://detnews.com/menu/stories/25171.htm

Queer as Folk [US]. Created by Ron Cowen and Daniel Lipman. Showtime, Showcase, USA, Canada, 2000–2005.

Queer Eye for the Straight Guy. Created by David Collins and David Metzler. Bravo 2003–2008.

Ramlow, Todd R. "Ceci n'est ce pas une lesbianne." *PopMatters,* June 18, 2002 (accessed November 30, 2004) http://www.popmatters.com/tv/reviews/b/buffy-the-vampire-slayer4.shtml

Raub, Kevin. "*Buffy the Vampire Slayer*'s Kindly Witch Flirts with Her Dark Side." *FHM,* June 2003: 132+.

The Real L Word. Created by Ilene Chaiken. Showtime, USA. 2010–.

Reed, Jennifer. "Public Lesbian Number One." *Feminist Media Studies,* 5.1 (2005): 23–35.

———. "Reading Gender Politics on *The L Word*: The Moira/Max Transitions." *Journal of Popular Film & Television* 37.4 (2009): 169–78.

Reznik, Shiri and Dafna Lemish. "Falling in love with High school musical: girls' talk about romantic perceptions." In *Mediated girlhoods : new explorations of girls' media culture,* ed., Mary Celeste Kearney. New York: Peter Lang, 2011, 151–170.

Rice, Lynette. "Willow Gay?" *Entertainment Weekly,* February 3, 2000. (Accessed July 24, 2006). http://www.ew.com/ew/report/0,6115,84966-3~-,00.html

Robinson, Paul. *Queer Wars: The New Gay Right and Its Critics.* Chicago and London: University of Chicago Press, 2005.

Roof, Judith. *A Lure of Knowledge: Lesbian Sexuality and Theory.* New York: Columbia University Press, 1991.

Roseanne. Created by Matt Williams. ABC, 1988–1997.

Rosenfeld, Megan. "Lifetime's Two-Mommy Weeper." *The Washington Post,* January 22, 2001: C1.

Ross, Sharon M. "Defining Teen Culture: The N Network." In *Teen Television: Essays on Programming and Fandom,* ed., Sharon Marie Ross and Louisa Ellen Stein. Jefferson, NC: McFarland. 2008. 61–77.

Ross, Sharon Marie, and Louisa Ellen Stein. *Teen Television: Essays on Programming and Fandom.* Jefferson, NC: McFarland. 2008.

Rubin, Gayle. "The Traffic in Women." In *Toward an Anthropology of Women,* ed. Rayna Reiter. New York and London: Monthly Review Press. 1975. 157–210.

Russo, Vito. *The Celluloid Closet: Homosexuality in the Movies.* Revised ed. New York: Harper, 1987.

Santos, Cindy. "Hospital Central's Lesbian Couple Shakes Up Primetime TV in Spain." October 12, 2005 (accessed July 24, 2007). http://www.Afterellen.com/TV/2005/10/centralhospital. html

Sassy. November 1978: Cover.

Schnuer, Jenna. "The Ellen DeGeneres Show: Upbeat Host Gains Fans, Feel-good Marketers." *Advertising Age* 76.20 (May 16, 2005): S1.

Schopenhauer, Arthur. *The World as Will and Representation,* vol. 1. Trans. E. F. J. Payne. New York: Dover, 1969.

Sconce, Jeffrey "What If?: Charting Television's New Textual Boundaries." In Lynn Spigel and Jan Olsson, eds. *Television after TV: Essays on a Medium in Transition.* Durham, NC.: Duke University Press, 2004, 93–112.

Scott, A. O. "Operation Desert Togs." Movie Review. *New York Times,* May 27, 2010. http://movies.nytimes.com/2010/05/27/movies/27sex.html

Sedgwick, Eve Kosofsky. *Epistemology of the Closet.* Berkeley: University of California Press, 1990.

———. *Touching Feeling: Affect, Pedagogy, Performativity.* Durham, NC, and London: Duke University Press, 2003.

Sedgwick, Eve Kosofsky, and Adam Frank, eds. *Shame and Its Sisters: A Silvan Tomkins Reader.* Durham, NC, and London: Duke University Press, 1995.

Seidman, Steven. *Beyond the Closet: The Transformation of Gay and Lesbian Life.* New York: Routledge, 2002.

"Semaj Taylor." Jackie's Blog. Bravotv.com. April 4, 2007 (accessed October 5, 2007). http://www.bravotv.com/blog/jackiewarner/2007/04/im_never_misunderstood_1.php?page=2

Sex and the City: The Movie. Dir. Michael Patrick King. New Line Cinema/HBO, 2008.

Sex and the City 2. Dir. Michael Patrick King. 2010. New Line Cinema/HBO, 2010.

Shales, Tom. "*Two Mothers*: A Wrenching True Life Story." *The Washington Post,* September 21, 1996: C01.

Simms, Meliors. "Lionel's a Lesbian: Queer Women Watching *Shortland Street.*" In *New Zealand Television: A Reader,* ed. John Farnsworth and Ian Hutchison. Palmerston North: Dunmore Press, 2002, 62–75.

Six Feet Under. Created by Alan Ball. Perf. Peter Krause, Michael C. Hall, and Frances Conroy. HBO, 2001–2005.

Smith, Liz. "Brooke's Biological Clock." *Newsday,* January 16, 2001: A11.

South of Nowhere. Created by Charles Randolph-Wright, Donna Deitch, Paul Hoen, Robert Townsend. The N, USA. 2005–2008.

Stanley, Alessandra. "Sex and the Gym: *Work Out* and the Gaying of Bravo." *New York Times* Online July 19, 2006 (accessed October 5, 2007). http://www.nytimes.com/2006/07/19/arts/television/19watc.html?_r=1&oref=slogin

Stillinside. "Thanks to *The L Word.*" *Showtime Message Boards.* November 3, 2007. Web. (accessed February 2, 2008). http://www.sho.com/site/message/thread.do?topicid=236020&boardid=226&groupid=12

Stockwell, Anne. "One Family's Value." *The Advocate,* January 30, 2001. (accessed September 25, 2002). http://www.advocate.com/html/stories/830/830_cvr_brooke.asp

Storm. "Response." *One More Month 'till the Next Season of* The L Word *Starts.* On blog post by Carmen Van Kerckhove. December 8, 2006. Web (accessed February 3, 2008). http://www.racialicious.com/2006/12/08/one-more-month-till-the-next-season-of-the-l-word-starts

Straayer, Chris. *Deviant Eyes, Deviant Bodies: Sexual Re-Orientations in Film and Video.* New York: Columbia University Press, 1996.

Sugar Rush. Created by Sean Grundy and Harry Bradbeer. Channel 4, UK. 2005–2006.

Survivor. Created by Charlie Parsons. CBS, 2000–.

Sweeney, Kathleen. "No Secrets, No Taboos: The Wild West of Millennial Girlhood." In Kathleen Sweeney, *Maiden USA: Girl Icons Come of Age.* Peter Lang: New York, 2008, 15–42.

Taylor, Ella. *Prime-Time Families: Television Culture in Postwar America.* Berkeley: University of California Press, 1989.

Taylor, John. "The Good Mother?" *New York,* September 27, 1993: 16–19.

Tenderwolf. "My Lesbian Role Models on *The L Word.*" *Showtime Message Boards.* February 2, 2004. Web (accessed September 28, 2011). http://www.sho.com/site/message/thread.do?topicid=48385&boardid=218&groupid=12

Thynne, Lizzie. "Being Seen: 'The Lesbian' in British Television Drama." In *Territories of Desire in Queer Culture: Refiguring Contemporary Boundaries,* ed., David Alderson and Linda Anderson. Manchester: Manchester University Press, 2000, 202–212.

"Timeline of Lesbian and Bisexual Regular and Recurring Characters on U.S. Television." *AfterEllen.com: Lesbian and Bisexual Women In Entertainment and the Media.* January 1, 2006. http://www.afterellen.com/TV/Timeline-TV.html

Tipping the Velvet. Directed by Geoffrey Sax. BBC, 2002.

Tomkins, Silvan S. *Affect Imagery Consciousness.* 4 vols. New York: Springer, 1962–1992.

Top Chef. Created by Dan Cutforth and Jane Lipsitz. Bravo, 2006–.

Torres, Sasha. "Television/Feminism: *Heartbeat* and Prime Time Lesbianism." In *The Lesbian and Gay Studies Reader*, ed., Henry Abelove, Michele Barale and David Halperin. London: Routledge, 1993, 176–185.

Tropiano, Stephen. *The Prime Time Closet: A History of Gays and Lesbians on TV.* New York Milwaukee, WI: Hal Leonard Corp., 2002.

Tucker, Ken. "The Ellen DeGeneres Show." EW.com December 13, 2010 (accessed May 12, 2012). http://www.ew.com/ew/article/0,,20448103,00.html

Turegano, Preston. "Controversial Custody Fight Brought Home by Several Excellent Dramatic Performances." *The San Diego Union-Tribune* January 21, 2001: TVWeek 6.

Turner, Guinevere. "Lipstick Los Angeles." *OUT Traveler Magazine,* December 2004. Web (accessed September 7, 2006). http://www.thelwordonlin.com /lipstick_LA.shtml

———. Personal Interview. March 28, 2005.

Turner, Victor. *From Ritual to Theatre: The Human Seriousness of Play.* New York: PAJ Publications, 1982.

TV Guide. May 7, 1977: Cover.

TV Guide. December 17, 1977: Cover.

"*Two Mothers* and Others." *The Washington Post,* September 22, 1996: Y03.

Two Mothers for Zachary. Dir. Peter Werner. Perf. Valerie Bertinelli, Colleen Flynn, Vanessa Redgrave. Avenue Pictures, 1996.

US Magazine. February 5, 1980: Cover.

US Magazine. May 15, 1979: Cover.

"Valerie Bertinelli." *Internet Movie Database.* May 11, 2001 http://us.imdb.com /BPublicity?Bertinelli,+Valerie

Virilio, Paul. *The Vision Machine.* Bloomington: Indiana University Press, 1994.

Vogue. September 1981: Cover.

Vorhees, John. "*Two Mothers*: Acting's Good, But Film Falters." *The Seattle Times,* September 22, 1996: 2.

Walter, Bronwen. "Gender, 'Race,' and Diaspora: Racialized Identities of Emigrant Irish Women." In *Thresholds in Feminist Geography: Difference, Methodology, Representation*, eds. John Paul Jones, Heidi J. Nast, Susan M. Roberts. Lanham, MD: Rowman and Littlefield, 1997, 339–60.

Walters, Suzanna Danuta. *All The Rage: The Story of Gay Visibility in America.* Chicago: The University of Chicago Press, 2001.

Warn, Sarah. "TV's Lesbian Baby Boom." Afterellen.com, January 2003 (accessed September 29, 2011). http://www.afterellen.com/archive/ellen/TV/lesbianbaby boom.html

———. "*Queer as Folk* Tackles Lesbians Who Sleep with Men––and Misses." Afterellen.com. July 2004 (accessed January 11, 2005). http://www.afterellen .com/TV/qaf/season4–72004.html

———."DVD Release of *Buffy* Season 7 Reminds Us of What We've Lost." AfterEllen.com. November 26, 2004 (accessed November 17, 2004). http://www .afterellen.com/TV/112004/buffy7-dvd.html

———. "Marissa Gets a Girlfriend on *The O.C.*" AfterEllen.com*: Lesbian and Bisexual Women In Entertainment and the Media*. December 8, 2004 (accessed December 16, 2005). http://www.afterellen.com/TV/122004/theoc.html

———. "*The O.C.*'s Alex Boosts Bisexual Visibility on TV." *AfterEllen.com: Lesbian and Bisexual Women In Entertainment and the Media*. January 17, 2005 (accessed December 16, 2005). http://www.afterellen.com/TV/2005/1/theoc.html

———. "A Disappointing End to *The OC*'s Lesbian Storyline." *AfterEllen.com: Lesbian and Bisexual Women In Entertainment and the Media*. March 21, 2005 (accessed December 16, 2005). http://www.afterellen.com/TV/2005/3/theoc .html

———. "Introduction." In *Reading The L Word*, ed., Kim Akass and Janet McCabe. London & New York: I. B. Tauris, 2006, 1–8.

———. "TV's Lesbian Baby Boom." *After Ellen* January 2003 (accessed September 29, 2011). http://www.afterellen.com/archive/ellen/TV/lesbian babyboom.html

Warner, Michael. *The Trouble with Normal: Sex, Politics, and the Ethics of Queer Life.* 1999. Cambridge, MA: Harvard University Press, 2003.

Webster's II New Riverside University Dictionary. New York: Houghton Mifflin Company, 1994: 1154.

Wertheimer, Ron. "In This Fight Over Custody, Parents Loved Each Other." *The New York Times* January 22, 2001: E10.

What Makes a Family? Dir. Maggie Greenwald. Perf. Brooke Shields, Cherry Jones, Anne Meara, Al Waxman. Barwood Films, 2001.

Whitman, Walt. *Leaves of Grass* [1855]. London and New York: Oxford University Press, 1998: 29–78.

Will & Grace. Created by David Kohan and Max Mutchnik. NBC, 1998–2006.

Willintoadmit. "You know you're an *L* addict when . . ." The L Word *Online Message Boards*. November 4, 2004. Web (accessed 2 February 2, 2008). http://www .mediablvd.com/forums/index.php?showtopic=20276

Williams, Linda. *Hard Core: Power, Pleasure, and the "Frenzy of the Visible."* Expanded ed. Berkeley: University of California Press, 1999.

Wilton, Tamsin. "Introduction: On Invisibility and Mortality." In *Immortal, Invisible: Lesbians and the Moving Image*, ed., Tamsin Wilton. London: Routledge, 1995. 1–19.

Wilkinson, Sue. "Bisexuality 'A La Mode.'" *Women's Studies International Forum* 19.3 (1996): 293–301.

Willig, Carla. *Introducing Qualitative Research in Psychology: Adventures in Theory and Method.* Buckinghamshire: Open University Press, 2001.

Wimberly, Travis. "Diversity." Web comment posted in reponse to Jill Dolan's "Fans of Lesbians on TV: *The L Word*'s Generations." *Flow TV*. May 8, 2005 (accessed May 12, 2012). http://flowtv.org/2005/04/fans-of-lesbians-on-tv-the-l-words -generations/

Wordswork. "Iranian Girl Playing a Latina?????" *AfterEllen Message Boards*. Nov. 16, 2004. Web (accessed 28 Sept. 2011). http://www.afterellen.com/node/761

Work Out. Created by Adam Karpel. Bravo, 2006–2008.

"Work Out." Bravotv.com. October 1, 2007 (accessed November 20, 2011). http://www.bravotv.com/Work_Out/about/index.shtml

Work Out Reunion: Watch What Happens. Bravo. May 15, 2007.

Wysocki, Anne Frances. "Seriously Visible." In *Eloquent Images: Word and Image in the Age of New Media*, ed., Mary E. Hocks and Michelle R. Kendrick. Cambridge, MA: MIT Press, 2003. 37–59.

Xena: Warrior Princess. Created by John Schulian and Robert G. Tapert. Perf. Lucy Lawless and Renée O'Connor. Syndicated, 1995–2001.

YouAreSoAnalog. "Why Does Everyone Hate Max?" *Showtime Message Boards.* Mar. 27, 2006. Web (accessed September 28, 2011). www.sho.com/site/message/thread.do?topicid=198625&boardid=4644&groupid=12

Young, Lola. *Fear of the Dark: Race, Gender and Sexuality in the Cinema.* London and New York: Routledge, 1996.

Young Miss. May 1979: Cover.

Zieger, Susan. "Sex and the Citizen in *Sex and the City*'s New York." In *Reading Sex and the City*, Kim Akass and Janet McCabe, eds. London and New York: I. B. Tauris, 2004, 96–111.

Index